# Springer Texts in Business and Economics

More information about this series at http://www.springer.com/series/10099

David L. Olson • Desheng Dash Wu

# Enterprise Risk Management Models

Second Edition

linear programming models, and data envelopment analysis. We also discuss data mining with respect to enterprise risk management. We close the modeling portion of the book with the use of business scorecard analysis in the context of supply chain enterprise risk management.

Chapters 11 through 15 discuss risk management contexts. Financial risk management has focused on banking, accounting, and finance.[1] There are many good organizations that have done excellent work to aid organizations dealing with those specific forms of risk. This book focuses on other aspects of risk, to include information systems and project management to supplement prior focus on supply chain perspectives.[2] We present more in-depth views of the perspective of supply chain risk management, to include frameworks and controls in the ERM process with respect to supply chains, information systems, and project management. We also discuss aspects of natural disaster management, as well as sustainability, and environmental damage aspects of risk management.

Operations research models have proven effective for over half a century. They have been and are being applied in risk management contexts worldwide. We hope that this book provides some view of how they can be applied by more readers faced with enterprise risk.

Lincoln, NE
Toronto, ON, Canada
September 2016

David L. Olson
Desheng Dash Wu

## Notes

1. Wu, D. D., & Olson, D. L. (2015). *Enterprise Risk Management in Finance*, New York: Palgrave Macmillan.
2. Olson, D. L., & Wu, D. (2015). *Enterprise Risk Management, 2nd ed.* Singapore: World Scientific.

# Acknowledgment

This work is supported by the Ministry of Science and Technology of China under Grant 2016YFC0503606, by National Natural Science Foundation of China (NSFC) grant [grant numbers 71471055 and 91546102] and by Chinese Academy of Sciences Frontier Scientific Research Key Project under Grant No. QYZDB-SSW-SYS021.

# Contents

# Enterprise Risk Management in Supply Chains

# 1

All human endeavors involve uncertainty and risk. Mitroff and Alpaslan (2003) categorized emergencies and crises into three categories: natural disasters, malicious activities, and systemic failures of human systems.[1] **Nature** does many things to us, disrupting our best-laid plans and undoing much of what humans have constructed. Natural disasters by definition are surprises, causing a great deal of damage and inconvenience. Nature inflicts disasters such as volcanic eruptions, tsunamis, hurricanes and tornados. Guertler and Spinler[2] noted a number of supply chain disruptions in recent years due to natural causes. In 2007 an earthquake damaged Toyota's major supplier for key parts, leading to shutdown of Toyota's Japanese factories as well as impacting Mitsubishi, Suzuki, and Honda. In 2010 the Icelandic volcanic activity shut down European air space for about a week, massively disrupting global supply chains. In 2011 the tsunami leading to the Fukushima disaster disrupted automakers and electronic supply chains, as well as many others.

While natural disasters come as surprises, we can be prepared. Events such as earthquakes, floods, fires and hurricanes are manifestations of the majesty of nature. In some cases, such as Mount Saint Helens or Hurricane Katrina,[3] we have premonitions to warn us, but we never completely know the extent of what is going to happen. Emergency management is a dynamic process conducted under stressful conditions, requiring flexible and rigorous planning, cooperation, and vigilance.

Some things we do to ourselves, to include revolutions, terrorist attacks and wars. **Malicious acts** are intentional on the part of fellow humans who are either excessively competitive or who suffer from character flaws. Wars fall within this category, although our perceptions of what is sanctioned or malicious are colored by our biases. Criminal activities such as product tampering or kidnapping and murder are clearly not condoned. Acts of terrorism are less easily classified, as what is terrorism to some of us is expression of political behavior to others. Similar gray categories exist in the business world. Marketing is highly competitive, and positive spinning of your product often tips over to malicious slander of competitor



D.L. Olson, D.D. Wu, *Enterprise Risk Management Models*, Springer Texts in Business and Economics, DOI 10.1007/978-3-662-53785-5_1

products. Malicious activity has even arisen within the area of information technology, in the form of identity theft or tampering with company records.

The third category is probably the most common source of crises: **unexpected consequences arising from overly complex systems.**[4] Some disasters combine human and natural causes—we dam up rivers to control floods, to irrigate, to generate power, and for recreation, as at Johnstown, PA at the turn of the twentieth Century. We have developed low-pollution, low-cost electricity through nuclear energy, as at Three-Mile Island in Pennsylvania and Chernobyl. The financial world is not immune to systemic failure. Financial risk importance was evidenced traumatically by events of 2007 and 2008, when the global financial community experienced a real estate bubble collapse from which most of the world's economies are still recovering. Human investment activity seems determined to create bubbles, despite our long history of suffering.[5] Financial investment seems to be a never-ending game of greedy players seeking to take advantage of each other, which Adam Smith assured us would lead to an optimal economic system. It is interesting that we pass through periods of trying one system, usually persisting until we encounter failure, and then move on to another system.[6]

## Unexpected Consequences

Charles Perrow contended that humans are creating technologies that are high risk because they are too complex, involving interactive complexity in tightly coupled systems. Examples include dam systems, which have provided a great deal of value to the American Northwest and Midwest, but which also create potential for disaster when dams might break; mines, which give access to precious metals and other needed materials but which have been known to collapse; and space activities, which demonstrate some of mankind's greatest achievements, as well as some of its most heartbreaking failures. Nuclear systems (power or weapon) and airline systems are designed to be highly reliable, with many processes imposed to provide checks and balances. Essentially, humans respond to high risk by creating redundant and more complex systems, which by their nature lead to a system prone to greater likelihood of systems failure.

Technological innovation is a manifestation of human progress, but efforts in this direction have yielded many issues. In the energy field, nuclear power was considered the solution to electrical supply 50 years ago. While it has proven to be a viable source of energy in France and other European countries, it has had problems in the US (Three Mile Island) and in the former Soviet Union (Chernobyl). There is a reticence on the part of citizens to nuclear power, and the issue of waste disposal defies solution. Even in Europe the trend is away from nuclear. The Federal Government in the US did not license new plants for decades, despite technological advances developed by national laboratories. Coal remains a major source of electrical energy fuel, although there are very strong questions concerning the need to replace it for carbon footprint reasons. Natural gas is one alternative. Wind power is another. Solar energy has been proposed. All of these alternatives can be seen to work physically, if not economically. The question of energy was further complicated with the recent large-scale adoption of *fracking*. This technique introduces risk and uncertainty not only to itself, but its inclusion changes decision-making regarding all sectors of energy.

All organizations need to prepare themselves to cope with crises from whatever source. In an ideal world, managers would identify everything bad that could happen to them, and develop a contingency plan for each of these sources of crisis. It is a good idea to be prepared. However, crises by definition are almost always the result of nature, malicious humans, or systems catching us unprepared (otherwise there may not have been a crisis). We need to consider what could go wrong, and think about what we might do to avoid problems. We cannot expect to cope with every contingency, however, and need to be able to respond to new challenges.

Enterprise risk management, especially in finance and accounting,[7] is well-covered by many sources. This book will review the types of risks faced within supply chains as identified by recent sources. We will also look at project management, information systems, emergency management, and sustainability aspects of supply chain risk. We will then look at processes proposed to enable organizations to identify, react to, and cope with challenges that have been encountered. This will include looking at risk mitigation options. One option explored in depth will be the application of value-focused analysis to supply chain risk. We will then seek to demonstrate points with cases from the literature. We will conclude this chapter with an overview.

## Supply Chain Risk Frameworks

There is a rapidly growing body of literature concerning risk management, to include special issues in Technovation,[8] Omega,[9] and Annals of Operations Research.[10] Special issues also have been devoted to sustainability and risk management.[11] This literature involves a number of approaches, including some frameworks, categorization of risks, processes, and mitigation strategies. Frameworks have been provided by many, to include Lavastre et al.[12] and Desai et al.[13] We begin with a general framework. Ritchie and Brindley[14] viewed five major components to a framework in managing supply chain risk.

### Risk Context and Drivers

Supply chains can be viewed as consisting of primary and secondary levels. The primary level chain involves those that have major involvement in delivery of goods and services (Wal-Mart itself and its suppliers). At the secondary level participants have a more indirect involvement (those who supply vendors who have contracts with Wal-Mart, or Wal-Mart's customers). The primary level participants are governed by contractual relationships, obviously tending to be more clearly stated. Risk drivers can arise from the external environment, from within an industry, from within a specific supply chain, from specific partner relationships, or from specific activities within the organization.

Risk drivers arising from the external environment will affect all organizations, and can include elements such as the potential collapse of the global financial system, or wars. Industry specific supply chains may have different degrees of exposure to risks. A regional grocery will be less impacted by recalls of Chinese products involving lead paint than will those supply chains carrying such items. Supply chain configuration can be the source of risks. Specific organizations can reduce industry risk by the way the make decisions with respect to vendor selection. Partner specific risks include consideration of financial solvency, product quality capabilities, and compatibility and capabilities of vendor information systems. The last level of risk drivers relate to internal organizational processes in risk assessment and response, and can be improved by better equipping and training of staff and improved managerial control through better information systems.

## Risk Management Influencers

This level involves actions taken by the organization to improve their risk position. The organization's attitude toward risk will affect its reward system, and mold how individuals within the organization will react to events. This attitude can be dynamic over time, responding to organizational success or decline.

## Decision Makers

Individuals within the organization have risk profiles. Some humans are more risk averse, others more risk seeking. Different organizations have different degrees of group decision making. More hierarchical organizations may isolate specific decisions to particular individuals or offices, while flatter organizations may stress greater levels of participation. Individual or group attitudes toward risk can be shaped by their recent experiences, as well as by the reward and penalty structure used by the organization.

## Risk Management Responses

Each organization must respond to risks, but there are many alternative ways in which the process used can be applied. Risk must first be identified. Monitoring and review requires measurement of organizational performance. Once risks are identified, responses must be selected. Risks can be mitigated by an implicit tradeoff between insurance and cost reduction. Most actions available to organizations involve knowing what risks the organization can cope with because of their expertise and capabilities, and which risks they should outsource to others at some cost. Some risks can be dealt with, others avoided.

## Performance Outcomes

Organizational performance measures can vary widely. Private for-profit organizations are generally measured in terms of profitability, short-run and long-run. Public organizations are held accountable in terms of effectiveness in delivering services as well as the cost of providing these services. Kleindorfer and Saad gave 8 key drivers of disruption/risk management in supply chains[15]:

| | |
|---|---|
| Corporate image | Regulatory compliance |
| Liability | Community relations |
| Employee health and safety | Customer relations |
| Cost reduction | Product improvement |

In normal times, there is more of a focus on high returns for private organizations, and lower taxes for public institutions. Risk events can make their preparation in dealing with risk exposure much more important, focusing on survival.

## Cases

The research literature is very heavily populated by studies of supply chain risk in recent years. Diabat et al.[16] presented a model of a food supply chain with five categories (macro concerning nature and political, demand, supply, product, and information management) of risk using interpretive structural modeling. Hachicha and Elmasalmi[17] proposed structural modeling and MICMAC (cross-impact) analysis for risk prioritization. Aqlan and Lam[18] applied optimization modeling to mitigate supply chain risks in a manufacturing environment. Davarzani et al.[19] considered economic/political risk in three companies in the automotive field, while Ceryno et al.[20] developed risk profiles in terms of drivers, sources, and events for automotive cases in Brazil. Trkman et al.[21] surveyed 89 supply chain companies, finding a predominant focus on risk avoidance rather than using risk management for value generation. These cases cited are only the tip of the iceberg, meant to give some flavor of the variety of supply chain domains that have been analyzed for risk.

## Models Applied

Many different types of models have been proposed in the literature. Because of the uncertainty involved, statistical analysis and simulation are very appropriate to consider supply chain risk. Bayesian analysis has been proposed to model supply chain risk.[22] Simulation was proposed in a number of studies, to include discrete-event simulation.[23] Colicchia et al.[24] applied simulation modeling to support risk management in supply chains. Simulation modeling of personnel system supply chains has been addressed.[25] System dynamics models have been widely used[26] and with respect to the bullwhip-effect.[27] Other modeling approaches have been applied to supply chain risk as well.[28] Optimization is widely used,[29] and even data mining.[30]

## Risk Categories Within Supply Chains

Supply chains involve many risks. Cucchiella and Gastaldi[31] divided supply chain risks into two categories: internal (involving such issues as capacity variations, regulations, information delays, and organizational factors) and external (market prices, actions of competitors, manufacturing yield and costs, supplier quality, and political issues). Specific supply chain risks considered by various studies are given in Table 1.1:

Supply chain organizations thus need to worry about risks from every direction. In any business, opportunities arise from the ability of that organization to deal with risks. Most natural risks are dealt with either through diversification and redundancy, or through insurance, both of which have inherent costs. As with any business decision, the organization needs to make a decision considering tradeoffs. Traditionally, this has involved the factors of costs and benefits. Society is more and more moving toward even more complex decision-making domains requiring consideration of ecological factors as well as factors of social equity.

Dealing with other external risks involves more opportunities to control risk sources. Some supply chains in the past have had influence on political systems. Arms firms like that of Alfred Nobel come to mind, as well as petroleum businesses, both of which have been accused of controlling political decisions. While most supply chain entities are not expected to be able to control political risks like wars and regulations, they do have the ability to create environments leading to labor unrest. Supply chain organizations have even greater expected influence over economic factors. While they are not expected to be able to control exchange rates, the benefit of monopolies or cartels is their ability to influence price. Business organizations also are responsible to develop technologies providing competitive advantage, and to develop product portfolios in dynamic markets with product life cycles. The risks arise from never-ending competition.

Internal risk management is more directly the responsibility of the supply chain organization and its participants. Any business organization is responsible to manage financial, production, and structural capacities. They are responsible for programs to provide adequate workplace safety, which has proven to be cost-beneficial to organizations as well as fulfilling social responsibilities. Within supply chains, there is need to coordinate activities with vendors, and to some degree with customers (supported by data obtained through bar-code cash register information providing instantaneous indication of demand). Information systems technology provides effective tools to keep on top of supply chain information exchange. Another factor of great importance is the responsibility of supply chain core

**Table 1.1** Supply chain risk categories

| Category | Risk | A | B | C | D | E | F | G |
|---|---|---|---|---|---|---|---|---|
| External | | | | | | | | |
| **Nature** | Natural disaster: flood, earthquake | X | X | | X | | X | X |
| | Plant fire | | | | X | | | |
| | Diseases, epidemics | | X | | | | X | |
| **Political system** | War, terrorism | X | | | X | | X | |
| | Labor disputes | X | X | | X | | X | X |
| | Customs and regulations | X | X | X | X | | X | X |
| **Competitor and market** | Price fluctuation | | | X | | | | |
| | Economic downturn | | X | | | | | |
| | Exchange rate risk | X | | | X | | | |
| | Consumer demand volatility | | X | X | | X | | |
| | Customer payment | X | | | | | | |
| | New technology | | X | X | | | | |
| | Obsolescence | X | | | X | | | |
| | Substitution alternatives | | | | X | | | |
| Internal | | | | | | | | |
| **Available capacity** | Cost | X | X | | | | | X |
| | Financial capacity/insurance | | X | X | | | | |
| | Structural capacity | X | X | X | X | | | X |
| | Supplier bankruptcy | | | | X | | | X |
| **Internal operation** | Forecast inaccuracy | X | X | | X | | | X |
| | Safety (worker accidents) | | X | | | | X | |
| | Agility/flexibility | | X | X | X | | | |
| | On-time delivery | | X | | X | | | X |
| | Quality | | X | | X | | | X |
| **Information system** | IS breakdown | X | | | | | | |
| | Integration | X | | | X | | X | |

**A**—Chopra and Sodhi (2004)[32]
**B**—Wu et al. (2006)[33]
**C**—Cucchiella and Gastaldi (2006)[34]
**D**—Blackhurst et al. (2008)[35]
**E**—Manuj and Mentzer (2008)[36]
**F**—Wagner and Body (2008)[37]
**G**—Lavastre et al. (2014)[38]

organizations to manage risks inherent in the tradeoff between wider participation made possible through Internet connections (providing a larger set of potential suppliers leading to lower costs) with the reliability provided by long-term relationships with a smaller set of suppliers that have proven to be reliable.

## Process

A process is a means to implement a risk management plan. Cucchiella and Gastaldi outlined a supply chain risk management process[39]:

- **Analysis**: examine supply chain structure, appropriate performance measures, and responsibilities
- **Identify sources of uncertainty**: focus on most important
- **Examine risks**: select risks in controllable sources of uncertainty
- **Manage risk**: develop strategies
- **Individualize most adequate real option**: select strategies for each risk
- **Implement**

This can be combined with a generic risk management process compatible with those provided by Hallikas et al., Khan and Burnes, Autry and Bobbitt, and by Manuj and Mentzer[40]:

- **Risk identification**
  - Perceiving hazards, identifying failures, recognizing adverse consequences
  - Security preparation and planning
- **Risk assessment** (estimation) **and evaluation**
  - Describing and quantifying risk, estimating probabilities\
  - Estimating risk significance, acceptability of risk acceptance, cost/benefit analysis
- **Selection of appropriate risk management strategy**
- **Implementation**
  - Security-related partnerships
  - Organizational adaptation
- **Risk monitoring/mitigation**
  - Communication and information technology security

Both of these views match the Kleindorfer and Saad risk management framework[41]:

1. The initial requirement is to specify the nature of underlying hazards leading to risks;
2. Risk needs to be quantified through disciplined risk assessment, to include establishing the linkages that trigger risks;
3. To manage risk effectively, approaches must fit the needs of the decision environment;
4. Appropriate management policies and actions must be integrating with on-going risk assessment and coordination.

In order to specify, assess and mitigate risks, Kleindorfer and Saad proposed ten principles derived from industrial and supply chain literatures:

1. Before expecting other supply chain members to control risk, the core activity must do so internally;
2. Diversification reduces risk—in supply chain contexts, this can include facility locations, sourcing options, logistics, and operational modes;
3. Robustness to disruption risks is determined by the weakest link;
4. Prevention is better than cure—loss avoidance and preemption are preferable to fixing problems after the fact;
5. Leanness and efficiency can lead to increased vulnerability
6. Backup systems, contingency plans, and maintaining slack can increase the ability to manage risk;
7. Collaborative information sharing and best practices are needed to identify vulnerabilities in the supply chain;
8. Linking risk assessment and quantification with risk management options is crucial to understand potential for harm and to evaluate prudent mitigation;
9. Modularity of process and product designs as well as other aspects of agility and flexibility can provide leverage to reduce risks, especially those involving raw material availability and component supply;
10. TQM principles such as Six-Sigma give leverage in achieving greater supply chain security and reduction of disruptive risks as well as reducing operating costs.

## Mitigation Strategies

There are many means available to control risks within supply chains. A fundamental strategy would be to try to do a great job in the fundamental supply chain performance measures of consistent fulfillment of orders, delivery dependability, and customer satisfaction. That basically amounts to doing a good job at what you do. Of course, many effective organizations have failed when faced with changing markets or catastrophic risks outlined in the last section as external risks. Some strategies proposed for supply chains are reviewed in Table 1.2:

Chopra and Sodhi developed a matrix to compare relative advantages or disadvantages of each strategy with respect to types of risks.[47] Adding capacity would be expected to reduce risk of needing more capacity of course, and also decrease risk of procurement and inventory problems, but increases the risk of delay. Adding inventory is very beneficial in reducing risk of delays, and reduces risk of disruption, procurement, and capacity, but incurs much greater risk of inventory-related risks such as out-dating, spoilage, carrying costs, etc. Having redundant suppliers is expected to be very effective at dealing with disruptions, and also can reduce procurement and inventory risk, but can increase the risk of excess

**Table 1.2** Supply chain mitigation strategies

| A | B | C | D | E |
|---|---|---|---|---|
| Add capacity | | | Expand where you have competitive advantage | |
| Add inventory | Buffers | | | Safety stock |
| Redundant suppliers | Multiple sources | Monitor suppliers | Drop troublesome suppliers | |
| Increase responsiveness | Information sharing | Contingency planning | | End-to-end visibility |
| Increase flexibility | Product differentiation | Late product differentiation | Delay resource commitment | Supply flexibility |
| Pool demand | | | | Multiple sourcing |
| Increase capability | | | Outsource low probability demand | |
| More customers | | | | |
| | Early supplier involvement | Information sharing | Sharing/transfer | Awareness |
| | Risk taking | Insurance | Hedge (insure, disperse globally) | Supplier development |
| | | | Drop troublesome customers | |

A—Chopra and Sodhi (2004)[42]
B—Khan and Burnes (2007)[43]
C—Wagner and Bode (2008)[44]
D—Manuj and Mentzer (2008)[45]
E—Oke and Gopalakrishnan (2009)[46]

capacity. Other strategies had no negative expected risk impacts (increasing responsiveness, increasing flexibility, aggregating demand, increasing capability, or increasing customer accounts), but could have negative cost implications. Talluri et al.[48] assessed such strategies via simulation.

Tang emphasized robustness.[49] He gave nine robust supply chain strategies, some of which were included in Table 1.2. He elaborated on the expected benefits of each strategy, both for normal operations as well as in dealing with major disruptions, outlined in Table 1.3, organized by purpose:

Cucchiella and Gastaldi gave similar strategies, with sources of supply chain research that investigated each.[50] Cucchiella and Gastaldi expanded Tang's list to include capacity expansion. Ritchie and Brindley included risk insurance, information sharing, and relationship development.[51]

**Table 1.3** Tang's Robust supply chain strategies

| Strategy | Purpose | Normal benefits | Disruption benefits |
|---|---|---|---|
| Strategic stock | Product availability | Better supply management | Quick response |
| Economic supply incentives | | | Can quickly adjust order quantities |
| Postponement | Product flexibility | | Can change product configurations quickly in response to actual demand |
| Flexible supply base | Supply flexibility | | Can shift production among suppliers quickly |
| Make-and-buy | | | Can shift production in-house or outsource |
| Flexible transportation | Transportation flexibility | | Can switch among modes as needed |
| Revenue management | Control product demand | Better demand management | Influence customer selection as needed |
| Dynamic assortment planning | | | Can influence product demand quickly |
| Silent product rollover | Control product exposure | Better manage both supply and demand | Quickly affect demand |

## Conclusions

Enterprise risk management began focusing on financial factors. After the corporate scandals in the U.S. in the early 2000s, accounting aspects grew in importance. This chapter discusses the importance of risk management in the context of supply chain management.

A representative risk framework based on the work of Ritchie and Brindley was presented. It rationally begins by identify causes (drivers) of risk, and influencers within the organization. Those responsible for decision making are identified, and a process outlined where risks, responses, and measures of outcomes are included.

There have been many cases involving supply chain risk management reported recently. Some were briefly reviewed, along with quantitative modeling. Typical risks faced by supply chains were extracted from sources, and categorized. A process of risk identification, assessment, strategy development and selection, implementation and monitoring is reviewed. Representative mitigation strategies were extracted from published sources.

Chapter 2 addresses the enterprise risk management process, describing use of risk matrices. Chapter 3 describes value-focused supply chain risk analysis, with examples demonstrated in Chap. 4. Chapter 5 provides simulation modeling of supply chain inventory. Chapter 6 deals with value at risk, Chap. 7 with chance constrained modeling, Chap. 8 with data envelopment analysis, and Chap. 9 with data mining from the perspective of enterprise risk management. Chapter 10 concludes the methods section of the book with balanced scorecards as tools to monitor implementation of risk management efforts. Domain specific issues for information systems are discussed in Chap. 11, for project management in Chap. 12, natural disaster response in Chap. 13, sustainability risk management in Chap. 14, and environmental damage and risk assessment in Chap. 15.

## Notes

1. Mitroff, I.I. and Alpaslan, M.C. (2003). Preparing for evil, *Harvard Business Review* 81:4, 109–115.
2. Guertler, B. and Spinler, S. (2015). Supply risk interrelationships and the derivation of key supply risk indicators, *Technological Forecasting & Social Change* 92, 224–236.
3. Kapucu, N. and Van Wart, M. (2008). Making matters worse: An anatomy of leadership failures in managing catastrophic events, *Administration & Society* 40(7): 711–740.
4. Perrow, C. (1984). *Normal Accidents: Living with High-Risk Technologies.* Princeton, NJ: Princeton University Press, 1999 reprint.
5. Laeven, L. and F. Valencia (2008) 'Systemic banking crises: A new database', International Monetary Fund Working Paper WP/08/224.
6. Wu, D.D. and Olson, D.L. (2015), *Enterprise Risk Management in Finance.* New York: Palgrave Macmillan.
7. Olson, D.L. and Wu, D.D. (2015). *Enterprise Risk Management 2nd ed..* Singapore: World Scientific.
8. Olson, D.L., Birge, J. and Linton, J. (2014). Special issue: Risk management in cleaner production. *Technovation* 34:8, 395–398.
9. Wu, D.D., Olson, D.L. and Dolgui, A. (2015). Decision making in enterprise risk management. *Omega* 57 Part A, 1–4.
10. Wu, D. (2016). Risk management and operations research: A review and introduction to the special issue. *Annals of Operations Research* 237(1–2), 1–3.
11. Wu, D.D., Olson, D.L. and Birge, J.R. (2013). Risk management in cleaner production. *Journal of Cleaner Production* 53, 1–6.
12. Lavastre, O., Gunasekaran, A. and Spalanzani, A. (2014). Effect of firm characteristic, supplier relationships and techniques used on supply chain risk management (SCRM): An empirical investigation on French industrial firms. *International Journal of Production Research* 52(110), 3381–3403.
13. Desai, K.J., Desai, M.S. and Ojode, L. (2015). Supply chain risk management framework: A fishbone analysis approach. *SAM Advanced Management Journal* 80(3), 34–56.
14. Ritchie, B. and Brindley, C. (2007a). An emergent framework for supply chain risk management and performance measurement, *Journal of the Operational Research Society* 58, 1398–1411; Ritchie, B. and Brindley, C. (2007b). Supply

chain risk management and performance: A guiding framework for future development, *International Journal of Operations & Production Management* 27:3, 303–322.
15. Kleindorfer, P.R. and Saad, G.H. (2005). Managing disruption risks in supply chains, *Production and Operations Management* 14:1, 53–68.
16. Diabat, A., Govindan, K. and Panicker, v.V. (2012). Supply chain risk management and its mitigation in a food industry. *International Journal of Production Research* 50(11), 3039–3050.
17. Hachicha, W. and Elmsalmi, M. (2014) An integrated approach based-struct6ural modeling rfor risk prioritization in supply network management. *Journal of Risk Research* 17(10), 1301–1324.
18. Aqlan, F. and Lam, S.S. (2015). Supply chain risk modelling and mitigation. *International Journal of Production Research* 53(18), 5640–5656.
19. Davarzani, H., Zanjirani Farahani, R., and Rahmandad, H. (2015). Understanding econo-political risks: Impact of sanctions on an automotive supply chain. *International Journal of Operations & Production Management* 35(11), 1567–1591.
20. Ceryno, P.S., Scavarda, L.F., and Klingebiel, K. (2015). Supply chain risk: Empirical research in the automotive industry. *Journal of Risk Research* 18(9), 1145–1164.
21. Trkman, P., de Oliveira, M.P.V. and McCormack, K. (2016). Valuie-oriented supply chain risk management: You get what you expect. *Industrial Management & Data Systems* 116(5), 1061–1083.
22. Burdeen, F., Shuaib, M., Wijekoon, K., Brown, A., Faulkner, W., Amundson, J., Jawahir, I.S., Goldsby, T.J., Iyengar, D. and Boden, B. (2014). Quantitative modeling and analysis of supply chain risks using Bayesian theory. *Journal of Manufacturing Technology Management* 631–654.
23. Elleuch, H., Hachicha, W., and Chabchoub, H. (2014). A combined approach for supply chain risk management: Description and application to a real hospital pharmaceutical case study. *Journal of Risk Research* 17(5), 641–663.
24. Colicchia, C., Dallari, F., and Melacini, M. (2011). A simulatin-based framework to evaluate strategies for managing global inbound supply risk. *International Journal of Logistics: Research & Applications* 14(6), 371–384.
25. Swenseth, S.R. and Olson, D.L. (2014). Simulation model of professional service personnel inventory. *International Journal of Services and Operations Management* 19(4), 451–467.
26. Ghadge, A., Dani, S., Chester, M. and Kalawsky, R. (2013). A systems approach for modelling supply chain risk. *Supply Chain Management* 18(5), 523–538.
27. Wangphanich, P., Kara, S. and Kayis, B. (2010). Analysis of the bullwhip effect in multi-product, multi-stage supply chain systems – a simulation approach. *International Journal of Production Research* 48(15), 4501–4517.
28. Wu, D. and Olson, D.L. (2011). Forward. *Annals of Operations Research* 185 (1), 1–3; Wu, D.D., Olson, D.L. and Birge, J. (2011) Guest editorial. *Computers and Operations Research* 39(4), 751–752; Wu, D., Olson, D.L. and Birge,

J. Introduction to special issue on enterprise risk management in operations. *International Journal of Production Economics* 134(1); Wu, D., Fang, S.-C., Olson, D.L. and Birge, J.R. (2012) Introduction to the special issue on optimizing risk management in services. *Optimization* 61(10–12), 1175–1177; Wu, D.D. and Olson, D.L. (2013) Computational simulation and risk analysis: An introduction of state of the art research.*Mathematical & Computer Modelling* 58, 1581–1587; Wu, D.D., Chen, S.-H. and Olson, D.L. (2014) Business intelligence in risk management: Some recent progresses. *Information Sciences* 256(20), 1–7.
29. Aqlan, F. and Lam, S.S. (2015). Supply chain risk modelling and mitigation. *International Journal of Production Research* 53(18), 5640–5656.
30. Ting, S.L., Tse, Y.K., Ho, G.T.S., Chung, S.H. and Pang, G. (2014). Mining logistics data to assure the quality in a sustainable food supply chain: A case in the red wine industry. *International Journal of Production Economics* 152, 200–209.
31. Cucchiella, F. and Gastaldi, M. (2006). Risk management in supply chain: A real option approach, *Journal of Manufacturing Technology Management* 17:6, 700–720.
32. Chopra, S. and Sodhi, M.S. (2004). Managing risk to avoid supply-chain breakdown, *MIT Sloan Management Review* 46:1, 53–61.
33. Wu, T., Blackhurst, J. and Chidambaram, V. (2006). A model for inbound supply risk analysis. *Computers in Industry* 57, 350–365. et al. (2006), op cit.
34. Cucchiella and Gastaldi (2006), op cit.
35. Blackhurst, J.V., Scheibe, K.P. and Johnson, D.J. (2008). Supplier risk assessment and monitoring for the automotive industry. *International Journal of Physical Distribution & Logistics Management* 38:2, 143–165.
36. Manuj, I. and Mentzer, J.T. (2008). Global supply chain risk management, *Journal of Business Logistics* 29:1, 133–155.
37. Wagner, S.M. and Bode, C. (2008). An empirical examination of supply chain performance along several dimensions of risk, *Journal of Business Logistics* 29:1, 307–325.
38. Lavastre, O., Gunasekaran, A. and Spalanzani, A. (2014). Effect of firm characteristics, supplier relationships and techniques used on supply chain risk management (SCRM): An empirical investigation on French industrial firms. *International Journal of Production Research* 52(11), 3381–3403.
39. Cucchiella and Gastaldi (2006), op cit.
40. Hallikas, J., Karvonen, I., Pulkkinen, U., Virolainen, V.-M. and Tuominen, M. (2004). Risk management processes in supplier networks, *International Journal of Production Economics* 90:1, 47–58; Khan and Burnes (2007), op cit.; Autry, C.W. and Bobbitt, L.M. (2008). Supply chain security orientation: Conceptual development and a proposed framework, *International Journal of Logistics Management* 19:1, 42–64; Manuj and Mentzer (2008), op cit.
41. Kleindorfer and Saad (2005), op cit.
42. Chopra and Sodhi (2004), op cit.

43. Kahn, O. and Burnes, B. (2007). Risk and supply chain management: Creating a research agenda. *International Journal of Logistics Management* 18(2): 197–216.
44. Wagner and Bodhi (2008), op cit.
45. Manuj and Mentzer (2008), op cit.
46. Oke, A., Gopalakrishnan, M. 2009. Managing Disruptions in Supply Chains: A Case Study of a Retail Supply Chain. *International Journal of Production Economics* 118(1); 168–174.
47. Chopra and Sodhi (2004), op cit.
48. Talluri, S., Kull, T.J., Yildiz, H. and Yoon, J. (2013) Assessing the efficiency of risk mitigation strategies in supply chains. *Journal of Business Logistics* 34(4), 253–269.
49. Tang, C.S. (2006). Robust strategies for mitigating supply chain disruptions, *International Journal of Logistics: Research and Applications* 9:1, 33–45.
50. Cucchiella and Gastaldi (2006), op cit.
51. Ritchie and Brindley (2007a), op cit.

# Risk Matrices

# 2

There is no doubt that risk management is an important and growing area in the uncertain world. Chapter 1 discussed a number of recent events where events made doing business highly challenging. Globalization offers many opportunities, but it also means less control, operating in a wider world where the actions of others intersect with our own. This chapter looks at enterprise risk management process, focusing on means to assess risks.

The Committee of Sponsoring Organizations of the Treadway Commission (COSO) is an accounting organization concerned with enterprise risk management (ERM). They define ERM as a process designed to identify potential events that may affect the organization, and manage risk to be within that organization's risk appetite in order to provide reasonable assurance of accomplishing the organization's objectives.[1] Risk identification and mitigation are a key component of an organization's ERM program. Table 2.1 outlines this risk framework:

This table is compatible with the overall risk management framework we gave in Chap. 1:

- Risk identification
- Risk assessment and evaluation
- Selection of risk management strategy
- Implementation
- Risk monitoring/mitigation

## Risk Management Process

An important step is to **set the risk appetite** for the organization. No organization can avoid risk. Nor should they insure against every risk. Organizations exist to take on risks in areas where they have developed the capability to cope with risk. However, they cannot cope with every risk, so top management needs to identify



D.L. Olson, D.D. Wu, *Enterprise Risk Management Models*, Springer Texts in Business and Economics, DOI 10.1007/978-3-662-53785-5_2

**Table 2.3** Product risk matrix

| | Likelihood of risk low | Likelihood of risk medium | Likelihood or risk high |
|---|---|---|---|
| Level of risk high | Hedge | Avoid | Avoid |
| Level of risk medium | Control internally | Hedge | Hedge |
| Level of risk low | Accept | Control internally | Control internally |

**Table 2.4** Product/technology risk assessment

| | 1- Fully experienced | 2- | 3- Significant change | 4- | 5- No experience | Score |
|---|---|---|---|---|---|---|
| Current development capability | | | X | | | 3 |
| Technological competency | | X | | | | 2 |
| Intellectual property protection | | | | X | | 4 |
| Manufacturing & service delivery system | X | | | | | 1 |
| Required knowledge | | | X | | | 3 |
| Necessary service | | X | | | | 2 |
| Expected quality | | | X | | | 3 |
| Total | | | | | | 18 |

**Table 2.5** Product/technology failure risk assessment

| | 1- Same as present | 2- | 3- Significant change | 4- | 5- Completely different | Score |
|---|---|---|---|---|---|---|
| Customer behavior | | | | X | | 4 |
| Distribution & sales | | | X | | | 3 |
| Competition | | | | | X | 5 |
| Brand promise | | | | | X | 5 |
| Current customer relationships | | | | | X | 5 |
| Knowledge of competitor behavior | | | | X | | 4 |
| Total | | | | | | 26 |

evaluation of both scales, historical data can be used to calibrate prediction of product success. Scaled measures for product/technology risk could be based on expert product manager evaluations as demonstrated in Table 2.4 for a proposed product, with higher scores associated with less attractive risk positions:

Table 2.5 demonstrates the development of risk assessment of the intended market.

**Table 2.6** Innovation product risk matrix—expert success probability assessments

| | Failure <10 | Failure 10–15 | Failure 15–20 | Failure 20–25 | Failure 25–30 |
|---|---|---|---|---|---|
| Technology 30–35 | 0.50 | 0.40 | 0.30 | 0.15 | 0.01 |
| Technology 25–30 | 0.65 | 0.50 | 0.45 | 0.30 | 0.05 |
| Technology 20–25 | 0.75 | 0.60 | 0.55 | 0.45 | 0.20 |
| Technology 15–20 | 0.80 | 0.70 | 0.65 | 0.55 | **0.30** |
| Technology 10–15 | 0.90 | 0.85 | 0.80 | 0.65 | 0.45 |
| Technology <10 | 0.95 | 0.90 | 0.85 | 0.70 | 0.60 |

Table 2.6 combines these scales, with risk assessment probabilities that should be developed by expert product managers based on historical data to the degree possible.

In Table 2.5, the combination of technology risk score of 18 with product failure risk score 26 is in bold, indicating a risk probability assessment of 0.30.

## Color Matrices

Risk matrices have been applied in many contexts. McIlwain[3] cited the application of clinical risk management in the United Kingdom arising from the National Health Service Litigation Authority creation in April 1995. This triggered systematic analysis of incident reporting on a frequency/severity grid comparing likelihood and consequence. Traffic light colors are often used to categorize risks into three (or more) categories, quickly identifying combinations of frequency and consequence calling for the greatest attention. Table 2.7 demonstrates the use of a risk matrix that could be based on historical data, with green assigned to a proportion of cases with serious incident rates below some threshold (say 0.01), red for high proportions (say 0.10 or greater), and amber in between.

While risk matrices have proven useful, they can be misused as can any tool. Cox[4] provided a critique of some of the many risk matrices in use. Positive examples were shown from the Federal Highway Administration for civil engineering administration (Table 2.8), and the Federal Aviation Administration applied to airport operation safety.

The Federal Aviation Administration risk matrix was quite similar, but used qualitative terms for the likelihood categories (frequent, probable, remote, extremely remote, and extremely improbable) and severity categories (no safety effect, minor, major, hazardous, and catastrophic). Cox identified some characteristics that should be present in risk matrices:

**Table 2.7** Risk matrix of medical events

| | Consequence insignificant | Consequence minor | Consequence moderate | Consequence major | Consequence catastrophic |
|---|---|---|---|---|---|
| Likelihood almost certain | Amber | Red | Red | Red | Red |
| Likelihood likely | Green | Amber | Red | Red | Red |
| Likelihood possible | Green | Amber | Amber | Amber | Red |
| Likelihood unlikely | Green | Green | Amber | Amber | Red |
| Likelihood rare | Green | Green | Green | Amber | Amber |

**Table 2.8** Risk matrix for Federal Highway Administration (2006)

| | Very low impact | Low impact | Medium impact | High impact | Very high impact |
|---|---|---|---|---|---|
| Very high probability | Green | Yellow | Red | Red | Red |
| High probability | Green | Yellow | Red | Red | Red |
| Medium probability | Green | Green | Yellow | Red | Red |
| Low probability | Green | Green | Yellow | Red | Red |
| Very low probability | Green | Green | Green | Yellow | Red |

Extracted from Cox (2008)

1. Under weak consistency conditions, no red cell should share an edge with a green cell
2. No red cell can occur in the left column or in the bottom row
3. There must be at least three colors
4. Too many colors give spurious resolution

Cox argued that risk ratings do not necessarily support good resource allocation decisions. This is due to the inherently subjective categorization of uncertain consequences. Thus Cox argues that theoretical results he presented demonstrate that quantitative and semi-quantitative risk matrices (using numbers instead of categories) cannot correctly reproduce risk ratings, especially if frequency and severity are negatively correlated. Levine suggested that scales in risk matrices are often more appropriately logarithmically scaled rather than linear.[5]

## Quantitative Risk Assessment

It would be ideal to go deeper than risk matrices allow, to be able to identify costs and benefits of risk actions. Risk matrices are simple and useful tools because most of the time, detailed cost and probability data is not available. However, if such data is available, more accurate risk assessment is possible.[6]

Risk can be characterized by the attributes of threat, vulnerability, and consequence, each of which can be expressed in terms of probability. Each of these is uncertain, and in fact these three aspects of risk may be correlated. A normative argument is that if these measures are important but are not known, the organization should invest in obtaining them. Levine demonstrated risk management of computer network security with an example comparing different types of attack in terms of frequency, consequence, and risk. Table 2.9 provides hypothetical data:

In Table 2.9, Risk is defined as the product of frequency and consequence, a common approach. The risk matrix in this case can overlay treatments with cells, as in Table 2.10.

In this case the most attention would be given to identity theft. The others either are relatively low consequence (web vandalism) or relatively low frequency (cyber espionage, denial of service). Looking at the quantitative scale of risk, a bit different outcome is obtained, with cyber espionage and identity theft both being very high, closely followed by denial of service. Web vandalism is lower on this scale. Generally, moving to a more quantitative metric is preferable, with the tradeoff of requiring more data with accuracy an important factor.

To demonstrate, assume the context of a construction firm with a portfolio of ten jobs, involving some risk to worker safety. The firm has a safety program that can be applied to reduce some of these risks to varying degrees on each job. Cox addressed four different levels of risk evaluation, depending upon the level of

**Table 2.9** Hypothetical computer network security data

| Attack type | Label | Frequency | Consequence | Risk |
|---|---|---|---|---|
| Cyber espionage | CE | $10^2$ per year | \$$10^7$ per event | \$$10^9$ per year |
| Denial of service | DS | $10^2$ per year | \$$10^6$ per event | \$$10^8$ per year |
| Identity theft | IT | $10^4$ per year | \$$10^5$ per event | \$$10^9$ per year |
| Web vandalism | WV | $10^3$ per year | \$$10^2$ per event | \$$10^5$ per year |

**Table 2.10** Risk matrix for computer network security

| | Consequence <\$$10^3$/event | Consequence \$$10^3$–≤\$$10^5$/event | Consequence ≥\$$10^6$/event |
|---|---|---|---|
| Frequency >$10^3$ per year | Green | Amber **IT** | Red |
| Frequency >$10^2$–$10^3$ per year | Green **WV** | Amber | Amber |
| Frequency ≤$10^2$ per year | Green | Green | Green **CE DS** |

**Table 2.11** Hypothetical construction data

| Job | Liability risk (k$) | Prob {injury} (frequency) | Expected loss (risk) | Reducible | Savings (k$) | Cost of reducing | RRPUC |
|---|---|---|---|---|---|---|---|
| 1 | 250 | 0.30 | 75.0 | 0.7 | 52.50 | 25 | 2.100 |
| 2 | 300 | 0.20 | 60.0 | 0.5 | 30.00 | 20 | 1.500 |
| 3 | 320 | 0.15 | 48.0 | 0.6 | 28.80 | 25 | 1.152 |
| 4 | 340 | 0.20 | 68.0 | 0.3 | 20.40 | 15 | 1.360 |
| 5 | 370 | 0.11 | 40.7 | 0.5 | 20.35 | 20 | 1.018 |
| 6 | 410 | 0.18 | 73.8 | 0.6 | 44.28 | 25 | 1.771 |
| 7 | 440 | 0.33 | 145.2 | 0.4 | 58.08 | 20 | 2.904 |
| 8 | 460 | 0.25 | 115.0 | 0.7 | 80.50 | 30 | 2.683 |
| 9 | 480 | 0.20 | 96.0 | 0.5 | 48.00 | 20 | 2.400 |
| 10 | 530 | 0.08 | 42.4 | 0.4 | 16.96 | 18 | 0.942 |

**Table 2.12** Hypothetical risk matrix

| | Liability risk low | Liability risk medium | Liability risk high |
|---|---|---|---|
| Prob{injury} high | Assign safety | Assign safety | Subcontract |
| Prob{injury} medium | Insurance only | Assign safety | Assign safety |
| Prob{injury} low | Insurance only | Insurance only | Assign safety |

data available. The risk matrices that we have been looking at require little quantitative data, although as we have demonstrated in Table 2.6, they are more convincing if they are based on quantitative input. Table 2.11 provides full raw data for the ten construction jobs:

In Table 2.11, column 2 is the potential liability due to injury in thousands of dollars. Column 3 is the probability of an injury if no special safety improvement is undertaken. Column 4 is the product of column 2 and column 3, the expected loss without action. Column 5 is the proportion of the injury probability that can be reduced by proposed action, which leads to savings in column 6 (the product of column 4 and column 5). Column 7 is the amount of budget that would be needed to reduce risk. Column 8 (RRPUC) is risk reduction per unit cost.

Table 2.12 gives the risk matrix in categorical terms, using the dimensions of probability of injury {below 0.19; 0.20–0.25; 0.26 and above) and liability risk {below 399; 400–599; 600 and above).

For each combination of injury probability and liability risk has a mitigation strategy assigned. Insurance is obtained in all cases (even for subcontracting). Assigning extra safety personnel costs additional expense. Subcontracting sacrifices quite a bit of expected profit, and thus is to be avoided except in extreme cases. This table demonstrates what Cox expressed as a limitation in that while the risk matrix is quick and easy, it is a simplification that can be improved upon. Cox suggested three indices, each requiring additional accurate inputs.

**Table 2.13** Ranking by index

| Risk index ranking | Budget (k$) | Risk reduction index ranking | Budget (k$) | RRPUC ranking | Budget (k$) |
|---|---|---|---|---|---|
| Job 7 | 20 | Job 8 | 30 | Job 7 | 20 |
| Job 8 | 30 | Job 7 | 20 | Job 8 | 30 |
| Job 9 | 20 | Job 1 | 25 | Job 9 | 20 |
| Job 1 | 25 | Job 9 | 20 | Job 1 | 25 |
| Job 6 | 25 | Job 6 | 25 | Job 6 | 25 |
| Job 4 | 15 | Job 2 | 20 | Job 2 | 20 |
| Job 2 | 20 | Job 3 | 25 | Job 4 | 15 |
| Job 3 | 25 | Job 4 | 15 | Job 3 | 25 |
| Job 10 | 18 | Job 5 | 20 | Job 5 | 20 |
| Job 5 | 20 | Job 10 | 18 | Job 10 | 18 |

**Table 2.14** Risk reductions achieved by index

| Budget | Risk index | Risk reduction index | RRPUC |
|---|---|---|---|
| $100k | 247.936 | 247.936 | 247.936 |
| $150k | 326.260 | 324.880 | 326.961 |

The first index is to use risk (the expected loss column in Table 2.11), the second risk reduction (savings column in Table 2.11), the third the risk reduction per unit cost (RRPUC column in Table 2.11). These would yield different rankings of which jobs should receive the greatest attention. In all three cases, the contention is that there is a risk reduction budget available to be applied, starting with the top-ranked job and adding jobs until the budget is exhausted. Table 2.13 shows rankings and budget required by job.

If there were a budget of $100k, using the risk ranking jobs 7, 8, 9, and 1 would be given extra safety effort, as well as a 20 % effort on job 6. With the risk reduction index as well as the RRPUC index, a different order of selection would be applied, here yielding the same set of jobs. For a budget of $150k, the risk index would provide full treatment to job 6, add job 4, and 75 % of job 2. The risk reduction index would also provide full treatment to job 6, add job 2, and provide 40 % coverage to job 3. The RRPUC index also would again provide full treatment to job 6, add job 2, and 2/3rds coverage to job 4. The idea of all three indices is much the same, but with more information provided. Table 2.14 shows the expected gains from these two budget levels for each index:

Given a budget of $100k, the risk index would reduce expected losses by $58.08k on job 7, $80.50k on job 8, $48k on job 9, $52.50k on job 1, and $8.856k on job 6, for total risk reduction of $247.936k. As we saw, this was the same for all three indices. But there is a difference given a budget of $150k. Here the risk index actually comes out a bit higher than the risk reduction index, but Cox has run simulations showing that risk reduction should provide a bit better performance. The RRPUC has to be at least as good as the other two, as its basis is the sorting key. The primary point is that there are ways to incorporate more complete information into risk management. The tradeoff is between the availability of information and accuracy of output.

## Strategy/Risk Matrix

Risk matrices can be applied to capture the essence of tradeoffs in risk and other measures of value. In this case, we apply a risk matrix to a construction industry study where the original authors applied an analytic hierarchy model.[7] The model is relatively straightforward. The construction context included a number of types of work, each with a relative rating of supply risk along with a similar weighting of strategic impact. Data is given in Table 2.15:

Figure 2.1 displays a scatter diagram of this data:

**Table 2.15** Construction work risk and impact

| Type | Supply risk | Strategic impact |
|---|---|---|
| Cement | 0.05 | 0.34 |
| Workforce | 0.09 | 0.40 |
| Aggregate | 0.11 | 0.58 |
| Transport | 0.12 | 0.18 |
| Demolition | 0.12 | 0.38 |
| Painting | 0.15 | 0.25 |
| Misc | 0.15 | 0.28 |
| Steel | 0.15 | 0.65 |
| Insulation | 0.16 | 0.18 |
| Travel | 0.17 | 0.29 |
| Cast iron | 0.18 | 0.23 |
| Excavation | 0.20 | 0.26 |
| Locksmith | 0.21 | 0.36 |
| Floor cover | 0.22 | 0.23 |
| Infrastructure | 0.23 | 0.58 |
| Sanitary | 0.23 | 0.70 |
| Ceilings | 0.25 | 0.24 |
| Geotechnical | 0.25 | 0.29 |
| Electrical | 0.25 | 0.57 |
| Climate | 0.26 | 0.34 |
| Aluminum | 0.31 | 0.24 |
| Formwork | 0.31 | 0.31 |
| Concrete | 0.46 | 0.92 |
| Mosaic | 0.51 | 0.26 |
| Carpentry | 0.54 | 0.24 |
| Special forming | 0.56 | 0.31 |
| Stone | 0.59 | 0.24 |
| Scaffolding | 0.62 | 0.29 |

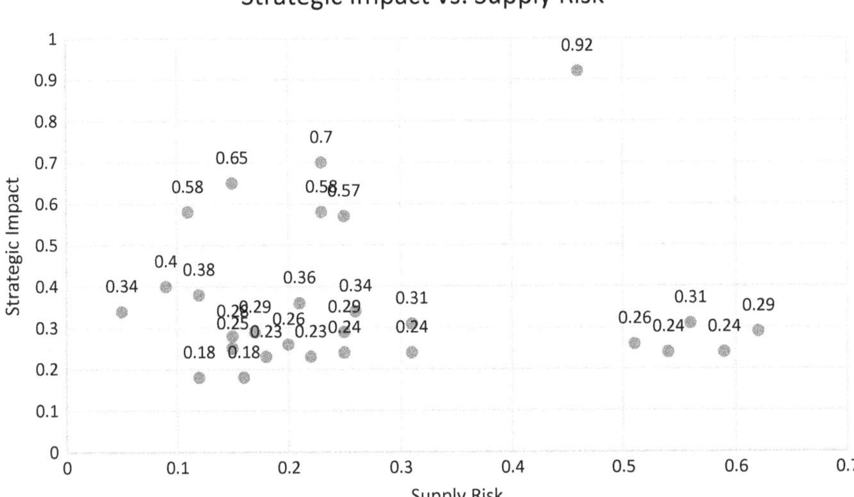


**Fig. 2.1** Strategic impact plotted against supply risk

**Table 2.16** Risk matrix of risk/strategic impact tradeoff

| | Supply risk ≤0.2 | Supply risk >0.2– ≤ 0.5 | Supply risk >0.5– ≤ 0.8 | Supply risk >0.8 |
|---|---|---|---|---|
| Strategic impact >0.8 | Add risk control | Outsource | Outsource | Outsource |
| Strategic impact >0.5– ≤ 0.8 | Add risk control | Add risk control | Outsource | Outsource |
| Strategic impact >0.2– ≤ 0.5 | Normal operation | Normal operation | Add risk control | Outsource |
| Strategic impact ≤0.2 | Normal operation | Normal operation | Normal operation | Add risk control |

Construction contexts could differ widely, but we will assume an operation where the greatest profit is expected from conducting operations normally. Risk can be reduced by spending extra money in the form of added inspection and safety supervisors, but this would eat into profit. The least profit would be expected from an option to outsource construction, placing the risk on subcontractors. The criteria can be sorted in a risk matrix considering both dimensions, as in Table 2.16:

In this case, this policy would result in outsourcing (subcontracting) concrete work, which has a supply risk rating of 0.46 and a very high strategic impact of 0.92. Added risk control would be adopted for ten other types of work: aggregate, steel, infrastructure, sanitary, electrical, mosaic, carpentry, special forming and scaffolding, and stone.

## Conclusions

The study of risk management has grown in the last decade in response to serious incidences threatening trust in business operations. The field is evolving, but the first step is generally considered to be application of a systematic process, beginning with consideration of the organization's risk appetite. Then risks facing the organization need to be identified, controls generated, and review of the risk management process along with historical documentation and records for improvement of the process.

Risk matrices are a means to consider the risk components of threat severity and probability. They have been used in a number of contexts, basic applications of which were reviewed. Cox and Levine provide useful critiques of the use of risk matrices. That same author also suggested more accurate quantitative analytic tools. An ideal approach would be to expend such measurement funds only if they enable reducing overall cost. The interesting aspect is that we don't really know. Thus we would argue that if you have accurate data (and it is usually worth measuring whatever you can), you should get as close to this ideal as you can. Risk matrices provide valuable initial tools when high levels of uncertainty are present. Quantitative risk assessment in the form of indices as demonstrated would be preferred if data to support it is available.

## Notes

1. Prasad, S.B. (2011) A matrixed assessment. *Internal Auditor* 68(6), 63–64.
2. Day, G.S. (2007). Is it real? Can we win? Is it worth doing? Managing risk and reward in an innovation portfolio, *Harvard Business Review* 85:12, 110–120.
3. McIlwain, J.C. (2006). A review: A decade of clinical risk management and risk tools, *Clinician in Management* 14:4, 189–199.
4. Cox, L.A. Jr. (2008). What's wrong with risk matrices? *Risk Analysis* 28:2, 497–512.
5. Levine, E.S. (2012). Improving risk matrices: The advantages of logarithmically scaled axes. *Journal of Risk Research* 15(2), 209–222.
6. Cox, L.A., Jr. (2012). Evaluating and improving risk formulas for allocating limited budgets to expensive risk-reduction opportunities. *Risk Analysis* 32(7), 1244–1252.
7. Ferreira, L.M.D.F., Arantes, A. and Kharlamov, A.A. (2015). Development of a purchasing portfolio model for the construct6ion industry: An empirical study. *Production Planning & Control* 26(5), 377–392.

# Value-Focused Supply Chain Risk Analysis 3

A fundamental premise of Keeney's book[1] is that decision makers should not settle for those alternatives that are thrust upon them. The conventional solution process is to generate alternative solutions to a problem, and then focus on objectives. This framework tends to suppose an environment where decision makers are powerless to do anything but choose among given alternatives. It is suggested that a more fruitful approach would be for decision makers to take more control over this process, and use objectives to create alternatives, based on what the decision makers would like to achieve, and why objectives are important.

## Hierarchy Structuring

Structuring translates an initially ill-defined problem into a set of well-defined elements, relations, and operations. This chapter is based on concepts presented in Keeney, and in Olson.[2]

Before we discuss hierarchies and their structure, we should give some basic definitions. Keeney and Raiffa[3] gave the following definitions:

**Objective**—the preferred direction of movement on some measure of value
**Attribute**—a dimension of measurement

Keeney and Raiffa distinguish between **utility** models, based upon tradeoffs of return and risk found in von Neumann-Morgenstern utility theory and the more general **value** models allowing tradeoffs among any set of objectives and sub-objectives. **Preferential independence** concerns whether the decision maker's preference among attainment levels on two criteria do not depend on changes in other attribute levels. **Attribute independence** is a statistical concept measured by correlation. Preferential independence is a property of the desires of the decision maker, not the alternatives available.



D.L. Olson, D.D. Wu, *Enterprise Risk Management Models*, Springer Texts in Business and Economics, DOI 10.1007/978-3-662-53785-5_3

**Table 3.1** Value hierarchy for supply chain risk

| Top Level | Second Level | Third Level |
|---|---|---|
| Product | Quality | |
| | Cost | Price |
| | | Investment required |
| | | Holding cost/service level tradeoff |
| | On-time delivery | |
| Service | Manufacturability | Outsourcing opportunity cost/risk tradeoff |
| | | Ability to expand production |
| | | New technology breakthroughs |
| | | Product obsolescence |
| | Deliverability | Transportation system |
| | | Insurance cost |
| Management | Communication | IS breakdown |
| | | Distorted information leading to bullwhip effect |
| | | Forecast accuracy |
| | | Integration |
| | | Viruses/bugs/hackers |
| | Flexibility | Agility of sources |
| | | Ability to replace sources as needed |
| | Safety | Plant disaster |
| | Labor | Risk of strikes, disputes |
| Political | Government | Customs and regulations |
| | War and Terrorism | |
| Economic | Overall economy | Economic downturn |
| | | Exchange rate risk |
| | Specific regional economy | Labor cost influence |
| | | Changes in competitive advantage |
| | Specific market | Price fluctuation |
| | | Customer demand volatility |
| | | Customer payment |
| Natural disaster | | Uncontrollable disaster |
| | | Diseases, epidemics |

ability of the supply chain to communicate, and to be agile in response to changes. There are also external risks, which we cluster into the three areas of political (regulation, as well as war and terrorism), economic (overall economic climate as well as the behavior of the specific market being served), and natural disaster. Each of these hierarchical elements can then be used to identify specific risks for a given supply chain situation. We use those identified in Table 3.1 to develop a value hierarchy.

The next step in multiple attribute analysis is to generate the alternatives. There are a number of decisions that might be made, to include vendor selection, plant siting, information system selection, or the decision to enter specific markets by region or country. For some of these, there may be binary decisions (enter a country's market or not), or there might be a number of variants (including different degrees of entering a specific market). In vendor selection and in plant siting, there may be very many alternatives. Usually, multiple attribute analysis focuses on two to seven alternatives that are selected as most appropriate through some screening process. Part of the benefit of value analysis is that better alternatives may be designed as part of the hierarchical development, seeking better solutions performing well on all features.

## Suggestions for Cases Where Preferential Independence Is Absent

If an independence assumption is found to be inappropriate, either a fundamental objective has been overlooked or means objectives are beings used as fundamental objectives. Therefore, identification of the absence of independence should lead to greater understanding of the decision maker's fundamental objectives.

## Multiattribute Analysis

The next step of the process is to conduct multiattribute analysis. There are a number of techniques that can be applied.[7] Multiattribute utility theory (MAUT) can be supported by software products such as Logical Decision, which are usually applied in more thorough and precise analyses. The simple multiattribute rating theory (SMART)[8] can be used with spreadsheet support, and is usually the easiest method to use. Analytic hierarchy process can also be applied, as was the case in all of the cases applying multiple objective analysis. Expert Choice software is available, but allows only seven branches, so is a bit more restrictive than MAUT, and much more restrictive than SMART. Furthermore, the number of pairwise comparisons required in AHP grows enormously with the number of branches. Still, users often are willing to apply AHP and feel confident in its results.[9] Here we will demonstrate using SMART for a decision involving site selection of a plant within a supply chain.

# The SMART Technique

Edwards proposed a ten step technique. Some of these steps include the process of identifying objectives and organization of these objectives into a hierarchy. Guidelines concerning the pruning of these objectives to a reasonable number were provided.

**Step 1: Identify the person or organization whose utilities are to be maximized** Edwards argued that MAUT could be applied to public decisions in the same manner as was proposed for individual decision making.

**Step 2: Identify the issue or issues** Utility depends on the context and purpose of the decision.

**Step 3: Identify the alternatives to be evaluated** This step would identify the outcomes of possible actions, a data gathering process.

**Step 4: Identify the relevant dimensions of value for evaluation of the alternatives** It is important to limit the dimensions of value to those that are important for this particular decision. This can be accomplished by restating and combining goals, or by omitting less important goals. Edwards argued that it was not necessary to have a complete list of goals. If the weight for a particular goal is quite low, that goal need not be included. There is no precise range of goals for all decisions. However, eight goals was considered sufficiently large for most cases, and fifteen too many.

**Step 5: Rank the dimensions in order of importance** For decisions made by one person, this step is fairly straightforward. Ranking is a decision task that is easier than developing weights, for instance. This task is usually more difficult in group environments. However, groups including diverse opinions can lead to a more thorough analysis of relative importance, as all sides of the issue are more likely to be voiced. An initial discussion could provide all group members with a common information base. This could be followed by identification of individual judgments of relative ranking.

**Step 6: Rate dimensions in importance, preserving ratios** The least important dimension would be assigned an importance of 10. The next-least-important dimension is assigned a number reflecting the ratio of relative importance to the least important dimension. This process is continued, checking implied ratios as each new judgment is made. Since this requires a growing number of comparisons, there is a very practical need to limit the number of dimensions (objectives). Edwards expected that different individuals in the group would have different relative ratings.

**Step 7: Sum the importance weights, and divide each by the sum** This step allows normalization of the relative importances into weights summing to 1.0.

**Step 8: Measure the location of each alternative being evaluated on each dimension** Dimensions were classified into the groups: subjective, partly subjective, and purely objective. For subjective dimensions, an expert in this field would estimate the value of an alternative on a 0–100 scale, with 0 as the minimum plausible value and 100 the maximum plausible value. For partly subjective dimensions, objective measures exist, but attainment values for specific alternatives must be estimated. Purely objective dimensions can be measured. Raiffa advocated identification of utility curves by dimension.[10] Edwards proposed the simpler expedient of connecting the maximum plausible and minimum plausible values with a straight line.[11] It was argued that the straight line approach would provide an acceptably accurate approximation.

**Step 9: Calculate utilities for alternatives** $U_j = \Sigma_k w_k u_{jk}$ where $U_j$ is the utility value for alternative j, $w_k$ is the normalized weight for objective k, and $u_{jk}$ is the scaled value for alternative j on dimension k. $\Sigma_k w_k = 1$. The $w_k$ values were obtained from Step 7 and the $u_{jk}$ values were generated in Step 8.

**Step 10: Decide** If a single alternative is to be selected, select the alternative with maximum $U_j$. If a budget constraint existed, rank order alternatives in the order of $U_j/C_j$ where $C_j$ is the cost of alternative j. Then alternatives are selected in order of highest ratio first until the budget is exhausted.

## Plant Siting Decision

Assume that a supply chain vendor is considering sites for a new production facility. Management has considered the factors that they feel are important in this decision (the criteria):

- Acquisition and building cost
- Expected cost per unit
- Work force ability to produce quality product
- Work force propensity for labor dispute
- Transportation system reliability
- Expandability
- Agility to changes in demand
- Information system linkage
- Insurance structure
- Tax structure
- Governmental stability
- Risk of disaster

Each of these factors need to be measured in some way. If possible, objective data would be preferred, but often subjective expert estimates are all that is available. The alternatives need to be identified as well. There are an infinite number of sites. But the number considered is always filtered down to a smaller number. Here we will start with ten options. Each of them has estimates performances on each of the twelve criteria listed (Table 3.2):

**Table 3.2** Plant siting data

| Location | A&B | UnitC | Quality | Labor | Trans | Expand |
|---|---|---|---|---|---|---|
| Alabama | $20 m | $5.50 | High | Moderate | 0.30 | Good |
| Utah | $23 m | $5.60 | High | Good | 0.28 | Poor |
| Oregon | $24 m | $5.40 | High | Low | 0.31 | Moderate |
| Mexico | $18 m | $3.40 | Moderate | Moderate | 0.25 | Good |
| Crete | $21 m | $6.20 | High | Low | 0.85 | Poor |
| Indonesia | $15 m | $2.80 | Moderate | Moderate | 0.70 | Fair |
| Vietnam | $12 m | $2.50 | Good | Good | 0.75 | Good |
| India | $13 m | $3.00 | Good | Good | 0.80 | Good |
| China #1 | $17 m | $3.10 | Good | Good | 0.60 | Fair |
| China #2 | $15 m | $3.20 | Good | Good | 0.55 | Good |

| Location | Agility | IS link | Insurance | Tax | Govt | Disaster |
|---|---|---|---|---|---|---|
| Alabama | 2 mos | Very good | $400 | $1000 | Very good | Hurricane |
| Utah | 3 mos | Very good | $350 | $1200 | Very good | Drought |
| Oregon | 1 mo | Very good | $450 | $1500 | Good | Flood |
| Mexico | 4 mos | Good | $300 | $1800 | Fair | Quake |
| Crete | 5 mos | Good | $600 | $3500 | Good | Quake |
| Indonesia | 3 mos | Poor | $700 | $800 | Fair | Monsoon |
| Vietnam | 2 mos | Good | $600 | $700 | Good | Monsoon |
| India | 3 mos | Very good | $700 | $900 | Very good | Monsoon |
| China #1 | 2 mos | Very good | $800 | $1200 | Very good | Quake |
| China #2 | 3 mos | Very good | $500 | $1300 | Very good | Quake |

Each of the choices involves some tradeoff. With twelve criteria, it will be rare that one alternative (of the final set of filtered choices) will dominate another, meaning that it is at least as good or better on all criteria measures, and strictly better on at least one criterion.

Each measure can now be assigned a value score on a 0–1 scale, with 0 being the worst performance imaginable, and 1 being the best performance imaginable. This reflects the decision maker's perception, a subjective value. For our data (Table 3.3), a possible set of values could be:

The SMART method now needs to identify relative weights for the importance of each criterion in the opinion of the decision maker or decision making group. This process begins by sorting the criteria by importance. One possible ranking:

- Work force ability to produce quality product
- Expected cost per unit
- Risk of disaster
- Agility to changes in demand
- Transportation system reliability
- Expandability
- Governmental stability
- Tax structure

**Table 3.3** Standardized scores for plant siting data

| Location | A&B | UnitC | Quality | Labor | Trans | Expand |
|---|---|---|---|---|---|---|
| Alabama | 0.60 | 0.40 | 0.90 | 0.30 | 0.90 | 1.0 |
| Utah | 0.30 | 0.35 | 0.90 | 0.80 | 0.95 | 0 |
| Oregon | 0.10 | 0.45 | 0.90 | 0.10 | 0.86 | 0.5 |
| Mexico | 0.70 | 0.80 | 0.40 | 0.30 | 1.00 | 1.0 |
| Crete | 0.50 | 0.20 | 0.90 | 0.10 | 0.30 | 0 |
| Indonesia | 0.80 | 0.90 | 0.40 | 0.30 | 0.55 | 0.3 |
| Vietnam | 0.90 | 0.95 | 0.60 | 0.80 | 0.50 | 1.0 |
| India | 0.85 | 0.87 | 0.60 | 0.80 | 0.40 | 1.0 |
| China #1 | 0.75 | 0.85 | 0.60 | 0.80 | 0.60 | 0.3 |
| China #2 | 0.80 | 0.83 | 0.60 | 0.80 | 0.70 | 1.0 |
| Location | Agility | IS link | Insurance | Tax | Govt | Disaster |
| Alabama | 0.8 | 1.0 | 0.70 | 0.80 | 1.0 | 0.5 |
| Utah | 0.6 | 1.0 | 0.80 | 0.70 | 1.0 | 0.9 |
| Oregon | 1.0 | 1.0 | 0.60 | 0.60 | 0.8 | 0.8 |
| Mexico | 0.4 | 0.7 | 1.00 | 0.40 | 0.4 | 0.4 |
| Crete | 0.2 | 0.7 | 0.50 | 0.00 | 0.8 | 0.3 |
| Indonesia | 0.6 | 0 | 0.30 | 0.90 | 0.4 | 0.7 |
| Vietnam | 0.8 | 0.7 | 0.50 | 1.00 | 0.8 | 0.7 |
| India | 0.6 | 1.0 | 0.30 | 0.85 | 1.0 | 0.7 |
| China #1 | 0.8 | 1.0 | 0.10 | 0.70 | 1.0 | 0.8 |
| China #2 | 0.6 | 1.0 | 0.55 | 0.65 | 1.0 | 0.4 |

Note that for the Disaster criterion, specifics for each locale can lead to different ratings for the same major risk category.

- Insurance structure
- Acquisition and building cost
- Information system linkage
- Work force propensity for labor dispute

The SMART method proceeds by assigning the most important criterion a value of 1.0, and then assessing relative importance by considering the proportional worth of moving from the worst to the best on the most important criterion (quality) and moving from the worst to the best on the criterion compared to it. For instance, the decision maker might judge moving from the worst possible unit cost to the best possible unit cost to be 0.8 as important as moving from the worst possible quality to the best possible quality. We assume the following ratings based on this procedure:

| Criterion | | Rating | Proportion |
|---|---|---|---|
| Work force ability to produce quality product | Quality | 1.00 | 0.167 |
| Expected cost per unit | UnitC | 0.80 | 0.133 |
| Risk of disaster | Disaster | 0.70 | 0.117 |

(continued)

| Agility to changes in demand | Agility | 0.65 | 0.108 |
|---|---|---|---|
| Transportation system reliability | Trans | 0.60 | 0.100 |
| Expandability | Expand | 0.58 | 0.097 |
| Government stability | Govt | 0.40 | 0.067 |
| Tax structure | Tax | 0.35 | 0.058 |
| Insurance structure | Insurance | 0.32 | 0.053 |
| Acquisition and building cost | A&B | 0.30 | 0.050 |
| Information system linkage | IS link | 0.20 | 0.033 |
| Work force propensity for labor dispute | Labor | 0.10 | 0.017 |

Proportion is obtained by dividing each rating by the sum of ratings (6.00). Overall value for each alternative site can then be ranked by the sumproduct of criterion relative importances times the matrix of scores on criteria.

| Location | A&B | UnitC | Quality | Labor | Trans | Expand | Agility | IS link | Insurance | Tax | Govt | Disaster |
|---|---|---|---|---|---|---|---|---|---|---|---|---|
| weight | 0.05 | 0.133 | 0.167 | 0.017 | 0.1 | 0.097 | 0.108 | 0.033 | 0.053 | 0.058 | 0.067 | 0.117 |
| Alabama | 0.6 | 0.4 | 0.9 | 0.3 | 0.9 | 1 | 0.8 | 1 | 0.7 | 0.8 | 1 | 0.5 |
| Utah | 0.3 | 0.35 | 0.9 | 0.8 | 0.95 | 0 | 0.6 | 1 | 0.8 | 0.7 | 1 | 0.9 |
| Oregon | 0.1 | 0.45 | 0.9 | 0.1 | 0.86 | 0.5 | 1 | 1 | 0.6 | 0.6 | 0.8 | 0.8 |
| Mexico | 0.7 | 0.8 | 0.4 | 0.3 | 1 | 1 | 0.4 | 0.7 | 1 | 0.4 | 0.4 | 0.4 |
| Crete | 0.5 | 0.2 | 0.9 | 0.1 | 0.3 | 0 | 0.2 | 0.7 | 0.5 | 0 | 0.8 | 0.3 |
| Indonesia | 0.8 | 0.9 | 0.4 | 0.3 | 0.55 | 0.3 | 0.6 | 0 | 0.3 | 0.9 | 0.4 | 0.7 |
| Vietnam | 0.9 | 0.95 | 0.6 | 0.8 | 0.5 | 1 | 0.8 | 0.7 | 0.5 | 1 | 0.8 | 0.7 |
| India | 0.85 | 0.87 | 0.6 | 0.8 | 0.4 | 1 | 0.6 | 1 | 0.3 | 0.85 | 1 | 0.7 |
| China #1 | 0.75 | 0.85 | 0.6 | 0.8 | 0.6 | 0.3 | 0.8 | 1 | 0.1 | 0.7 | 1 | 0.8 |
| China #2 | 0.8 | 0.83 | 0.6 | 0.8 | 0.7 | 1 | 0.6 | 1 | 0.55 | 0.65 | 1 | 0.4 |

This analysis ranks the alternatives as follows:

| Rank | Site | Score |
|---|---|---|
| 1 | Vietnam | 0.762 |
| 2 | Alabama | 0.754 |
| 3 | India | 0.721 |
| 4 | China #2 | 0.710 |
| 5 | Oregon | 0.706 |
| 6 | China #1 | 0.679 |
| 7 | Utah | 0.674 |
| 8 | Mexico | 0.626 |
| 9 | Indonesia | 0.557 |
| 10 | Crete | 0.394 |

This indicates a close result for Vietnam and Alabama, with the first seven sites all reasonably close as well. There are a couple of approaches. More detailed comparisons might be made between Vietnam and Alabama. Another approach is to look at characteristics that these alternatives were rated low on, with the idea that maybe the site's characteristics could be improved.

## Conclusions

Structuring of a value hierarchy is a relatively subjective activity, with a great deal of possible latitude. It is good to have a complete hierarchy, including everything that could be of importance to the decision maker. However, this yields unworkable analyses. Hierarchies should focus on those criteria that are important in discriminating among available alternatives. The key to hierarchy structuring is to identify those criteria that are most important to the decision maker, and that will help the decision maker make the required choice.

This chapter presented the value-focused approach, and the SMART method. These were demonstrated in the context of the supply chain risk management decision of selecting a plant location for production of a component. The methods apply for any decision involving multiple criteria.

## Notes

1. Keeney, R.L. (1992). *Value-Focused Thinking: A Path to Creative Decisionmaking*. Cambridge, MA: Harvard University Press.
2. Olson, D.L. (1996). *Decision Aids for Selection Problems*. New York: Springer.
3. Keeney, R.L. & Raiffa, H. (1976). *Decisions with Multiple Objectives: Preferences and Value Tradeoffs*. New York: John Wiley & Sons.
4. Saaty, T.L. (1988). *Decision Making for Leaders: The Analytic Hierarchy Process for Decisions in a Complex World*. Pittsburgh: RWS Publications.
5. Keeney, R.L., Renn, O. and von Winterfeldt, D. (1987). Structuring Germany's energy objectives, *Energy Policy* 15, 352–362.
6. Neiger, D., Rotaru, K and Churilov, L. (2009). Supply chain risk identification with value-focused process engineering, *Journal of Operations Management* 27, 154–168.
7. Olson (1996), op cit.
8. Edwards, W. (1977). How to use multiattribute utility measurement for social decisionmaking, *IEEE Transactions on Systems, Man, and Cybernetics*, SMC-7:5, 326–340.
9. Olson, D.L., Moshkovich, H.M., Schellenberger, R. and Mechitov, A.I. (1995). Consistency and Accuracy in Decision Aids: Experiments with Four Multiattribute Systems, *Decision Sciences* **26**:6, 723–749; Olson, D.L., Mechitov, A.I. and Moshkovich, H. (1998). Cognitive Effort and Learning Features of Decision Aids: Review of Experiments, *Journal of Decision Systems* **7**:2, 129–146.
10. Raiffa, H. (1968). *Decision Analysis*. Reading, MA: Addison-Wesley.
11. Edwards, W. (1977), op cit.

# 4 Examples of Supply Chain Decisions Trading Off Criteria

We encountered five recent cases in supply chain risk management that applied multiple criteria analysis models to supply chain risk management decisions. We present value analysis and SMART models, using the contexts of the other studies as a basis. We have simplified the longer models with the intent of presenting the essence of the decision context, while demonstrating value analysis. In this chapter we review these five cases, which usually applied analysis to evaluate alternative suppliers, either relatively as sources of various types of risk, or in a selection decision.

## Case 1: Öztűrk and Özçelik (2014)[1]

This study focused on a method to identify suppliers with emphasis on sustainable awareness. They utilized the triple bottom line paradigm, considering sustainability along with social and financial aspects. These authors used TOPSIS,[2] which has the relative advantage over SMART of being applicable to large numbers of alternatives. But the treatment of criteria, weights, and scores is common to TOPSIS and SMART. They also used fuzzy modeling, and a group context, but since they converted fuzzy input to crisp numbers and used a group decision set of preferences, the method works the same once numbers are modified. Based on the data provided in their paper, we can infer the following risk order. We provided specific swing weights in Table 4.1:

Scores for suppliers (which we made up) on each criterion are given below, along with resultant value scores in Table 4.2:

Supplier 1 has stronger characteristics with respect to quality, environmental issues and safety, but is expensive. Supplier 2 has good quality, moderate risk and moderate cost. Supplier 3 has lower quality, higher risk, and lowest cost. With this set of scores and one particular set of weights, supplier 2, who emphasizes quality, has the highest score. Value analysis provides a means to utilize these scores to identify areas of potential improvement.


D.L. Olson, D.D. Wu, *Enterprise Risk Management Models*, Springer Texts in Business and Economics, DOI 10.1007/978-3-662-53785-5_4

**Table 4.4** Case 2 Scores

| Risk | Weights | Supplier1 | Supplier2 | Supplier3 |
|---|---|---|---|---|
| Env3: Natural disasters | **0.184** | 0.70 | **0.80** | 0.30 |
| Env4: Economic downturns | **0.123** | **0.60** | 0.50 | 0.20 |
| Dem1: Sudden demand fluctuation | **0.099** | 0.70 | **0.90** | 0.10 |
| Env2: Political instability | **0.077** | **0.95** | 0.80 | 0.20 |
| Dem2: Market changes | **0.075** | 0.70 | **0.80** | 0.40 |
| Sup4: Sudden hike in costs | **0.066** | 0.50 | **0.70** | 0.30 |
| Env1: Terrorism | **0.055** | **0.80** | 0.50 | 0.10 |
| Sup1: Outsourcing risks | **0.053** | **1.00** | 1.00 | 0.30 |
| Dem4: Forecasting errors | **0.050** | 0.70 | 0.80 | 0.40 |
| Sup2: Supplier insolvency | **0.050** | 0.60 | **0.80** | 0.30 |
| Proc1: Machine failure | **0.037** | 0.90 | **0.95** | 0.50 |
| Sup3: Supply quality | **0.029** | 0.90 | **1.00** | 0.40 |
| Proc3: Quality problems | **0.028** | 0.95 | **1.00** | 0.50 |
| Dem3: Competition change | **0.026** | 0.80 | **0.90** | 0.50 |
| Proc2: Labor strike | **0.020** | **0.80** | 0.40 | 0.50 |
| Proc4: Technological change | **0.015** | 0.70 | 0.50 | **1.00** |
| Env5: Social & cultural grievances | **0.013** | **0.70** | 0.60 | 0.20 |
| **Value scores** | | 0.735 | **0.765** | 0.296 |

relatively inferior except for the ability to adapt to technological change. Furthermore, this set of criteria focused on risk, without emphasis on cost advantage. Suppliers usually can't do much about these types of risks—they are inherent in location. It is possible that such risks might be valuable to consider in site location decisions.

## Case 3: Onat, Gumus, Kucukvar and Tatari (2006)[4]

This study used TOPSIS and intuitionist fuzzy multi-criteria decision making modeling to evaluate alternative vehicle technologies. They compared seven types of vehicles with 16 criteria (using the triple bottom line paradigm of economic, social, and environmental) as in Table 4.5:

The seven vehicle types were:

- Internal combustion vehicles (ICV)
- Hybrid electric vehicles (HEV)
- Plug-in electric range 10 miles (P10)
- Plug-in electric range 20 miles (P20)
- Plug-in electric range 30 miles (P30)
- Plug-in electric range 40 miles (P40)
- Battery elective vehicles (BEV)

Table 4.6 gives scores and shows value calculations:

**Table 4.5** Case 3 Weight development

| Criteria | Rank | Based on 1st | Weight |
|---|---|---|---|
| Env7: Total GHG emissions | 1–2 | 100 | 0.084 |
| Env9: Water withdrawal | 1–2 | 100 | 0.084 |
| Env8: Total energy consumption | 3 | 99 | 0.083 |
| Soc1: Employment | 4 | 96 | 0.081 |
| Soc3: Injuries | 5 | 85 | 0.072 |
| Econ1: Foreign Purchases | 6–9 | 79 | 0.066 |
| Econ3: GDP | 6–9 | 79 | 0.066 |
| Env5: Carbon fossil fuel | 6–9 | 79 | 0.066 |
| Env6: Carbon electricity | 6–9 | 79 | 0.066 |
| Env3: Forestry | 10 | 74 | 0.062 |
| Env4: Cropland | 11–12 | 68 | 0.057 |
| Env10: Hazard waste | 11–12 | 68 | 0.057 |
| Soc2: Tax | 13 | 63 | 0.053 |
| Econ2: Profit | 14 | 58 | 0.049 |
| Env2: Grazing | 15 | 48 | 0.04 |
| Env1: Fishery | 16 | 13 | 0.011 |
| **Total** | | 1188 | |

**Table 4.6** Case 3 scoring

| | Weight | ICV | HEV | P10 | P20 | P30 | P40 | BEV |
|---|---|---|---|---|---|---|---|---|
| Env7 | 0.084 | **1.00** | .40 | .30 | .25 | .30 | .35 | .70 |
| Env9 | 0.084 | .40 | .30 | .60 | .70 | .80 | .90 | **1.00** |
| Env8 | 0.083 | **.90** | .40 | .50 | .60 | .70 | .80 | .85 |
| Soc1 | 0.081 | .60 | .58 | .40 | .45 | .50 | .70 | **.90** |
| Soc3 | 0.072 | .70 | .75 | .50 | .55 | .65 | .75 | **.80** |
| Econ1 | 0.066 | **.50** | .40 | .34 | .30 | .32 | .36 | .38 |
| Econ3 | 0.066 | .40 | .38 | .30 | .36 | .37 | .39 | **.60** |
| Env5 | 0.066 | **.60** | .40 | .38 | .34 | .34 | .34 | .50 |
| Env6 | 0.066 | .60 | .50 | .35 | .37 | .40 | .48 | **.70** |
| Env3 | 0.062 | .40 | .45 | .30 | .35 | .60 | .70 | **.90** |
| Env4 | 0.057 | .60 | .50 | .40 | .45 | .55 | .65 | **.80** |
| Env10 | 0.057 | **1.00** | .60 | .40 | .30 | .25 | .20 | .10 |
| Soc2 | 0.053 | **.80** | .70 | .60 | .50 | .40 | .30 | .35. |
| Econ2 | 0.049 | .60 | .55 | .50 | .53 | .70 | .75 | **.90** |
| Env2 | 0.040 | **.70** | **.70** | .50 | .60 | .60 | .65 | **.70** |
| Env1 | 0.011 | .60 | .55 | .40 | .55 | .60 | .70 | **.90** |
| **Value** | | 0.652 | 0.493 | 0.421 | 0.443 | 0.501 | 0.564 | **0.677** |

## Value Analysis

In this case, there were clear distinguishing performance scores, and each of the alternatives has some compensating advantage. There were quite a few criteria. While it is often best to focus on fewer criteria, if there are a number of measurable items falling into clear categories, as is the case here, it can work. In this case criterion Env1 (related to fisheries) there is very little impact, and in fact the small weight of 0.011 is further minimized by the range of scores of the seven alternatives (0.4–0.9).

Alternative BEV scores highest, and is best on many metrics, weak on hazardous waste, tax, and foreign purchases. Alternative ICV is very close to BEV in weighted score, with strenchts in GHG emission, hazardous waste, and energy consumption while having slight weakness on water withdrawal and GDP impact. The HEV vehicle has few strengths, although it is best on grazing impact, which has a low weight. The plug-ins are best on nothing, although none are dominated (as often is the case with many criteria). As to value analysis, looking at weaknesses provides guidance for design improvement for any of the alternatives.

## Case 4: Infante, de Mendonça, Purcidinio and Valle (2013)[5]

This study used ELECTRE multi-criteria decision making modeling to evaluate oil and gas companies, again using the triple bottom line. They compared the biggest five global oil and gas companies with two economic, ten environmental, and three social criteria as in Table 4.7:

**Table 4.7** Infante et al. criteria

| Criteria | | | |
|---|---|---|---|
| Econ1 | Total production | Economic value/day | Max |
| Econ2 | Investment impact | qualitative | Max |
| Env1 | Direct energy consumption | Barrels/year | Min |
| Env2 | Water withdrawal | Barrels/year | Min |
| Env3 | Greenhouse gas emission | Tons/barrel/year | Min |
| Env4 | Indirect greenhouse gas emission | Tons/barrel/year | Min |
| Env5 | Sulpher oxide emission | Tons/barrel/year | Min |
| Env6 | Nitrous oxide emission | Tons/barrel/year | Min |
| Env7 | Water discharge | Volume & quality | Min |
| Env8 | Waste | Tons/barrel/year | Min |
| Env9 | Spill volume | Volume | Min |
| Env10 | Expenditure—environmental protection | Dollar/barrel/year | Max |
| Soc1 | Workforce employed | Employees | Max |
| Soc2 | Work-related deaths | Deaths/employee | Min |
| Soc3 | Work-related illness | Rate/hour | Min |

Infante et al. evaluated firms over time, with scores provided for each year from 2005 through 2010. We will base our scores to reflect 2010 numbers in their data. The matrix of scores for each criterion by option are given below, along with calculation of overall value score. Table 4.8 shows input measures from the original article:

Infante et al. utilized equal weights, and then demonstrated sensitivity to weights in some variants. Based on ELECTRE approaches, scores were generated in one of the metrics that method offers, with a score of 0 below some minimum (a q parameter) and 1 at or above some maximum (a p parameter). The scores in Table 4.9 reflect a linear formulation for input measures between q and p.

**Table 4.8** Case 4 Measures

| | q | p | PetroB | BP | RDS | ExMob | Chev |
|---|---|---|---|---|---|---|---|
| Econ1 | 0.207 | 0.413 | 1.956 | 3.499 | 1.793 | 3.980 | 2.616 |
| Econ2 | 0.253 | 0.507 | 5 | 3 | 2 | 5 | 2 |
| Env1 | 42.372 | 72.831 | 756.832 | 706.766 | 895.208 | 929.227 | 1002.963 |
| Env2 | 39.322 | 71.767 | 255.085 | 221.129 | 498.953 | 195.662 | 286.909 |
| Env3 | 12.610 | 24.439 | 82.390 | 89.247 | 124.973 | 91.065 | 49.147 |
| Env4 | 3.080 | 6.097 | 1.334 | 6.025 | 22.345 | 11.727 | 8.949 |
| Env5 | 23.365 | 44.129 | 196.139 | 56.743 | 302.825 | 126.586 | 136.751 |
| Env6 | 18.390 | 35.578 | 319.702 | 130.055 | 250.98 | 96.311 | 131.620 |
| Env7 | 41.967 | 77.967 | 264.318 | 57.400 | 438.226 | 156.468 | 309.987 |
| Env8 | 78.333 | 152.598 | 663.428 | 325.166 | 2311.411 | 417.909 | 193.904 |
| Env9 | 44.993 | 82.034 | 404.551 | 204.825 | 449.155 | 172.132 | 268.284 |
| Env10 | 191626 | 383251 | 1459916 | 1870477 | 5161248 | 3192585 | 2023640 |
| Soc1 | 3113.581 | 6311.123 | 72088.4 | 86460 | 90045 | 81300 | 58712 |
| Soc2 | 0.022 | 0.045 | 0.143 | 0.006 | 0.087 | 0.047 | 0.062 |
| Soc3 | 0.066 | 0.138 | 0.597 | 0.354 | 0.720 | 0.324 | 0.318 |

**Table 4.9** Case 4 Scores

| | PetroB | BP | RDS | ExMob | Chev |
|---|---|---|---|---|---|
| Econ1 | 0.489 | 0.875 | 0.448 | 0.995 | 0.654 |
| Econ2 | 1 | 0.5 | 0.25 | 1 | 0.250 |
| Env1 | 0.811 | 0.977 | 0.349 | 0.236 | 0 |
| Env2 | 0.816 | 0.930 | 0.003 | 1 | 0.710 |
| Env3 | 0.537 | 0.439 | 0 | 0.413 | 1 |
| Env4 | 0.933 | 0.699 | 0 | 0.414 | 0.553 |
| Env5 | 0.415 | 0.973 | 0 | 0.694 | 0.653 |
| Env6 | 0 | 0.850 | 0.245 | 1 | 0.842 |
| Env7 | 0.388 | 0.979 | 0 | 0.696 | 0.257 |
| Env8 | 0.743 | 0.930 | 0 | 0.879 | 1 |
| Env9 | 0.318 | 0.984 | 0.169 | 1 | 0.772 |
| Env10 | 0 | 0.106 | 1 | 0.484 | 0.150 |
| Soc1 | 0.442 | 0.729 | 0.801 | 0.626 | 0.174 |
| Soc2 | 0 | 0.940 | 0.130 | 0.530 | 0.380 |
| Soc3 | 0.258 | 0.865 | 0 | 0.940 | 0.955 |

**Table 4.13** Case 5 Value calculation with subjective scores

| | weights | Procurement | Warehouse | OrderCycle | Manufact. | Trans. |
|---|---|---|---|---|---|---|
| On-time delivery | 0.36 | 0 | 0.5 | 1 | 0.5 | 0 |
| Completeness | 0.29 | 0 | 0.5 | 1 | 1 | 1 |
| Correctness | 0.21 | 1 | 1 | 1 | 1 | 0.5 |
| Defect free | 0.14 | 0.5 | 1 | 1 | 1 | 0 |
| **Value scores** | | **0.28** | **0.675** | **1** | **0.82** | **0.395** |

Gaudenzi and Borghesi gave two sets of scores to evaluate risks within their departments. Scores based on managerial input as well as a model used by Gaudenzi and Borghesi are demonstrated with both sets of weights generated above. Scores here are presented in a positivist perspective, with 1.0 representing the best performance. Therefore low resulting scores are associated with the most problematic departments.

The first set of value scores reflect weights emphasizing on-time delivery, with manager subjective scores shown in Table 4.13:

The scores themselves highlight where risks exist (0 indicates high risk, 0.5 medium level risk). The value scores give something that could be used to assess overall relative performance by department. Order cycle has no problems, so it has to score best. Manufacturing seems to have their risks well under control. Procurement and transportation departments are more troublesome.

The second set uses the same weights, but scores based on model inputs (see Table 4.14):

The implications are similar, except that the warehousing department shows up as facing much more risk.

We can repeat the analysis using weights emphasizing completeness. Using managerial subjective scores (Table 4.15):

This set of weights gives the transport department a better performance rating, but otherwise similar performance to the earlier analysis.

Finally, we use the model scores for weights emphasizing completeness (Table 4.16):

Here the warehouse department appears to face the greatest risk, followed by the procurement department.

The Guadenzi and Borghesi article presents an interesting application of multiple criteria analysis to something akin to business scorecard analysis, extending it to provide a potential departmental assessment of relative degree of risk faced.

## Value Analysis

This application differs, because its intent is to provide a balanced scorecard type of model. This can be very useful, and interesting. But value analysis applies only to

**Table 4.14** Case 5 Value calculation with model inputs

| | Weights | Procurement | Warehouse | OrderCycle | Manufact. | Trans. |
|---|---|---|---|---|---|---|
| On-time delivery | 0.36 | 0 | 0 | 1 | 0.5 | 0 |
| Completeness | 0.29 | 0 | 0 | 1 | 1 | 1 |
| Correctness | 0.21 | 1 | 1 | 0.5 | 1 | 0.5 |
| Defect free | 0.14 | 1 | 0.5 | 1 | 1 | 0 |
| **Value scores** | | **0.35** | **0.28** | **0.895** | **0.82** | **0.395** |

**Table 4.15** Case 5 Value calculations emphasizing completeness and subjective scores

| | Weights | Procurement | Warehouse | OrderCycle | Manufact. | Trans. |
|---|---|---|---|---|---|---|
| On-time delivery | 0.22 | 0 | 0.5 | 1 | 0.5 | 0 |
| Completeness | 0.43 | 0 | 0.5 | 1 | 1 | 1 |
| Correctness | 0.21 | 1 | 1 | 1 | 1 | 0.5 |
| Defect free | 0.14 | 0.5 | 1 | 1 | 1 | 0 |
| **Value scores** | | **0.28** | **0.675** | **1** | **0.89** | **0.535** |

**Table 4.16** Case 5 Value calculations emphasizing completeness with model scores

| | weights | Procurement | Warehouse | OrderCycle | Manufact. | Trans. |
|---|---|---|---|---|---|---|
| On-time delivery | 0.22 | 0 | 0 | 1 | 0.5 | 0 |
| Completeness | 0.43 | 0 | 0 | 1 | 1 | 1 |
| Correctness | 0.21 | 1 | 1 | 0.5 | 1 | 0.5 |
| Defect free | 0.14 | 1 | 0.5 | 1 | 1 | 0 |
| **Value scores** | | **0.35** | **0.28** | **0.895** | **0.89** | **0.535** |

hierarchical development, because Gaudenzi and Borghesi apply AHP to performance measurement.

## Conclusions

The cases presented here all applied multiple criteria models. This type of model provides a very good framework to describe specific aspects of risk and to assess where they exist, as well as considering their relative performance. The value scores might be usable as a means to select preferred alternatives or as performance metrics. Through value analysis, they can direct attention to features that call for the greatest improvement.

Value analysis can provide useful support to decision making by first focusing on hierarchical development. In all five cases presented here, this was accomplished in the original articles. Nonetheless, it is important to consider over-arching objectives, as well as means objectives in light of over-arching objective accomplishment.

Two aspects of value analysis should be considered. First, if scores on available alternatives are equivalent on a specific criterion, this criterion will not matter for this set of alternatives. However, it may matter if new alternatives are added, or existing alternatives improved. Second, a benefit of value analysis is improvement of existing alternatives. The score matrix provides useful comparisons of relative alternative performance. If decision makers are not satisfied with existing alternatives, they might seek additional choices through expanding their search or designing them. The criteria with the greatest weights might provide an area of search, and the ideal scores provide a design standard.

## Notes

1. Öztűrk, B.A. and Özçelik, F. (2014). Sustainable supplier selection with a fuzzy multi-criteria decision making method based on triple bottom line. *Business and Economics Research Journal* 5(3), 129–147.
2. Olson, D.L. (2005). Comparison of weights in TOPSIS models. *Mathematical and Computer Modelling* 40(7–8), 721–727.

that a simultaneous solution is usually necessary. Typically, the objective is to minimize total inventory costs.

Total inventory cost can include four components: holding costs, ordering costs, shortage costs, and purchasing costs. **Holding costs**, or *carrying costs*, represent costs associated with maintaining inventory. These costs include interest incurred or the opportunity cost of having capital tied up in inventories; storage costs such as insurance, taxes, rental fees, utilities, and other maintenance costs of storage space; warehousing or storage operation costs, including handling, record keeping, information processing, and actual physical inventory expenses; and costs associated with deterioration, shrinkage, obsolescence, and damage. Total holding costs are dependent on how many items are stored and for how long they are stored. Therefore, holding costs are expressed in terms of *dollars associated with carrying one unit of inventory for unit of time*

**Ordering costs** represent costs associated with replenishing inventories. These costs are not dependent on how many items are ordered at a time, but on the number of orders that are prepared. Ordering costs include overhead, clerical work, data processing, and other expenses that are incurred in searching for supply sources, as well as costs associated with purchasing, expediting, transporting, receiving, and inspecting. In manufacturing operations, **setup cost** is the equivalent to ordering cost. Set-up costs are incurred when a factory production line has to be shut down in order to reorganize machinery and tools for a new production run. Set-up costs include the cost of labor and other time-related costs required to prepare for the new product run. We usually assume that the ordering or setup cost is constant and is expressed in terms of *dollars per order.*

**Shortage costs**, or *stock-out costs*, are those costs that occur when demand exceeds available inventory in stock. A shortage may be handled as a *backorder*, in which a customer waits until the item is available, or as a *lost sale*. In either case, a shortage represents lost profit and possible loss of future sales. Shortage costs depend on how much shortage has occurred and sometimes for how long. Shortage costs are expressed in terms of *dollar cost per unit of short item.*

**Purchasing costs** are what firms pay for the material or goods. In most inventory models, the price of materials is the same regardless of the quantity purchased; in this case, purchasing costs can be ignored. However, when price varies by quantity purchased, called the ***quantity discount*** case, inventory analysis must be adjusted to account for this difference.

## Basic Inventory Simulation Model

Many models contain variables that change continuously over time. One example would be a model of a retail store's inventory. The number of items change gradually (though discretely) over an extended time period; however, for all intents and purposes, they may be treated as continuous. As customer demand is fulfilled, inventory is depleted, leading to factory orders to replenish the stock. As orders are received from suppliers, the inventory increases. Over time, particularly if orders are relatively small and frequent as we see in just-in-time environments, the inventory level can be represented by a smooth, continuous, function.

We can build a simple inventory simulation model beginning with a spreadsheet model as shown in Table 5.1. Model parameters include a holding rate of 0.8 per item per day, an order rate of 300 for each order placed, a purchase price of 90, and a sales price of 130. The decision variables are when to order (when the end of day quantity drops below the reorder point (ROP), and the quantity ordered (Q). The model itself has a row for each day (here 30 days are modeled). Each day has a starting inventory (column B) and a probabilistic demand (column C) generated from a normal distribution with a mean of 100 and a standard deviation of 10. Demand is made integer. Sales (column D) are equal to the minimum of the starting quantity and demand. End of day inventory (column E) is the maximum of 0 or starting inventory minus demand. The quantity ordered at the end of each day in column F (here assumed to be on hand at the beginning of the next day) is 0 if ending inventory exceeds ROP, or Q if ending inventory drops at or below ROP.

Profit and shortage are calculated to the right of the basic inventory model. Column G calculates holding cost by multiplying the parameter is cell B2 times the ending inventory quantity for each day, and summing over the 30 days in cell G5. Order costs are calculated by day as $300 if an order is placed that day, and 0 otherwise, with the monthly total ordering cost accumulated in cell H5. Cell I5 calculates total purchasing cost, cell J5 total revenue, and cell H3 calculates net profit considering the value of starting inventory and ending inventory. Column K identifies sales lost (SHORT), with cell K5 accumulating these for the month.

Crystal Ball simulation software allows introduction of three types of special variables. Probabilistic variables (assumption cells in Crystal Ball terminology) are modeled in column C using a normal distribution (CB.Normal (mean, std)). Decision variables are modeled for ROP (cell E1) and Q (cell E2). Crystal Ball allows setting minimum and maximum levels for decision variables, as well as step size. Here we used ROP values of 80, 100, 120, and 140, and Q values of 100, 110, 120, 130 and 140. The third type of variable is a forecast cell. We have forecast cells for net profit (H3) and for sales lost (cell K3).

The Crystal Ball simulation can be set to run for up to 10,000 repetitions for combination of decision variables. We selected 1000 repetitions. Output is given for forecast cells. Figure 5.1 shows net profit for the combination of an ROP of 140 and a Q of 140.

Tabular output is also provided as in Table 5.2.

Similar output is given for the other forecast variable, SHORT (Fig. 5.2; Table 5.3).

Crystal Ball also provides a comparison over all decision variable values, as given in Table 5.4.

The implication here is that the best decision for the basic model parameters would be an ROP of 120 and a Q of 130, yielding an expected net profit of $101,446 for the month. The shortage for this combination had a mean of 3.43 items per day, with a distribution shown in Fig. 5.3. The probability of shortage was 0.4385.

**Table 5.1** Basic inventory model

| | A | B | C | D | E | F | G | H | I | J | K |
|---|---|---|---|---|---|---|---|---|---|---|---|
| 1 | holdrate | 0.8 | | ROP | 140 | | | | | | |
| 2 | orderrate | 300 | | Q | 140 | | | | | | |
| 3 | purchase | 90 | | | | | net | 110359.2 | | short | 0 |
| 4 | sell | 130 | | | | | | | | | |
| 5 | | | | | | | 2440.8 | 6600 | 277200 | 388050 | |
| 6 | day | Start | demand | Sales | end | order | holdcost | ordercost | purchase | revenue | SHORT |
| 7 | 1 | 100 | 85 | 85 | 15 | 140 | 12 | 300 | 12600 | 11050 | 0 |
| 8 | 2 | 155 | 84 | 84 | 71 | 140 | 56.8 | 300 | 12600 | 10920 | 0 |
| 9 | 3 | 211 | 104 | 104 | 107 | 140 | 85.6 | 300 | 12600 | 13520 | 0 |
| 10 | 4 | 247 | 105 | 105 | 142 | 0 | 113.6 | 0 | 0 | 13650 | 0 |
| 11 | 5 | 142 | 104 | 104 | 38 | 140 | 30.4 | 300 | 12600 | 13520 | 0 |
| 12 | 6 | 178 | 116 | 116 | 62 | 140 | 49.6 | 300 | 12600 | 15080 | 0 |
| 13 | 7 | 202 | 105 | 105 | 97 | 140 | 77.6 | 300 | 12600 | 13650 | 0 |
| 14 | 8 | 237 | 94 | 94 | 143 | 0 | 114.4 | 0 | 0 | 12220 | 0 |
| 15 | 9 | 143 | 83 | 83 | 60 | 140 | 48 | 300 | 12600 | 10790 | 0 |
| 16 | 10 | 200 | 94 | 94 | 106 | 140 | 84.8 | 300 | 12600 | 12220 | 0 |
| 17 | 11 | 246 | 115 | 115 | 131 | 140 | 104.8 | 300 | 12600 | 14950 | 0 |
| 18 | 12 | 271 | 128 | 128 | 143 | 0 | 114.4 | 0 | 0 | 16640 | 0 |
| 19 | 13 | 143 | 107 | 107 | 36 | 140 | 28.8 | 300 | 12600 | 13910 | 0 |
| 20 | 14 | 176 | 110 | 110 | 66 | 140 | 52.8 | 300 | 12600 | 14300 | 0 |
| 21 | 15 | 206 | 102 | 102 | 104 | 140 | 83.2 | 300 | 12600 | 13260 | 0 |
| 22 | 16 | 244 | 96 | 96 | 148 | 0 | 118.4 | 0 | 0 | 12480 | 0 |
| 23 | 17 | 148 | 91 | 91 | 57 | 140 | 45.6 | 300 | 12600 | 11830 | 0 |
| 24 | 18 | 197 | 102 | 102 | 95 | 140 | 76 | 300 | 12600 | 13260 | 0 |
| 25 | 19 | 235 | 104 | 104 | 131 | 140 | 104.8 | 300 | 12600 | 13520 | 0 |

| | | | | | | | | | | | |
|---|---|---|---|---|---|---|---|---|---|---|---|
| 26 | 20 | 271 | 96 | 96 | 175 | 0 | 140 | 0 | 0 | 12480 | 0 |
| 27 | 21 | 175 | 103 | 103 | 72 | 140 | 57.6 | 300 | 12600 | 13390 | 0 |
| 28 | 22 | 212 | 98 | 98 | 114 | 140 | 91.2 | 300 | 12600 | 12740 | 0 |
| 29 | 23 | 254 | 97 | 97 | 157 | 0 | 125.6 | 0 | 0 | 12610 | 0 |
| 30 | 24 | 157 | 103 | 103 | 54 | 140 | 43.2 | 300 | 12600 | 13390 | 0 |
| 31 | 25 | 194 | 86 | 86 | 108 | 140 | 86.4 | 300 | 12600 | 11180 | 0 |
| 32 | 26 | 248 | 105 | 105 | 143 | 0 | 114.4 | 0 | 0 | 13650 | 0 |
| 33 | 27 | 143 | 89 | 89 | 54 | 140 | 43.2 | 300 | 12600 | 11570 | 0 |
| 34 | 28 | 194 | 106 | 106 | 88 | 140 | 70.4 | 300 | 12600 | 13780 | 0 |
| 35 | 29 | 228 | 89 | 89 | 139 | 140 | 111.2 | 300 | 12600 | 11570 | 0 |
| 36 | 30 | 279 | 84 | 84 | 195 | 0 | 156 | 0 | 0 | 10920 | 0 |

**Table 5.4** Comparative net profit for all values of ROP, Q. ©Oracle. Used with permission

| Trend Chart / Overlay Chart / Forecast Chart | Q (100.00) | Q (110.00) | Q (120.00) | Q (130.00) | Q (140.00) | |
|---|---|---|---|---|---|---|
| ROP (80.00) | 99,530 | 99,948 | 99,918 | 100,159 | 101,331 | *1* |
| ROP (100.00) | 99,627 | 100,701 | 101,051 | 101,972 | 101,512 | *2* |
| ROP (120.00) | 99,519 | 100,429 | 100,919 | **101,446** | 101,252 | *3* |
| ROP (140.00) | 99,525 | 99,894 | 100,586 | 100,712 | 100,805 | *4* |
| | *1* | *2* | *3* | *4* | *5* | |

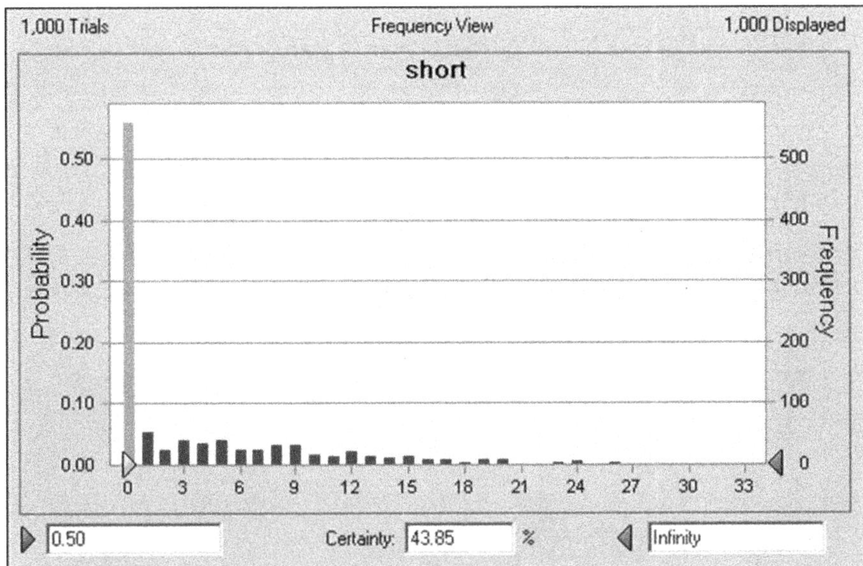


**Fig. 5.3** SHORT for R = 120, Q = 130. ©Oracle. Used with permission

Continuous variables are often called state variables. A continuous simulation model defines equations for relationships among state variables so that the dynamic behavior of the system over time can be studied. To simulate continuous systems, we use an activity-scanning approach whereby time is decomposed into small increments. The defining equations are used to determine how the state variables change during an increment of time. A specific type of continuous simulation is called system dynamics, which dates back to the early 1960s and a classic work by Jay Forrester of M.I.T.[1] System dynamics focuses on the structure and behavior of systems that are composed of interactions among variables and feedback loops. A system dynamics model usually takes the form of an influence diagram that shows the relationships and interactions among a set of variables.

System dynamics models have been widely used to model supply chains, especially with respect to the bullwhip phenomenon,[2] which has to do with the dramatic increase in inventories across supply chains when uncertainty in demand appears. Many papers have dealt with the bullwhip effect through system dynamics models.[3] These models have been used to evaluate lean systems,[4] Kanban systems,[5] and JIT systems,[6] They also have been used to model vendor management inventory in supply chains.[7]

We present a four echelon supply chain model, consisting of a vendor providing raw materials, an assembly operation to create the product, a warehouse, and a set of five retailers. We will model two systems—one a push system, the other pull in the sense that upstream activity depends on downstream demand. We will present the pull system first.

| | A | B | C | D | E |
|---|---|---|---|---|---|
| 1 | RevP | 100 | ROPven | 20 | |
| 2 | Cost | 70 | Qven | 50 | |
| 3 | Hold | 1 | | | |
| 4 | | Vendor | Vendor | | |
| 5 | | Start | Prod | Send | End |
| 6 | Time | | | | |
| 7 | 1 | 40 | =IF(E7<=$D$1,$D$2,0) | =IF(J7<=$I$1,$D$2,0) | =MAX(0,B7-D7) |
| 8 | =A7+1 | =E7 | =IF(E8<=$D$1,$D$2,0) | =IF(J8<=$I$1,$D$2,0) | =MAX(0,B8-D8) |
| 9 | =A8+1 | =E8+C7 | =IF(E9<=$D$1,$D$2,0) | =IF(J9<=$I$1,$D$2,0) | =MAX(0,B9-D9) |
| 10 | =A9+1 | =E9+C8 | =IF(E10<=$D$1,$D$2,0) | =IF(J10<=$I$1,$D$2,0) | =MAX(0,B10-D10) |
| 11 | =A10+1 | =E10+C9 | =IF(E11<=$D$1,$D$2,0) | =IF(J11<=$I$1,$D$2,0) | =MAX(0,B11-D11) |
| 12 | =A11+1 | =E11+C10 | =IF(E12<=$D$1,$D$2,0) | =IF(J12<=$I$1,$D$2,0) | =MAX(0,B12-D12) |
| 13 | =A12+1 | =E12+C11 | =IF(E13<=$D$1,$D$2,0) | =IF(J13<=$I$1,$D$2,0) | =MAX(0,B13-D13) |
| 14 | =A13+1 | =E13+C12 | =IF(E14<=$D$1,$D$2,0) | =IF(J14<=$I$1,$D$2,0) | =MAX(0,B14-D14) |
| 15 | =A14+1 | =E14+C13 | =IF(E15<=$D$1,$D$2,0) | =IF(J15<=$I$1,$D$2,0) | =MAX(0,B15-D15) |
| 16 | =A15+1 | =E15+C14 | =IF(E16<=$D$1,$D$2,0) | =IF(J16<=$I$1,$D$2,0) | =MAX(0,B16-D16) |
| 17 | =A16+1 | =E16+C15 | =IF(E17<=$D$1,$D$2,0) | =IF(J17<=$I$1,$D$2,0) | =MAX(0,B17-D17) |
| 18 | =A17+1 | =E17+C16 | =IF(E18<=$D$1,$D$2,0) | =IF(J18<=$I$1,$D$2,0) | =MAX(0,B18-D18) |
| 19 | =A18+1 | =E18+C17 | =IF(E19<=$D$1,$D$2,0) | =IF(J19<=$I$1,$D$2,0) | =MAX(0,B19-D19) |
| 20 | =A19+1 | =E19+C18 | =IF(E20<=$D$1,$D$2,0) | =IF(J20<=$I$1,$D$2,0) | =MAX(0,B20-D20) |
| 21 | =A20+1 | =E20+C19 | =IF(E21<=$D$1,$D$2,0) | =IF(J21<=$I$1,$D$2,0) | =MAX(0,B21-D21) |
| 22 | =A21+1 | =E21+C20 | =IF(E22<=$D$1,$D$2,0) | =IF(J22<=$I$1,$D$2,0) | =MAX(0,B22-D22) |
| 23 | =A22+1 | =E22+C21 | =IF(E23<=$D$1,$D$2,0) | =IF(J23<=$I$1,$D$2,0) | =MAX(0,B23-D23) |
| 24 | =A23+1 | =E23+C22 | =IF(E24<=$D$1,$D$2,0) | =IF(J24<=$I$1,$D$2,0) | =MAX(0,B24-D24) |
| 25 | =A24+1 | =E24+C23 | =IF(E25<=$D$1,$D$2,0) | =IF(J25<=$I$1,$D$2,0) | =MAX(0,B25-D25) |
| 26 | =A25+1 | =E25+C24 | =IF(E26<=$D$1,$D$2,0) | =IF(J26<=$I$1,$D$2,0) | =MAX(0,B26-D26) |
| 27 | =A26+1 | =E26+C25 | =IF(E27<=$D$1,$D$2,0) | =IF(J27<=$I$1,$D$2,0) | =MAX(0,B27-D27) |
| 28 | =A27+1 | =E27+C26 | =IF(E28<=$D$1,$D$2,0) | =IF(J28<=$I$1,$D$2,0) | =MAX(0,B28-D28) |
| 29 | =A28+1 | =E28+C27 | =IF(E29<=$D$1,$D$2,0) | =IF(J29<=$I$1,$D$2,0) | =MAX(0,B29-D29) |
| 30 | =A29+1 | =E29+C28 | =IF(E30<=$D$1,$D$2,0) | =IF(J30<=$I$1,$D$2,0) | =MAX(0,B30-D30) |
| 31 | =A30+1 | =E30+C29 | =IF(E31<=$D$1,$D$2,0) | =IF(J31<=$I$1,$D$2,0) | =MAX(0,B31-D31) |
| 32 | =A31+1 | =E31+C30 | =IF(E32<=$D$1,$D$2,0) | =IF(J32<=$I$1,$D$2,0) | =MAX(0,B32-D32) |
| 33 | =A32+1 | =E32+C31 | =IF(E33<=$D$1,$D$2,0) | =IF(J33<=$I$1,$D$2,0) | =MAX(0,B33-D33) |
| 34 | =A33+1 | =E33+C32 | =IF(E34<=$D$1,$D$2,0) | =IF(J34<=$I$1,$D$2,0) | =MAX(0,B34-D34) |
| 35 | =A34+1 | =E34+C33 | =IF(E35<=$D$1,$D$2,0) | =IF(J35<=$I$1,$D$2,0) | =MAX(0,B35-D35) |
| 36 | =A35+1 | =E35+C34 | =IF(E36<=$D$1,$D$2,0) | =IF(J36<=$I$1,$D$2,0) | =MAX(0,B36-D36) |
| 37 | | | | | =SUM(E7:E36) |

**Fig. 5.4** Factory model

## Pull System

The basic model uses a forecasting system based on exponential smoothing to drive decisions to send material down the supply chain. We use EXCEL modeling, along with Crystal Ball software to do simulation repetitions, following Evans and Olson (2004).[8] The formulas for the factory portion of the model are given in Fig. 5.4.

Figure 5.4 models a month of daily activity. Sales of products at retail generate $100 in revenue for the core organization, at a cost of $70 per item. Holding costs are $1 at the retail level ($0.50 at wholesale, $0.40 at assembly, $0.25 at vendors). Daily orders are shipped from each element, at a daily cost of $1000 from factory to assembler, $700 from assembler to warehouse, $300 from warehouse to retailers. Vendors produce 50 items of material per day if inventory drops to 20 items or less. If not, they do not produce. They send material to the assembly operation if called by that element, which is modeled in Fig. 5.5 (only the first 5 days are shown). Vendor ending inventory is shown in column E, with cell E37 adding total monthly inventory.

The assembly operation calls for replenishment of 30 units from the vendor whenever their inventory of finished goods drops to 20 or less. Each daily delivery

| | | | | | | |
|---|---|---|---|---|---|---|
| 10 | 4 | =J9 | =D9 | =G9 | =MIN(F10,M9) | =F10+H10-I10 |
| 11 | 5 | =J10 | =D10 | =G10 | =MIN(F11,M10) | =F11+H11-I11 |

**Fig. 5.5** Core assembly model

| | A | K | L | M | N | O | P |
|---|---|---|---|---|---|---|---|
| 1 | | | | WholMin | 20 | | |
| 2 | | | | WholMax | 25 | | |
| 3 | | | | | | | |
| 4 | | Whol | | | | | |
| 5 | Day | Start | Demand | Order | End | Short | Sent |
| 6 | | | | 0 | | | |
| 7 | 1 | =20 | =20 | =IF(O7>0,$N$1+INT(0.7*O7),IF(N7>$N$2,0,$N$2-N7)) | =K7-P7 | =IF(L7>K7,L7-K7,0) | MIN(K7,L7) |
| 8 | 2 | =N7+I7 | =T7+Y7+AD7+AI7+AM7 | =IF(O8>0,$N$1+INT(0.7*O8),IF(N8>$N$2,0,$N$2-N8)) | =K8-P8 | =IF(L8>K8,L8-K8,0) | MIN(K8,L8) |
| 9 | 3 | =N8+I8 | =T8+Y8+AD8+AI8+AM8 | =IF(O9>0,$N$1+INT(0.7*O9),IF(N9>$N$2,0,$N$2-N9)) | =K9-P9 | =IF(L9>K9,L9-K9,0) | MIN(K9,L9) |
| 10 | 4 | =N9+I9 | =T9+Y9+AD9+AI9+AM9 | =IF(O10>0,$N$1+INT(0.7*O10),IF(N10>$N$2,0,$N$2-N10)) | =K10-P10 | =IF(L10>K10,L10-K10,0) | MIN(K10,L10) |
| 11 | 5 | =N10+I10 | =T10+Y10+AD10+AI10+AM10 | =IF(O11>0,$N$1+INT(0.7*O11),IF(N11>$N$2,0,$N$2-N11)) | =K11-P11 | =IF(L11>K11,L11-K11,0) | MIN(K11,L11) |

**Fig. 5.6** Wholesale model

is 30 units, and is received at the beginning of the next day's operations. The assembly operation takes one day, and goods are available to send that evening. Column J shows ending inventory to equal what starting inventory plus what was processed that day minus what was sent to wholesale. Figure 5.6 shows the model of the wholesale operation.

The wholesale operation feeds retail demand, which is shown in column L. They feed retailers up to the amount they have in stock. They order from the assembler if they have less than 25 items. If they stock out, they order 20 items plus 70 % of what they were unable to fill (this is essentially an exponential smoothing forecast). If they still have stock on hand, the order to fill up to 25 items. Figure 5.7 shows one of the five retailer operations (the other four are identical).

Retailers face a highly variable demand with a mean of 4. They fill what orders they have stock for. Shortfall is measured in column U. They order if their end of day inventory falls to 4 or less. The amount ordered is 4 plus 70 % of shortfall, up to a maximum of 8 units.

This model is run of Crystal Ball to generate a measure of overall system profit. Here the profit formula is $175 times sales minus holding costs minus transportation costs. Holding costs at the factory were $0.25 times sum of ending inventory, at the assembler $0.40 times sum of ending inventory, at the warehouse 0.50 times ending inventory, and at the retailers $1 times sum of ending inventories. Shipping costs were $1000 per day from factory to assembler, $700 per day from assembler to warehouse, and $300 per day from warehouse to retailer. The results of 1000 repetitions are shown in Fig. 5.8.

Here average profit for a month is $5942, with a minimum a loss of $8699 and a maximum a gain of $18,922. There was a 0.0861 probability of a negative profit. The amount of shortage across the system is shown in Fig. 5.9. The average was 138.76, with a range of 33 to 279 over the 1000 simulation repetitions.

| | A | Q | R | S | T | U |
|---|---|---|---|---|---|---|
| 1 | | start | 4 | | order | ROP+.7short |
| 2 | | rop | 4 | | | to Tmax |
| 3 | | Tmax | 8 | | | |
| 4 | | | | | | |
| 5 | | R1 | | | | |
| 6 | | start | demand | end | order | short |
| 7 | | =$R$1 | =INT(CB.Exponential(0.25)) | =MAX(0,Q7-R7) | =IF(S7<=$R$2,4+INT(0.7*U7),IF(S7>$R$3,0,$R$3-S7)) | =IF(R7>Q7,R7-Q7,0) |
| 8 | | =S7+MIN(P7,T7) | =INT(CB.Exponential(0.25)) | =MAX(0,Q8-R8) | =IF(S8<=$R$2,4+INT(0.7*U8),IF(S8>$R$3,0,$R$3-S8)) | =IF(R8>Q8,R8-Q8,0) |
| 9 | | =S8+MIN(P8,T8) | =INT(CB.Exponential(0.25)) | =MAX(0,Q9-R9) | =IF(S9<=$R$2,4+INT(0.7*U9),IF(S9>$R$3,0,$R$3-S9)) | =IF(R9>Q9,R9-Q9,0) |
| 10 | | =S9+MIN(P9,T9) | =INT(CB.Exponential(0.25)) | =MAX(0,Q10-R10) | =IF(S10<=$R$2,4+INT(0.7*U10),IF(S10>$R$3,0,$R$3-S10)) | =IF(R10>Q10,R10-Q10,0) |
| 11 | | =S10+MIN(P10,T10) | =INT(CB.Exponential(0.25)) | =MAX(0,Q11-R11) | =IF(S11<=$R$2,4+INT(0.7*U11),IF(S11>$R$3,0,$R$3-S11)) | =IF(R11>Q11,R11-Q11,0) |

**Fig. 5.7** Retailing model

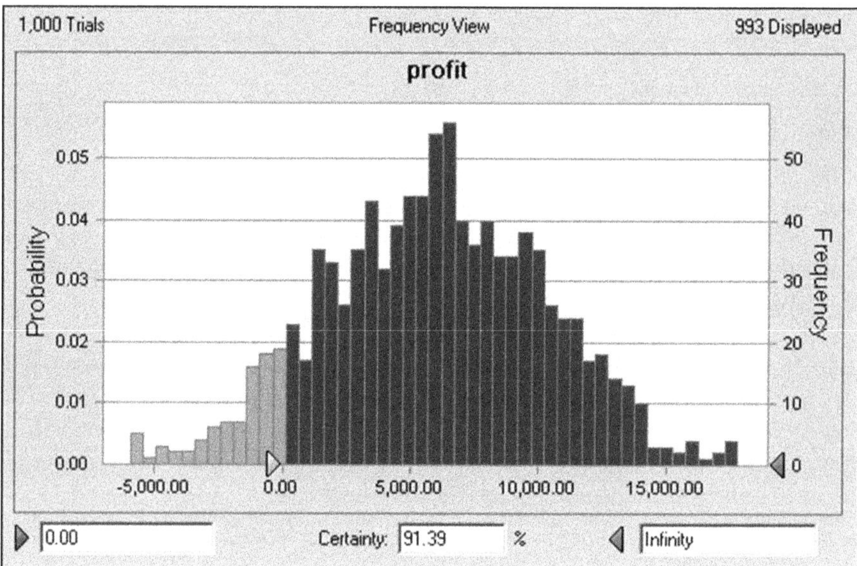


**Fig. 5.8** Overall system profit for basic model. ©Oracle. Used with permission

The central limit theorem can be shown to have effect, as the sum of the five retailer shortfalls has a normally shaped distribution. Figure 5.10 shows shortfall at the wholesale level, which had only one entity.

The average wholesale shortages was 15.73, with a minimum of 0 and a maximum of 82. Crystal Ball output indicates a probability of shortfall of 0.9720, meaning a 0.0280 probability of going the entire month without having shortage at the wholesale level.

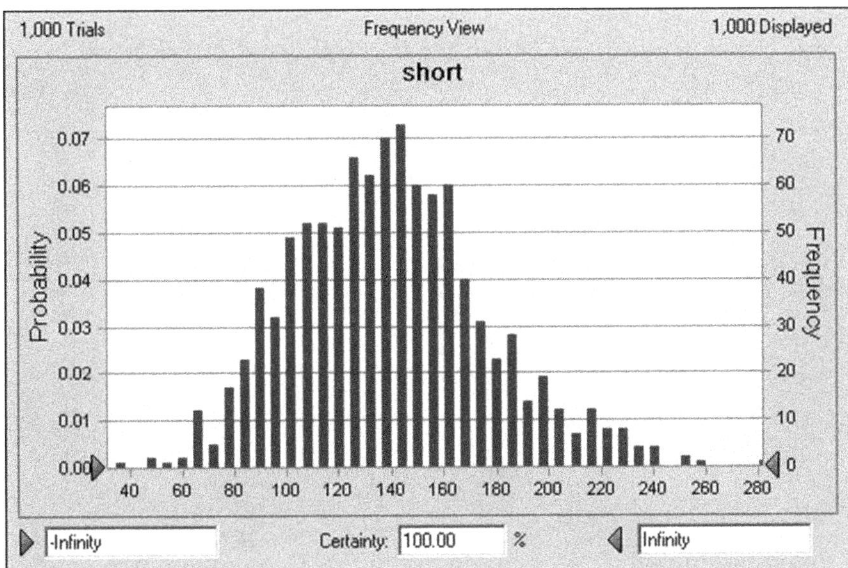


Fig. 5.9 Retail shortages for basic model. ©Oracle. Used with permission

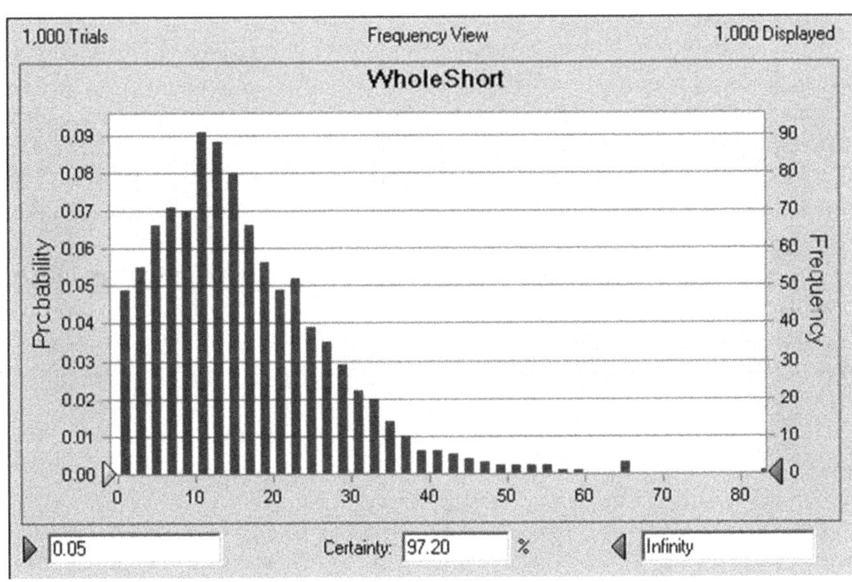


Fig. 5.10 Wholesale shortages for basic model. ©Oracle. Used with permission

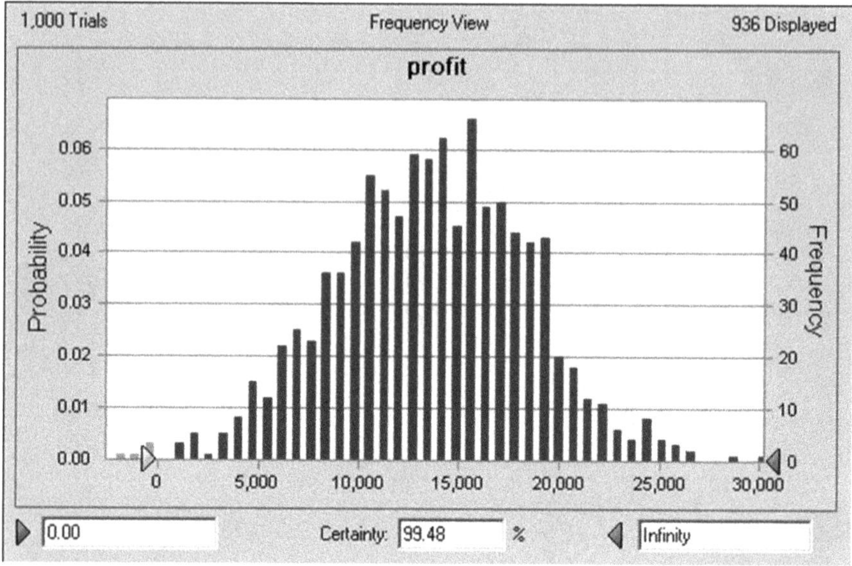


Fig. 5.11 Push system profit. ©Oracle. Used with permission

## Push System

The difference in this model is that production at the factory (column C in Fig. 5.4) is a constant 20 per day, the amount sent from the factory to the assembler (column D in Fig. 5.4) is also 20 per day, the amount ordered by the wholesaler (column M in Fig. 5.6) is 20, the amount sent by the wholesaler to retailers (column P in Fig. 5.6) is a constant 20, and the amount ordered by the wholesaler (column T in Fig. 5.7) is a constant 20.

This system proved to be more profitable and safer for the given conditions. Profit is shown in Fig. 5.11.

The average profit was $13,561, almost double that of the more variable push system. Minimum profit was a loss of $2221, with the probability of loss 0.0052. Maximum profit was $29,772. Figure 5.12 shows shortfall at the retail level.

The average shortfall was only 100.32, much less than the 137.16 for the pull model. Shortfall at the wholesale level (Fig. 5.13) was an average of 21.54, ranging from 0 to 67.

For this set of assumed values, the push system performed better. But that establishes nothing, as for other conditions, and other means of coordination, a pull system could do better.

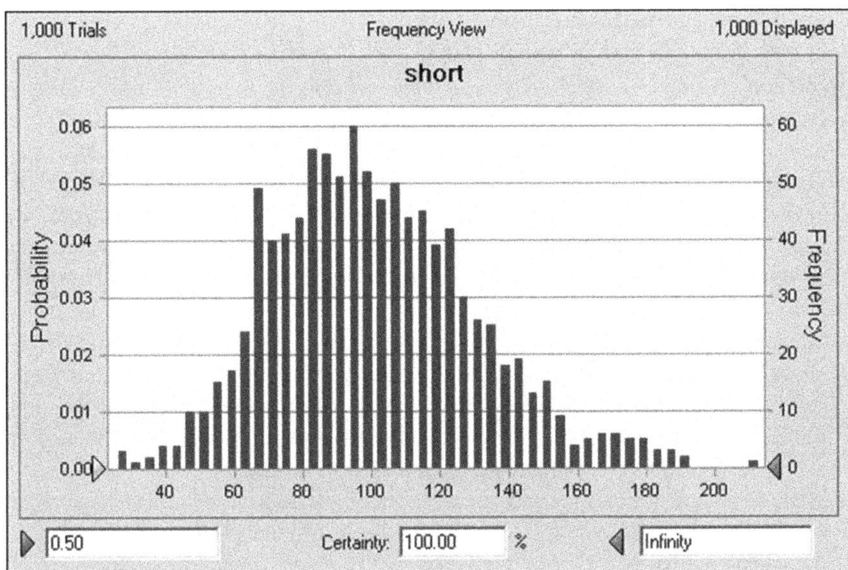


**Fig. 5.12** Retail shortages for the push model. ©Oracle. Used with permission

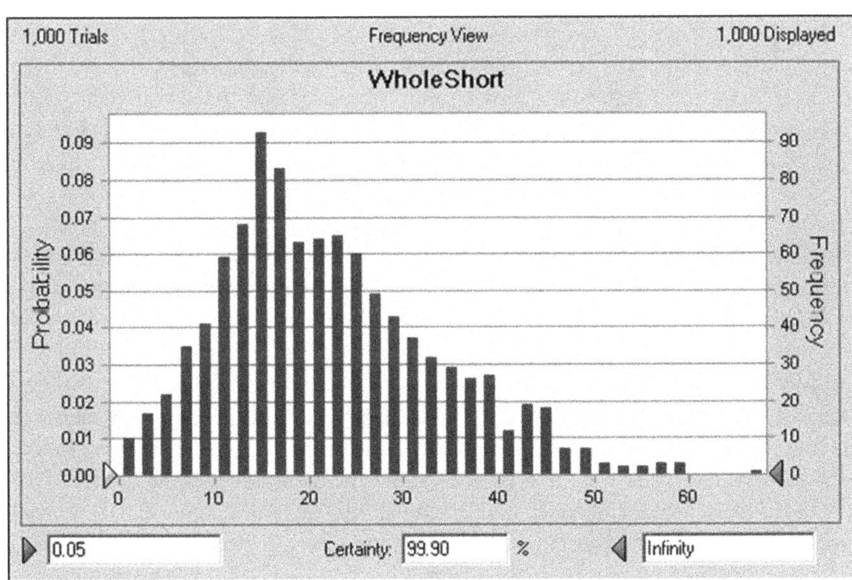


**Fig. 5.13** Wholesale shortages for the push model. ©Oracle. Used with permission

## Monte Carlo Simulation for Analysis

Simulation models are sets of assumptions concerning the relationship among model components. Simulations can be time-oriented (for instance, involving the number of events such as demands in a day) or process-oriented (for instance, involving queuing systems of arrivals and services). Uncertainty can be included by using probabilistic inputs for elements such as demands, inter-arrival times, or service times. These probabilistic inputs need to be described by probability distributions with specified parameters. Probability distributions can include normal distributions (with parameters for mean and variance), exponential distributions (with parameter for a mean), lognormal (parameters mean and variance), or any of a number of other distributions. A simulation run is a sample from an infinite population of possible results for a given model. After a simulation model is built, the number of trials is established. Statistical methods are used to validate simulation models and design simulation experiments.

Many financial simulation models can be accomplished on spreadsheets, such as Excel. There are a number of commercial add-on products that can be added to Excel, such as @Risk or Crystal Ball, that vastly extend the simulation power of spreadsheet models. These add-ons make it very easy to replicate simulation runs, and include the ability to correlate variables, expeditiously select from standard distributions, aggregate and display output, and other useful functions.

In supply chain outsourcing decisions, a number of factors can involve uncertainty, and simulation can be useful in gaining better understanding of systems.[9] We begin by looking at expected distributions of prices for the component to be outsourced from each location. China C in this case has the lowest estimated price, but it has a wide expected distribution of exchange rate fluctuation. These distributions will affect the actual realized price for the outsourced component. The Chinese C vendor is also rated as having relatively high probabilities of failure in product compliance with contractual standards, in vendor financial survival, and in political stability of host country. The simulation is modeled to generate 1000 samples of actual realized price after exchange rate variance, to include having to rely upon an expensive ($5 per unit) price in case of outsourcing vendor failure.

Monte Carlo simulation output is exemplified in Fig. 5.14, which shows the distribution of prices for the hypothetical Chinese outsourcing vendor C, which was the low price vendor very nearly half of the time. Figure 5.15 shows the same for the Taiwanese vendor, and Fig. 5.16 for the safer but expensive German vendor.

The Chinese vendor C has a higher probability of failure (over 0.31 from all sources combined, compared to 0.30 for Indonesia). This raises its mean cost, because in case of failure, the $5 per unit default price is used. There is a cluster around the contracted cost of $0.60, with a minimum dropping slightly below 0 due to exchange rate variance, a mean of $0.78 and a maximum of $1.58 given survival in all three aspects of risk modeled. There is a spike showing a default price of $5.00 per unit in 0.3134 of the cases. Thus while the contractual price is lowest for this alternative, the average price after consideration of failure is $2.10.

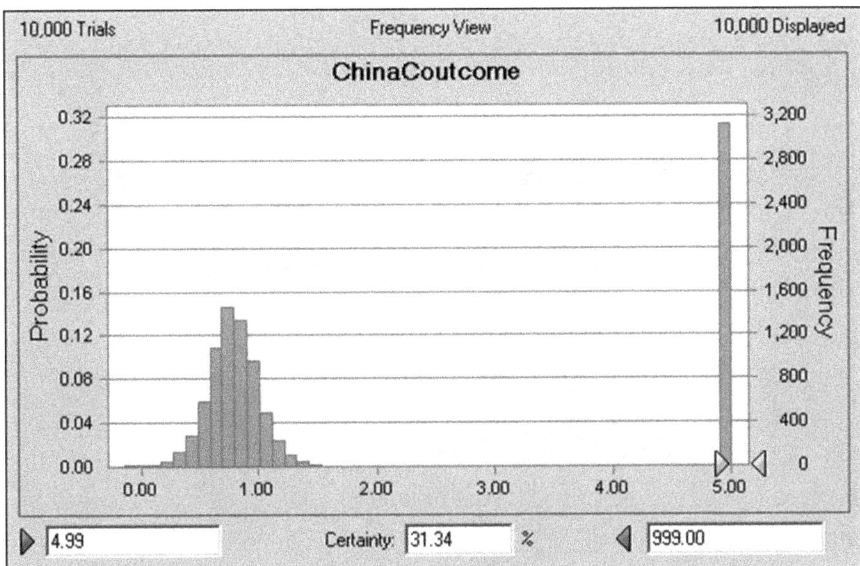


**Fig. 5.14** Distribution of results for Chinese vendor C costs. ©Oracle. Used with permission

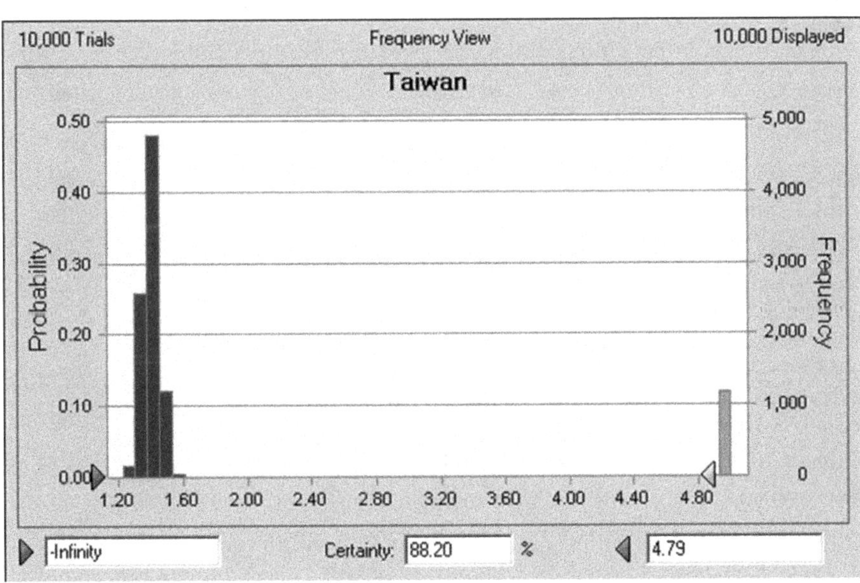


**Fig. 5.15** Distribution of results for Taiwanese vendor costs. ©Oracle. Used with permission

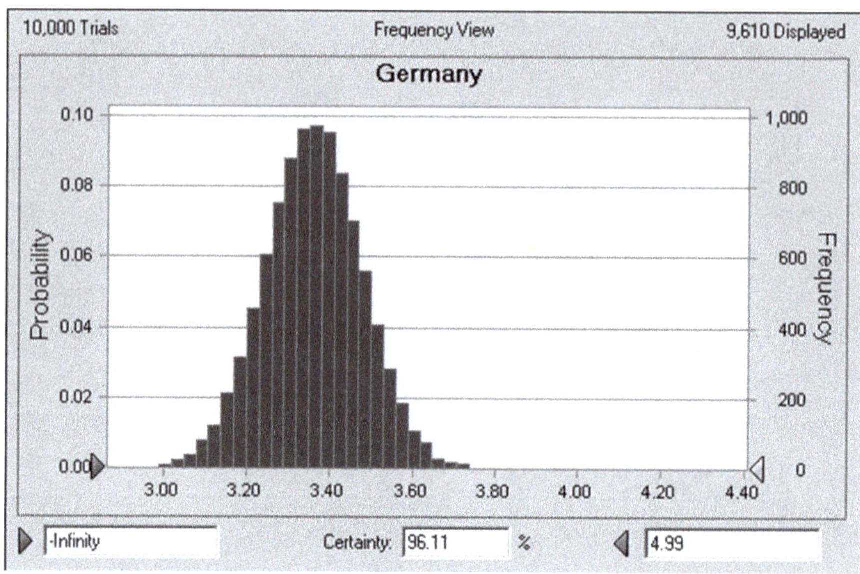


**Fig. 5.16** Distribution of results for Germany vendor costs. ©Oracle. Used with permission

**Table 5.5** Simulation output

| Vendor | Mean Cost | Min Cost | Max Cost | Probability of Failure | Probability Low | AvgCost if didn't fail | Average overall |
|---|---|---|---|---|---|---|---|
| China B | 0.70 | -0.01 | 1.84 | 0.2220 | 0.1370 | 0.91 | 1.82 |
| Taiwan | 1.36 | 1.22 | 1.60 | 0.1180 | 0.0033 | 1.41 | 1.83 |
| China C | 0.60 | 0.05 | 1.58 | 0.3134 | 0.4939 | 0.78 | 2.10 |
| China A | 0.82 | -0.01 | 2.16 | 0.2731 | 0.0188 | 1.07 | 2.14 |
| Indonesia | 0.80 | 0.22 | 1.61 | 0.2971 | 0.1781 | 0.96 | 2.16 |
| Arizona | 1.80 | 1.80 | 1.80 | 0.2083 | 0.0001 | 2.71 | 2.47 |
| Vietnam | 0.85 | 0.40 | 1.49 | 0.3943 | 0.1687 | 0.94 | 2.54 |
| Alabama | 2.05 | 2.05 | 2.05 | 0.2472 | 0 | | 2.78 |
| Ohio | 2.50 | 2.50 | 2.50 | 0.2867 | 0 | | 3.22 |
| Germany | 3.20 | 2.90 | 3.81 | 0.0389 | 0 | | 3.42 |

Note: Average Overall assumes cost of $5 to Supply Chain should Vendor Fail

Table 5.5 shows comparative output. Simulation provides a more complete picture of the uncertainties involved.

Probabilities of being the low-cost alternative are also shown. The greatest probability was for China C at 0.4939, with Indonesia next at 0.1781. The expensive (but safer) alternatives of Germany and Alabama both were never low (and thus were dominated in the DEA model). But Germany had a very high probability of survival, and in the simulation could appear as the best choice (rarely).

## Conclusion

Simulation is the most flexible management science modeling technique. It allows making literally any assumption you want, although the trade-off is that you have to work very hard to interpret results in a meaningful way relative to your decision.

Because of the variability inherent in risk analysis, simulation is an obviously valuable tool for risk analysis. There are two basic simulation applications in business. Waiting line models involve queuing systems, and software such as Arena (or many others) are very appropriate for that type of modeling. The other type is supportable by spreadsheet tools such as Crystal Ball, demonstrated in this chapter. Spreadsheet simulation is highly appropriate for inventory modeling as in push/pull models. Spreadsheet models also are very useful for system dynamic simulations. We will see more Crystal Ball simulation models in chapters covering value at risk and chance constrained models.

## Notes

1. Forrester, J.W. (1961). *Industrial Dynamics*. Cambridge, MA: MIT Press.
2. Sterman, J. (1989). Modelling managerial behavior: Misperceptions of feedback in a dynamic decision making experiment. *Management Science* 35:3, 321–339.
3. Huang, H.-Y., Chou, Y.-C. and Chang, S. (2009). A dynamic system model for proactive control of dynamic events in full-load states of manufacturing chains. *International Journal of Production Research* 47(9), 2485–2506; Demarzo, P.M., Fishman, M.J., He, Z. and Wang, N. (2012). Dynamic agency and the q theory of investment. *The Journal of Finance* LXVII(6), 2295–2340.
4. Agyapong-Kodua, K., Ajaefobi, J.O. and Weston, R.H. (2009). Modelling dynamic value streams in support of process design and evaluation. *International Journal of Computer Integrated Manufacturing* 22(5), 411–427.
5. Claudio, D. and Krishnamurthy, A. (2009). Kanban-based pull systems with advance demand information. *International Journal of Production Research* 47(12), 3139–3160.
6. Chakravarty, F. (2013). Managing a supply chain's web of risk. *Strategy & Leadership* 41(2), 39–45.
7. Mishra, M. and Chan, F.T.S. (2012). Impact evaluation of supply chain initiatives: A system simulation methodology. *International Journal of Production Research* 50(6), 1554–1567.
8. Evans, J.R. and Olson, D.L. (2002). *Introduction to Simulation and Risk Analysis* 2nd ed. Englewood Cliffs, NJ: Prentice-Hall.
9. Wu, D. and Olson, D.L. (2008), Supply chain risk, simulation and vendor selection, *International Journal of Production Economics*, 114:2, 646–655.

# 6 Value at Risk Models

Value at risk (VaR) is one of the most widely used models in risk management. It is based on probability and statistics.[1] VaR can be characterized as a maximum expected loss, given some time horizon and within a given confidence interval. Its utility is in providing a measure of risk that illustrates the risk inherent in a portfolio with multiple risk factors, such as portfolios held by large banks, which are diversified across many risk factors and product types. VaR is used to estimate the boundaries of risk for a portfolio over a given time period, for an assumed probability distribution of market performance. The purpose is to diagnose risk exposure.

## Definition

Value at risk describes the probability distribution for the value (earnings or losses) of an investment (firm, portfolio, etc.). The mean is a point estimate of a statistic, showing historical central tendency. Value at risk is also a point estimate, but offset from the mean. It requires specification of a given probability level, and then provides the point estimate of the return or better expected to occur at the prescribed probability. For instance, Fig. 6.1 gives the normal distribution for a statistic with a mean of 10 and a standard deviation of 4 (Crystal Ball was used, with 10,000 replications).

This indicates a 0.95 probability (for all practical purposes) of a return of at least 3.42. The precise calculation can be made in Excel, using the NormInv function for a probability of 0.05, a mean of 10, and a standard deviation of 4, yielding a return of 3.420585, which is practically the same as the simulation result shown in Fig. 6.1. Thus the value of the investment at the specified risk level of 0.05 is 3.42. The interpretation is that there is a 0.05 probability that things would be worse than the value at this risk level. Thus the greater the degree of assurance, the lower the value at risk return. The value at the risk level of 0.01 would only be 0.694609.



D.L. Olson, D.D. Wu, *Enterprise Risk Management Models*, Springer Texts in Business and Economics, DOI 10.1007/978-3-662-53785-5_6

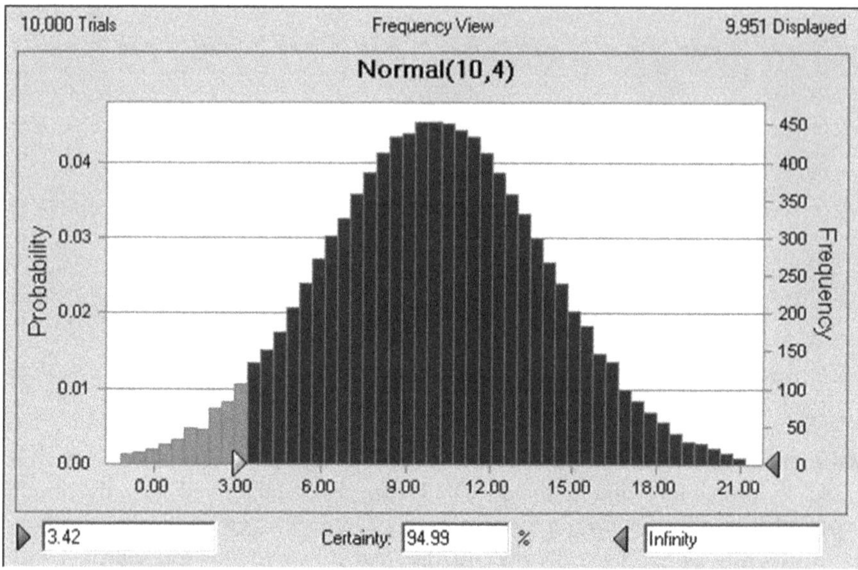


**Fig. 6.1** Normal distribution (10,4). ©Oracle. used with permission

## The Basel Accords

VaR is globally accepted by regulatory bodies responsible for supervision of banking activities. These regulatory bodies, in broad terms, enforce regulatory practices as outlined by the Basel Committee on Banking Supervision of the Bank for International Settlements (BIS). The regulator that has responsibility for financial institutions in Canada is the Office of the Superintendent of Financial Institutions (OSFI), and OSFI typically follows practices and criteria as proposed by the Basel Committee.

### Basel I

Basel I was promulgated in 1988, focusing on credit risk. A key agreement of the Basel Committee is the Basel Capital Accord (generally referred to as "Basel" or the "Basel Accord"), which has been updated several times since 1988. In the 1996 (updated, 1998) Amendment to the Basel Accord, banks were encouraged to use internal models to measure Value at Risk, and the numbers produced by these internal models support capital charges to ensure the capital adequacy, or liquidity, of the bank. Some elements of the minimum standard established by Basel are:

- VaR should be computed daily, using a 99th percentile, one-tailed confidence interval.
- A minimum price shock equivalent to ten trading days be used. This is called the "holding period" and simulates a 10-day period of liquidating assets in a period of market crisis.
- The model should incorporate a historical observation period of at least 1 year.
- The capital charge is set at a minimum of three times the average of the daily value-at-risk of the preceding 60 business days.

In 2001 the Basel Committee on Banking Supervision published principles for management and supervision of operational risks for banks and domestic authorities supervising them.

## Basel II

Basel II was published in 2009 to deal with operational risk management of banking. Banks and financial institutions were bound to use internal and external data, scenario analysis, and qualitative criteria. Banks were required to compute capital charges on a yearly basis and to calculate 99.9 % confidence levels (one in one thousand events as opposed to the earlier one in one hundred events). Basel II included standards in the form of three pillars:

1. **Minimum capital requirements.**
2. **Supervisory review**, to include categorization of risks as systemic, pension related, concentration, strategic, reputation, liquidity, and legal.
3. **Market discipline**, to include enhancements to strengthen disclosure requirements for securitizations, off-balance sheet exposures, and trading activities.

## Basel III

Basel III was a comprehensive set of reform measures published in 2011 with phased implementation dates. The aim was to strengthen regulation, supervision, and risk management of the banking sectors.

Pillar 1 dealt with capital, risk coverage, and containing leverage:

- **Capital requirements** to improve bank ability to absorb shocks from financial and economic stress:
  Common equity $\geq$ 0.045 of risk-weighted assets
- **Leverage requirements** to improve risk management and governance:
  Tier1 capital $\geq$ 0.03 of total exposure
- **Liquidity requirements** to strengthen bank transparency and disclosure:
  High quality liquid assets $\geq$ total net liquidity outflows over 30 days

Pillar 2 dealt with risk management and supervision.
Pillar 3 dealt with market discipline through disclosure requirements.

## The Use of Value at Risk

In practice, these minimum standards mean that the VaR that is produced by the Market Risk Operations area is multiplied first by the square root of 10 (to simulate 10 days holding) and then multiplied by a minimum capital multiplier of 3 to establish capital held against regulatory requirements.

In summary, VaR provides the worst expected loss at the 99 % confidence level. That is, a 99 % confidence interval produces a measure of loss that will be exceeded only 1 % of the time. But this does mean there will likely be a larger loss than the VaR calculation two or three times in a year. This is compensated for by the inclusion of the multiplicative factors, above, and the implementation of Stress Testing, which falls outside the scope of the activities of Market Risk Operations.

Various approaches can be used to compute VaR, of which three are widely used: Historical Simulation, Variance-covariance approach, and Monte Carlo simulation. Variance-covariance approach is used for investment portfolios, but it does not usually work well for portfolios involving options that are close to delta neutral. Monte Carlo simulation solves the problem of non-linearity approximation if model error is not significant, but it suffers some technical difficulties such as how to deal with time-varying parameters and how to generate maturation values for instruments that mature before the VaR horizon. We present Historical Simulation and Variance-covariance approach in the following two sections. We will demonstrate Monte Carlo Simulation in a later section of this chapter.

## Historical Simulation

Historical simulation is a good tool to estimate VAR in most banks. Observations of day-over-day changes in market conditions are captured. These market conditions are represented using upwards of 100,000 points daily of observed and implied Market Data. This historical market data is captured and used to generate historical 'shocks' to current spot market data. This shocked market data is used to price the Bank's trading positions as against changing market conditions, and these revalued positions then are compared against the base case (using spot data). This simulates a theoretical profit or loss. Each day of historically observed data produces a theoretical profit/loss number in this way, and all of these theoretical P&L numbers produce a distribution of theoretical profits/losses. The (1-day) VaR can then be read as the 99th percentile of this distribution.

The primary advantage of historical simulation is ease of use and implementation. In Market Risk Operations, historical data is collected and reviewed on a regular basis, before it is added to the historical data set. Since this data corresponds to historical events, it can be reviewed in a straightforward manner. Also, the historical nature of the data allows for some clarity of explanation of VaR numbers. For instance, the Bank's VaR may be driven by widening credit spreads, or by decreasing equity volatilities, or both, and this will be visible in actual historical data. Additionally, historical data implicitly contains correlations and non-linear effects (e.g. gamma, vega and cross-effects).

The most obvious disadvantage of historical simulation is the assumption that the past presents a reasonable simulation of future events. Additionally, a large bank usually holds a large portfolio, and there can be considerable operational overhead involved in producing a VaR against a large portfolio with dependencies on a large and varied number of model inputs. All the same, other VaR methods, such as variance-covariance (VCV) and Monte Carlo simulation, produce essentially the same objections. The main alternative to historical simulation is to make assumptions about the probability distributions of the returns on the market variables and calculate the probability distribution of the change in the value of the portfolio analytically. This is known as the variance-covariance approach. VCV is a parametric approach and contains the assumption of normality, and the assumption of the stability of correlation and at the same time. Monte Carlo simulation provides another tool to these two methods. Monte Carlo methods are dependent on decisions regarding model calibration, which have effectively the same problems. No VaR methodology is without simplifying assumptions, and several different methods are in use at institutions worldwide. The literature on volatility estimation is large and seemingly subject to unending growth, especially in acronyms.[2]

## Variance-Covariance Approach

VCV Models portfolio returns as a multivariate normal distribution. We can use a position vector containing cash flow present values to represent all components of the portfolio and describe the portfolio. VCV approach concerns most the return and covariance matrix($Q$) representing the risk attributes of the portfolio over the chosen horizon. The standard deviation of portfolio value ($\sigma$), also called volatility, is computed:

$$\sigma = \sqrt{h^t Q h} \tag{1}$$

The volatility ($\sigma$) is then scaled to find the desired centile of portfolio value that is the predicted maximum loss for the portfolio or VaR:

$$\begin{aligned} &VaR = \sigma f(Y) \\ &where: \quad f(Y) \ is\ the\ scale\ factor\ for\ centile\ Y. \end{aligned} \tag{2}$$

For example, for a multivariate normal return distribution, $f(Y) = 2.33$ for $\mathrm{Y} = 1\ \%$.

It is then easy to calculate VaR from the standard deviation (1-day VaR = 2.33 s). The simplest assumption is that daily gains/losses are normally distributed and independent. The $N$-day VaR equals $\sqrt{N}$ times the one-day VaR. When there is autocorrelation equal to r the multiplier is increased from $N$ to

$$N + 2(N-1)\rho + 2(N-2)\rho^2 + 2(N-3)\rho^3 + \ldots 2\rho^{n-1}$$

Besides being easy to compute, VCV also lends itself readily to the calculation of the calculation of the marginal risk (Marginal VaR), Incremental VaR and Component VaR of candidate trades. For a Portfolio where an amount $x_i$ is invested in the $i$th component of the portfolio, these three VaR measures are computed as:

- Marginal VaR: $\frac{\partial \text{VaR}}{\partial x_i}$
- Incremental VaR: Incremental effect of $i$th component on VaR
- Component VaR $x_i \frac{\partial \text{VaR}}{\partial x_i}$

VCV uses delta-approximation, which means the representative cash flow vector is a linear approximation of positions. In some cases, a second-order term in the cash flow representation is included to improve this approximation.[3] However, this does not always improve the risk estimate and can only be done with the sacrifice of some of the computational efficiency. In general, VCV works well in calculating linear instruments such as forward, interest rate SWAP, but works quite badly in non-linear instruments such as various options.

## Monte Carlo Simulation of VaR

Simulation models are sets of assumptions concerning the relationship among model components. Simulations can be time-oriented (for instance, involving the number of events such as demands in a day) or process-oriented (for instance, involving queuing systems of arrivals and services). Uncertainty can be included by using probabilistic inputs for elements such as demands, inter-arrival times, or service times. These probabilistic inputs need to be described by probability distributions with specified parameters. Probability distributions can include normal distributions (with parameters for mean and variance), exponential distributions (with parameter for a mean), lognormal (parameters mean and variance), or any of a number of other distributions. A simulation run is a sample from an infinite population of possible results for a given model. After a simulation model is built, a selected number of trials is established. Statistical methods are used to validate simulation models and design simulation experiments.

Many financial simulation models can be accomplished on spreadsheets, such as Excel. There are a number of commercial add-on products that can be added to Excel, such as @Risk or Crystal Ball, that vastly extend the simulation power of spreadsheet models.[4] These add-ons make it very easy to replicate simulation runs, and include the ability to correlate variables, expeditiously select from standard distributions, aggregate and display output, and other useful functions.

## The Simulation Process

Using simulation effectively requires careful attention to the modeling and implementation process. The simulation process consists of five essential steps:

**Develop a conceptual model of the system or problem under study**. This step begins with understanding and defining the problem, identifying the goals and objectives of the study, determining the important input variables, and defining output measures. It might also include a detailed logical description of the system that is being studied. Simulation models should be made as simple as possible to focus on critical factors that make a difference in the decision. The cardinal rule of modeling is to build simple models first, then embellish and enrich them as necessary.

1. **Build the simulation model**. This includes developing appropriate formulas or equations, collecting any necessary data, determining the probability distributions of uncertain variables, and constructing a format for recording the results. This might entail designing a spreadsheet, developing a computer program, or formulating the model according to the syntax of a special computer simulation language (which we discuss further in Chap. 7).
2. **Verify and validate the model**. Verification refers to the process of ensuring that the model is free from logical errors; that is, that it does what it is intended to do. Validation ensures that it is a reasonable representation of the actual system or problem. These are important steps to lend credibility to simulation models and gain acceptance from managers and other users. These approaches are described further in the next section.
3. **Design experiments using the model**. This step entails determining the values of the controllable variables to be studied or the questions to be answered in order to address the decision maker's objectives.
4. **Perform the experiments and analyze the results**. Run the appropriate simulations to obtain the information required to make an informed decision.

As with any modeling effort, this approach is not necessarily serial. Often, you must return to pervious steps as new information arises or as results suggest modifications to the model. Therefore, simulation is an evolutionary process that must involve not only analysts and model developers, but also the users of the results.

## Demonstration of VaR Simulation

We use an example Monte Carlo simulation model published by Beneda[5] to demonstrate simulation of VaR and other forms of risk. Beneda considered four risk categories, each with different characteristics of data availability:

- Financial risk—controllable (interest rates, commodity prices, currency exchange)
- Pure risk—controllable (property loss and liability)
- Operational—uncontrollable (costs, input shortages)
- Strategic—uncontrollable (product obsolescence, competition)

Beneda's model involved forward sale (45 days forward) of an investment (CD) with a price that was expected to follow the uniform distribution ranging from 90 to 110. Half of these sales (20,000 units) were in Canada, which involved an exchange rate variation that was probabilistic (uniformly distributed from −0.008 to −0.004). The expected price of the CD was normally distributed with mean 0.8139, standard deviation 0.13139. Operating expenses associated with the Canadian operation were normally distributed with mean $1,925,000 and standard deviation $192,500. The other half of sales were in the US. There was risk of customer liability lawsuits (2, Poisson distribution), with expected severity per lawsuit that was lognormally distributed with mean $320,000, standard deviation $700,000. Operational risks associated with US operations were normally distributed with mean $1,275,000, standard deviation $127,500. The Excel spreadsheet model for this is given in Table 6.1.

In Crystal Ball, entries in cells B2, B3, B7, B10, B21, B22 and B23 were entered as assumptions with the parameters given in column C. Prediction cells were defined for cells B17 (Canadian net income) and B29 (Total net income after tax). Results for cell B17 are given in Fig. 6.2, with a probability of 0.9 prescribed in Crystal Ball so that we can identify the VaR at the 0.05 level.

Statistics are given in Table 6.2.

The value at risk at the 0.95 level for this investment was −540,245.40, meaning that there was a 0.05 probability of doing worse than losing $540,245.50 in US dollars. The overall investment outcome is shown in Fig. 6.3.

Statistics are given in Table 6.3.

On average, the investment paid off, with a positive value of $96,022.98. However, the worst case of 500 was a loss of over $14 million. (The best was a gain of over $1.265 million.) The value at risk shows a loss of $1.14 million, and Fig. 6.3 shows that the distribution of this result is highly skewed (note the skewness measures for Figs. 6.2 and 6.3).

Beneda proposed a model reflecting hedging with futures contracts, and insurance for customer liability lawsuits. Using the hedged price in cell B4, and insurance against customer suits of $640,000, the after-tax profit is shown in Fig. 6.4.

Mean profit dropped to $84,656 (standard deviation $170,720), with minimum −$393,977 (maximum gain $582,837). The value at risk at the 0.05 level was a loss

**Table 6.1** Excel model of investment

| | A | B | C |
|---|---|---|---|
| 1 | Financial risk | Formulas | Distribution |
| 2 | Expected basis | −0.006 | Uniform(−0.008,−0.004) |
| 3 | Expected price per CD | 0.8139 | Normal(0.8139,0.13139) |
| 4 | March futures price | 0.8149 | |
| 5 | Expected basis 45 days | =B2 | |
| 6 | Expected CD futures | 0.8125 | |
| 7 | Operating expenses | 1.925 | Normal(1,925,000,192,500) |
| 8 | Sales | 20,000 | |
| 9 | | | |
| 10 | Price $US | 100 | Uniform(90,110) |
| 11 | Sales | 20,000 | |
| 12 | Current | 0.8121 | |
| 13 | Receipts | =B10 * B11/B12 | |
| 14 | Expected exchange rate | =B3 | |
| 15 | Revenues | =B13 * B14 | |
| 16 | COGS | =B7 * 1,000,000 | |
| 17 | Operating income | =B15 − B16 | |
| 18 | | | |
| 19 | Local sales | 20,000 | |
| 20 | Local revenues | =B10 * B19 | |
| 21 | Lawsuit frequency | 2 | Poisson(2) |
| 22 | Lawsuit severity | 320,000 | Lognormal(320,000,700,000) |
| 23 | Operational risk | 1,275,000 | Normal(1,275,000,127,500) |
| 24 | Losses | =B21 * B22 + B23 | |
| 25 | Local income | =B20 − B24 | |
| 26 | | | |
| 27 | Total income | =B17 + B25 | |
| 28 | Taxes | =0.35 * B27 | |
| 29 | After Tax Income | =B27 − B28 | |

of $205,301. Thus there was an expected cost of hedging (mean profit dropped from $96,022 to $84,656), but the worst case was much improved (loss of over $14 million to loss of $393,977) and value at risk improved from a loss of over $1.14 million to a loss of $205 thousand.

## Conclusions

Value at risk is a useful concept in terms of assessing probabilities of investment alternatives. It is a point estimator, like the mean (which could be viewed as the value at risk for a probability of 0.5). It is only as valid as the assumptions made, which include the distributions used in the model and the parameter estimates. This

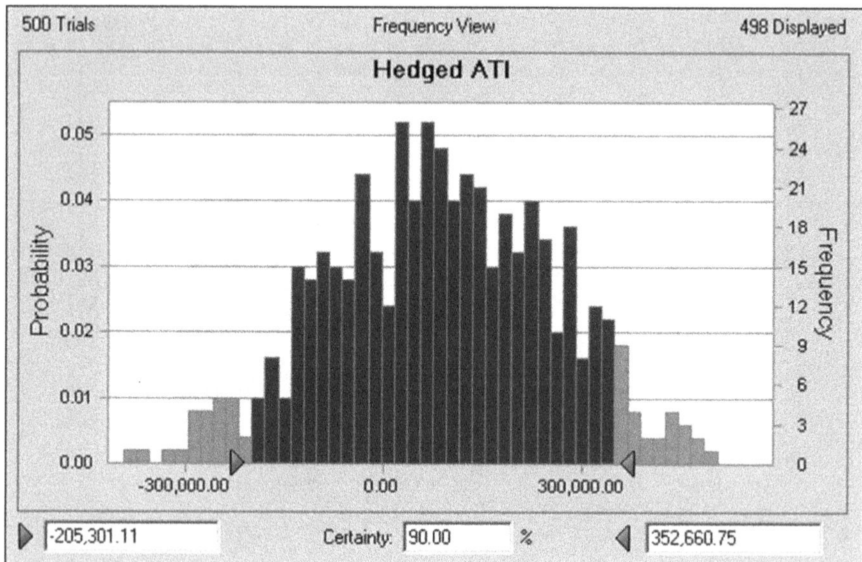


**Fig. 6.4** After-tax profit with hedging and insurance. ©Oracle. used with permission

incur large losses assuming a specified confidence level. CVaR has been applied to financial trading portfolios,[7] implemented through scenario analysis,[8] and applied via system dynamics.[9] A popular refinement is to use copulas, multivariate distributions permitting the linkage of a huge number of distributions.[10] Copulas have been implemented through simulation modeling[11] as well as through analytic modeling.[12]

We will show how specified confidence levels can be modeled through chance constraints in the next chapter. It is possible to maximize portfolio return subject to constraints including Conditional Value-at-Risk (CVaR) and other downside risk measures, both absolute and relative to a benchmark (market and liability-based). Simulation CVaR based optimization models can also be developed.

## Notes

1. Jorion, P. (1997). *Value at Risk: The New Benchmark for Controlling Market Risk*. New York: McGraw-Hill.
2. Danielson, J. and de Vries, C.G. (1997). Extreme returns, tail estimation, and value-at-risk. Working Paper, University of Iceland (http://www.hag.hi.is/~jond/research); Fallon, W. (1996). Calculating value-at-risk. Working Paper, Columbia University (bfallon@groucho.gsb.columbia.edu); Garman, M.B. (1996). Improving on VaR. *Risk* 9, No. 5.
3. JP Morgan (1996). *RiskMetrics™-technical document,* 4th ed.
4. Evans, J.R. and Olson, D.L. (2002). *Introduction to Simulation and Risk Analysis 2nd ed.* Upper Saddle River, NJ: Prentice Hall.

5. Beneda, N. (2004). Managing an asset management firm's risk portfolio, *Journal of Asset Management* 5:5, 327–337.
6. Rockafellar, R.T. and Uryassev, S. (2002). Conditional value-at-risk for general loss distributions. *Journal of Banking & Finance* 26:7, 1443–1471.
7. Al Janabi, M.A.M. (2009). Corporate treasury market price risk management: A practical approach for strategic decision-making. *Journal of Corporate Treasury Management* 3(1), 55–63.
8. Sawik, T. (2011). Selection of a dynamic supply portfolio in make-to-order environment with risks. *Computers & Operations Research* 38(4), 782–796.
9. Mehrjoo, M. and Pasek, Z.J. (2016). Risk assessment for the supply chain of fast fashion apparel industry: A system dynamics framework. *International Journal of Production Research* 54(1), 28–48.
10. Guégan, D. and Hassani, B.K. (2012). Operational risk: A Basel II++ step before Basel III. *Journal of Risk Management in Financial Institutions* 6(1), 37–53.
11. Hsu, C.-P., Huang, C.-W. and Chiou, W.-J. (2012). Effectiveness of copula-extreme value theory in estimating value-at-risk: Empirical evidence from Asian emerging markets. *Review of Quantitative Finance & Accounting* 39(4), 447–468.
12. Kaki, A., Salo, A. and Talluri, S. (2014). Scenario-based modeling of interdependent demand and supply uncertainties. *IEEE Transactions on Engineering Management* 61(1), 101–113.

# 7 Chance Constrained Models

Chance constrained programming was developed as a means of describing constraints in mathematical programming models in the form of probability levels of attainment.[1] Consideration of chance constraints allows decision makers to consider mathematical programming objectives in terms of the probability of their attainment. If $\alpha$ is a predetermined confidence level desired by a decision maker, the implication is that a constraint will be violated at most $(1-\alpha)$ of all possible cases.

Chance constraints are thus special types of constraints in mathematical programming models, where there is some objective to be optimized subject to constraints. A typical mathematical programming formulation might be:

$$\begin{aligned}&\text{Maximize } f(X)\\&\text{Subject to}: Ax \leq b\end{aligned}$$

The objective function *f(X)* can be profit, with the function consisting of *n* variables *X* as the quantities of products produced and *f(X)* including profit contribution rate constants. There can be any number *m* of constraints in *Ax*, each limited by some constant *b*. Chance constraints can be included in *Ax*, leading to a number of possible chance constraint model forms. Charnes and Cooper presented three formulations[2]:

$$\begin{aligned}&(1)\ \text{Maximize the expected value of a probabilistic function}\\&\quad\ \text{Maximize E[Y] (where } Y = f(X))\\&\quad\ \text{Subject to}: \Pr\{Ax \leq b\} \geq \alpha\end{aligned}$$

Any coefficient of this model (*Y*, *A*, *b*) may be probabilistic. The intent of this formulation would be to maximize (or minimize) a function while assuring $\alpha$ probability that a constraint is met. While the expected value of a function usually involves a linear functional form, chance constraints will usually be nonlinear. This



D.L. Olson, D.D. Wu, *Enterprise Risk Management Models*, Springer Texts in Business and Economics, DOI 10.1007/978-3-662-53785-5_7

- $r_p$ is percent return on a portfolio over the holding period.
- $Ax \leq b$, the feasible region in decision space

In the investor's decision problem (1), the quantity $r_p$ to be maximized is a random variable because $r_p$ is a function of the individual-security $r_i$ random variables. Therefore, (1) is a *stochastic programming problem*. Stochastic programming models are similar to deterministic optimization problems where the parameters are known only within certain bounds but take advantage of the fact that probability distributions governing the data are known or can be estimated. To solve a stochastic programming problem, we need convert the stochastic programming to an equivalent *deterministic programming problem*. A popular way of doing this is to use utility function $U(\cdot)]$, which maps stochastic terms into their deterministic equivalents. For example, by use of the means $\mu_i$, variances $\sigma_{ii}$ and covariances $\sigma_{ij}$ of the $r_i$, a portfolio selection problem is to maximize expected utility.

$$E[U(r_p)] = E[r_p] - \lambda Var[r_p],$$

where $\lambda \geq 0$ a risk reversion coefficient and may be different from different investors. In other words, a portfolio selection problem can be modeled by a trade-off between the mean and variance of random variable $r_p$:

$$\text{Max } E[U(r_p)] = E[r_p] - \lambda Var[r_p],$$

$$\lambda \geq 0$$

$$Ax \leq b$$

Assuming $[U(r_p)]$ is Taylor series expandable, the validity of $E[U(r_p)]$ and thus the above problem can be guaranteed if $[U(r_p)]$ Taylor series expandable of $\mathbf{r} = (r_1, \ldots, r_n)$ follows the multinormal distribution. Another alternative to Markowitz's mean variance framework, chance constrained programming was employed to model the portfolio selection problem. We will demonstrate the utilization of chance constrained programming to model the portfolio selection problem in the next section.

## Demonstration of Chance Constrained Programming

The following example was taken from Lee and Olson (2006).[12] The Hal Chase Investment Planning Agency is in business to help investors optimize their return from investment, to include consideration of risk. Through the use of nonlinear programming models, Hal Chase can control risk.

Hal deals with three investment mediums: a stock fund, a bond fund, and his own Sports and Casino Investment Plan (SCIP). The stock fund is a mutual fund investing in openly traded stocks. The bond fund focuses on the bond market,

**Table 7.1** Hal chase investment data

| | Stock **S** | Bond **B** | SCIP **G** |
|---|---|---|---|
| Average return | 0.148 | 0.060 | 0.152 |
| Variance | 0.014697 | 0.000155 | 0.160791 |
| Covariance with S | | 0.000468 | −0.002222 |
| Covariance with B | | | −0.000227 |

which has a much stabler return, although significantly lower expected return. SCIP is a high-risk scheme, often resulting in heavy losses, but occasionally coming through with spectacular gains. In fact, Hal takes a strong interest in SCIP, personally studying investment opportunities and placing investments daily. The return on these mediums, as well as their variance and correlation, are given in Table 7.1:

Note that there is a predictable relationship between the relative performance of the investment opportunities, so the covariance terms report the tendency of investments to do better or worse given that another investment did better or worse. This indicates that variables **S** and **B** tend to go up and down together (although with a fairly weak relationship), while variable **G** tends to move opposite to the other two investment opportunities.

Hal can develop a mathematical programming model to reflect an investor's desire to avoid risk. Hal assumes that return on investments are normally distributed around the average returns reported above. He bases this on painstaking research he has done with these three investment opportunities.

## Maximize Expected Value of Probabilistic Function

Using this form, the objective is to maximize return:

$$\text{Expected return} = 0.148\,\mathbf{S} + 0.060\,\mathbf{B} + 0.152\,\mathbf{G}$$

subject to staying within budget:

$$\text{Budget} = 1\,\mathbf{S} + 1\,\mathbf{B} + 1\,\mathbf{G} \leq 1000$$

having a probability of positive return greater than a specified probability:

$$\Pr\{\text{Expected return} \geq 0\} \geq \alpha$$

with all variables greater than or equal to 0:

$$\mathbf{S}, \mathbf{B}, \mathbf{G} \geq 0$$

The solution will depend on the confidence limit α. Using EXCEL, and varying α from 0.5, 0.8, 0.9 and 0.95, we obtain the solutions given in Table 7.2:

**Table 7.2** Results for chance constrained formulation (1)

| Probability {return ≥ 0} | α | Stock | Bond | Gamble | Expected return |
|---|---|---|---|---|---|
| 0.50 | 0 | – | – | 1000.00 | 152.00 |
| 0.80 | 0.253 | 379.91 | – | 620.09 | 150.48 |
| 0.90 | 0.842 | 556.75 | – | 443.25 | 149.77 |
| 0.95 | 1.282 | 622.18 | – | 377.82 | 149.51 |
| 0.99 | 2.054 | 668.92 | – | 331.08 | 149.32 |

The probability determines the penalty function α. At a probability of 0.80, the one-tailed normal z-function is 0.253, and thus the chance constrained is:

$$0.148\mathbf{S} + 0.060\mathbf{B} + 0.152\mathbf{G} - 0.253{*}\mathrm{SQRT}\big(0.014697\mathbf{S}^2 + 0.000936\mathbf{SB} - 0.004444\mathbf{SG} + 0.000155\mathbf{B}^2 - 0.000454\mathbf{BG} + 0.160791\mathbf{G}^2$$

The only difference in the constraint set for the different rows of Table 7.2 is that α is varied. The affect is seen is that investment is shifted from the high risk gamble to a bit safer stock. The stock return has low enough variance to assure the specified probabilities given. Had it been higher, the even safer bond would have entered into the solution at higher specified probability levels.

## Minimize Variance

With this chance constrained form, Hal is risk averse. He wants to minimize risk subject to attaining a prescribed level of gain. The variance-covariance matrix measures risk in one form, and Hal wants to minimize this function.

$$\mathrm{Min}\ 0.014697\mathbf{S}^2 + 0.000936\mathbf{SB} - 0.004444\mathbf{SG} + 0.000155\mathbf{B}^2 - 0.000454\mathbf{BG} + 0.160791\mathbf{G}^2$$

This function can be constrained to reflect other restrictions on the decision. For instance, there typically is some budget of available capital to invest.

$$\mathbf{S} + \mathbf{B} + \mathbf{G} \leq 1000 \quad \text{for a \$1000 budget}$$

Finally, Hal only wants to minimize variance given that he attains a prescribed expected return. Hal wants to explore four expected return levels: \$50/\$1000 invested, \$100/\$1000 invested, \$150/\$1000 invested, and \$200/\$1000 invested. Note that these four levels reflect expected returns of 5, 10, 15, and 20 %.

$$0.148\ \mathbf{S} + 0.06\ \mathbf{B} + 0.152\ \mathbf{G} \geq r \quad \text{where } r = 50,\ 100,\ 150,\ \text{and } 200$$

## Solution Procedure

The EXCEL input file will start off with the objective, MIN followed by the list of variables. Then we include the constraint set. The constraints can be stated as you want, but the partial derivatives of the variables need to consider each constraint stated in less-than-or-equal-to form. Therefore, the original model is transformed to:

$$\begin{aligned}
&\text{Min } .014697\mathbf{S}^2 + .000936\mathbf{SB} - .004444\mathbf{SG} + .000155\mathbf{B}^2 - .000454\mathbf{BG} + .160791\mathbf{G}^2] \\
&\text{st } \mathbf{S} + \mathbf{B} + \mathbf{G} \leq 1000 \qquad \text{budget constraint} \\
&\quad 0.148\ \mathbf{S} + 0.06\ \mathbf{B} + 0.152\ \mathbf{G} \geq 50 \qquad \text{gain constraint} \\
&\qquad \mathbf{S},\ \mathbf{B},\ \mathbf{G} \geq 0
\end{aligned}$$

The solution for each of the four gain levels are given in Table 7.3:

The first solution indicates that the lowest variance with an expected return of \$50 per \$1000 invested would be to invest \$825.30 in **B** (the bond fund), \$3.17 in **G** (the risky alternative), and keeping the 171.53 slack. The variance is \$106.002. This will yield an average return of 5 % on the money invested. Increasing specified gain to \$100 yields the designed expected return of \$100 with a variance of \$2928.51. Raising expected gain to 150 yields the prescribed \$150 with a variance of \$42,761.06. Clearly this is a high risk solution. But it also is near the maximum expected return (if all \$1000 was placed on the riskiest alternative, **G**, the expected return would be maximized at \$152 per \$1000 invested). A model specifying a gain of \$200 yields an infeasible solution, and thus by running multiple models, we can identify the maximum gain available (matching the linear programming model without chance constraints). It can easily be seen that lower variance is obtained by investing in bonds, then shifting to stocks, and finally to the high-risk gamble option.

## Maximize Probability of Satisfying Chance Constraint

The third chance constrained form is implicitly attained by using the first form example above, stepping up α until the model becomes infeasible. When the probability of satisfying the chance constraint was set too high, a null solution

**Table 7.3** Results for chance constrained formulation (2)

| Specified Gain | Variance | Stock | Bond | Gamble |
|---|---|---|---|---|
| ≥50 | 106.00 | – | 825.30 | 3.17 |
| ≥100 | 2928.51 | 406.31 | 547.55 | 46.14 |
| ≥150 | 42,761 | 500.00 | – | 500.00 |
| ≥152 | 160,791 | – | – | 1000.00 |

Table 7.4 Results for chance constrained formulation (3)

| α | Stock | Bond | Gamble | Expected return |
|---|---|---|---|---|
| 3 | 157.84 | 821.59 | 20.57 | 75.78 |
| 4 | 73.21 | 914.93 | 11.86 | 67.53 |
| 4.5 | 406.31 | 547.55 | 46.14 | 64.17 |
| 4.8 | 500.00 | – | 500.00 | 61.48 |
| 4.9 and up | – | – | – | 0 |

was generated (don't invest anything—keep all the $1000). Table 7.4 shows solutions obtained, with the highest α yielding a solution being 4.8, associated with a probability very close to 1.0 (0.999999 according to EXCEL).

## Real Stock Data

To check the validity of the ideas presented, we took real stock data from the Internet, taking daily stock prices for six dispersed, large firms, as well as the S&P500 index. Data was manipulated to obtain daily rates of return over the period 1999 through 2008 (2639 observations—dividing closing price by closing price of prior day).

$$r = \frac{V_t}{V_{t-1}}$$

where $V_t$ = return for day $t$ and $V_{t-1}$ = return for the prior day. (The arithmetic return yields identical results, only subtracting 1 from each data point.)

$$r_{arith} = \frac{V_t - V_{t-1}}{V_{t-1}}$$

We first looked at possible distributions. Figure 7.1 shows the Crystal Ball best fit for all data (using the Chi-square criterion—same result for Kolmogorov-Smirnov or Anderson criteria), while Fig. 7.2 shows fit with the logistic distribution, and Fig. 7.3 with the normal distribution:

The parameters for the student-t distribution fit was a scale of 0.01, and 2.841 degrees of freedom. For the logistic distribution, the scale parameter was 0.01.

The data had a slight negative skew, with a skewness score of −1.87. It had a high degree of kurtosis (73.65), and thus much more peaked than a normal distribution. This demonstrates "fat tail" distributions that are often associated with financial returns. Figures 7.1, 7.2, 7.3 clearly show how the normal assumption is too spread out for probabilities close to 0.5, and too narrow for the extremes (tails). The logistic distribution gives a better fit, but student-t distribution does better yet.

Table 7.5 shows means standard deviations, and covariances of these investments.

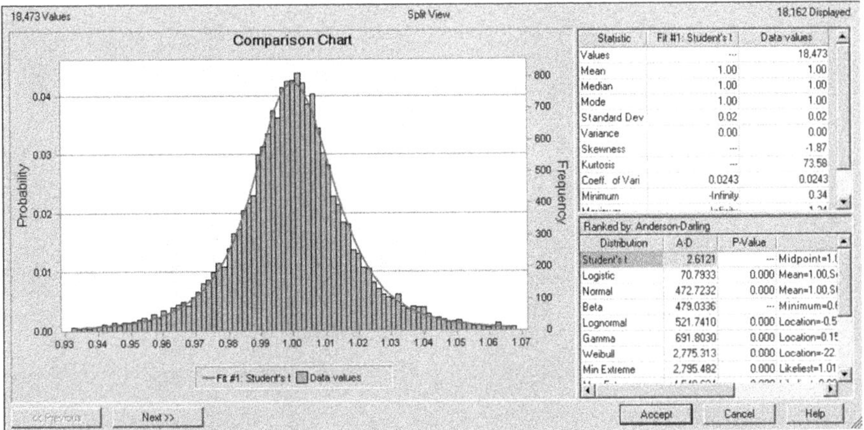


**Fig. 7.1** Data distribution fit student-t. ©Oracle. used with permission

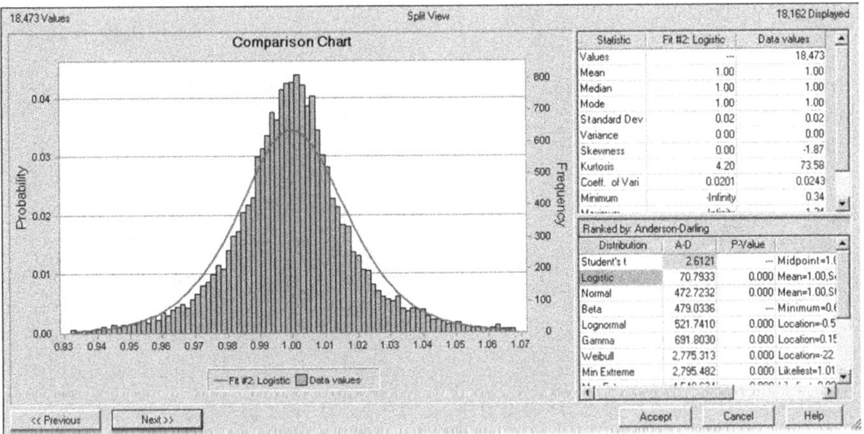


**Fig. 7.2** Logistic fit. ©Oracle. used with permission

An alternative statistic for returns is the logarithmic return, or continuously compounded return, using the formula:

$$r_{log} = \ln\left(\frac{V_f}{V_i}\right)$$

The student's t distribution again had the best fit, followed by logistic and normal (see Fig. 7.4):

This data yields slightly different data, as shown in Table 7.6.

Like the arithmetic return, the logarithmic return is centered on 0. There is a difference (slight) between logarithmic return covariances and arithmetic return covariances. The best distribution fit was obtained with the original data (identical

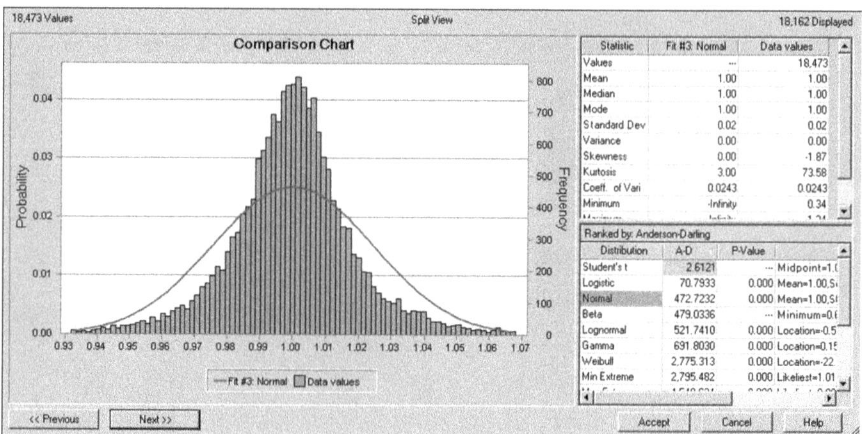


**Fig. 7.3** Normal model fit to data. ©Oracle. used with permission

**Table 7.5** Daily data

| | Ford | IBM | Pfizer | SAP | WalMart | XOM | S&P |
|---|---|---|---|---|---|---|---|
| Mean | 1.00084 | 1.00033 | 0.99935 | 0.99993 | 1.00021 | 1.00012 | 0.99952 |
| Std. Dev | 0.03246 | 0.02257 | 0.02326 | 0.03137 | 0.02102 | 0.02034 | 0.01391 |
| Min | 0.62822 | 0.49101 | 0.34294 | 0.81797 | 0.53203 | 0.51134 | 0.90965 |
| Max | 1.29518 | 1.13160 | 1.10172 | 1.33720 | 1.11073 | 1.17191 | 1.11580 |
| Cov(Ford) | 0.00105 | 0.00019 | 0.00014 | 0.00020 | 0.00016 | 0.00015 | 0.00022 |
| Cov(IBM) | | 0.00051 | 0.00009 | 0.00016 | 0.00013 | 0.00012 | 0.00018 |
| Cov(Pfizer) | | | 0.00054 | 0.00011 | 0.00014 | 0.00014 | 0.00014 |
| Cov(SAP) | | | | 0.00098 | 0.00010 | 0.00016 | 0.00016 |
| Cov(WM) | | | | | 0.00044 | 0.00011 | 0.00014 |
| Cov(XOM) | | | | | | 0.00041 | 0.00015 |
| Cov(S&P) | | | | | | | 0.00019 |

to arithmetic return), so we used that data for our chance constrained calculations. If logarithmic return data was preferred, the data in Table 7.6 could be used in the chance constrained formulations.

## Chance Constrained Model Results

We ran the data into chance constrained models assuming a normal distribution for data, using means, variances, and covariances from Table 7.5. The model included a budget limit of \$1000, all variables $\geq 0$, (chance constrained to have no loss), obtaining results shown in Table 7.7.

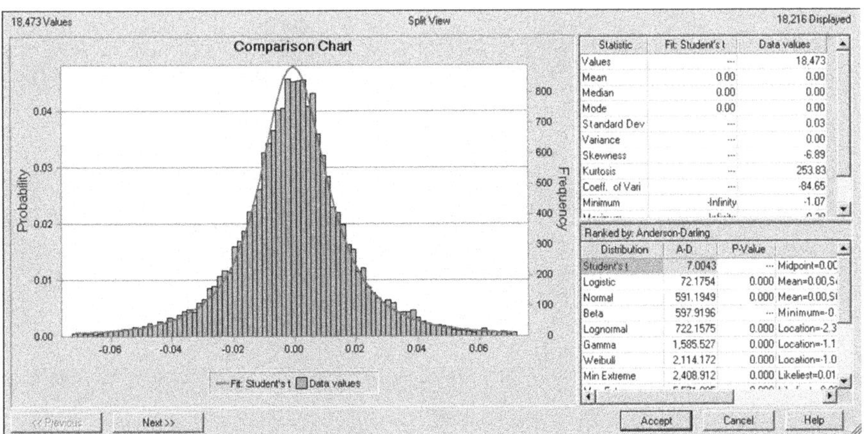


**Fig. 7.4** Distribution comparison from Crystal Ball. ©Oracle. used with permission

Maximizing return is a linear programming model, with an obvious solution of investing all available funds in the option with the greatest return (Ford). This has the greatest expected return, but also the highest variance.

Minimizing variance is equivalent to chance constrained form (2). The solution avoided Ford (which had a high variance), and spread the investment out among the other options, but had a small loss.

A series of models using chance constrained form (1) were run. Maximizing expected return subject to investment $\leq$1000 as well as adding the chance constraint Pr{return $\geq$ 970} was run for both normal and t-distributions.

Max expected return
s.t. Sum investment $\leq$ 1000
Pr{return $\geq$ 970} $\geq$ 0.95
All investments $\geq$ 0

It can be seen in Table 7.6 that the t-distribution was less restrictive, resulting in more investment in the riskier Ford option, but having a slightly higher variance (standard deviation). The chance constraint was binding in both assumptions (normal and Student-t). There was a 0.9 probability return of 979.50, and a 0.8 probability of return of 988.09 by t-distribution. Further chance constraint models were run assuming t-distribution. For the model:

Max expected return
s.t. Sum investment $\leq$ 1000
Pr{return $\geq$ 970} $\geq$ 0.95
Pr{return $\geq$ 980} $\geq$ 0.9
All investments $\geq$ 0

**Table 7.6** Daily data for logarithmic return

| | Ford | IBM | Pfizer | SAP | WalMart | XOM | S&P |
|---|---|---|---|---|---|---|---|
| Mean | −0.00029 | 0.00015 | −0.00084 | −0.00038 | 0.00006 | −0.00017 | −0.00068 |
| Std. Dev | 0.03278 | 0.02455 | 0.02852 | 0.03087 | 0.02254 | 0.02219 | 0.01392 |
| Min | −0.46486 | −0.71130 | −1.07021 | −0.20093 | −0.63105 | −0.67073 | −0.09470 |
| Max | 0.25865 | 0.12364 | 0.09687 | 0.29058 | 0.10502 | 0.15863 | 0.10957 |
| Cov(Ford) | 0.00107 | 0.00019 | 0.00013 | 0.00020 | 0.00016 | 0.00015 | 0.00022 |
| Cov(IBM) | | 0.00060 | 0.00009 | 0.00015 | 0.00013 | 0.00012 | 0.00018 |
| Cov(Pfizer) | | | 0.00081 | 0.00011 | 0.00014 | 0.00013 | 0.00014 |
| Cov(SAP) | | | | 0.00095 | 0.00010 | 0.00016 | 0.00016 |
| Cov(WM) | | | | | 0.00051 | 0.00011 | 0.00014 |
| Cov(XOM) | | | | | | 0.00049 | 0.00015 |
| Cov(S&P) | | | | | | | 0.00019 |

**Table 7.7** Model results

| Model | Ford | IBM | Pfizer | SAP | WM | XOM | S&P | Return | Stdev |
|---|---|---|---|---|---|---|---|---|---|
| Max return | 1000.000 | – | – | – | – | – | – | 1000.84 | 32.404 |
| Min variance | – | 45.987 | 90.869 | 30.811 | 127.508 | 116.004 | 588.821 | 999.76 | 13.156 |
| Normal **Pr{>970}>0.95** | 398.381 | 283.785 | – | – | 222.557 | 95.277 | – | 1000.49 | 18.534 |
| t **Pr{>970}>0.95** | 607.162 | 296.818 | – | – | 96.020 | – | – | 1000.63 | 23.035 |
| t Pr{>970}>0.95 **Pr{>980}>0.9** | 581.627 | 301.528 | – | – | 116.845 | – | – | 1000.61 | 22.475 |
| t Pr{>970}>0.95 Pr{>980}>0.9 **Pr{>990}>0.8** | 438.405 | 279.287 | – | – | 220.254 | 62.054 | – | 1000.51 | 19.320 |
| Max Pr{>1000} | 16.275 | 109.867 | 105.586 | 38.748 | 174.570 | 172.244 | 382.711 | 999.91 | 13.310 |

The bold emphasis signifies the instance with high variance

# Data Envelopment Analysis in Enterprise Risk Management

# 8

Charnes, Cooper and Rhodes[1] first introduced DEA (CCR) for efficiency analysis of Decision-making Units (DMU). DEA can be used for modeling operational processes, and its empirical orientation and absence of *a priori* assumptions have resulted in its use in a number of studies involving efficient frontier estimation in both nonprofit and in private sectors. DEA is widely applied in banking[2] and insurance.[3] DEA has become a leading approach for efficiency analysis in many fields, such as supply chain management,[4] petroleum distribution system design,[5] and government services.[6] DEA and multicriteria decision making models have been compared and extended.[7]

Moskowitz et al.[8] presented a vendor selection scenario involving nine vendors with stochastic measures given over 12 criteria. This model was used by Wu and Olson[9] in comparing DEA with multiple criteria analysis. We start with discussion of the advanced ERM technology, i.e., value-at-risk (VaR) and view it as a tool to conduct risk management in enterprises.

While risk needs to be managed, taking risks is fundamental to doing business. Profit by necessity requires accepting some risk.[10] ERM provides tools to rationally manage these risks. We will demonstrate multiple criteria and DEA models in the enterprise risk management context with a hypothetical nuclear waste repository site location problem.

## Basic Data

For a set of data including a supply chain needing to select a repository for waste dump siting, we have 12 alternatives with four criteria. Criteria considered include cost, expected lives lost, risk of catastrophe, and civic improvement. Expected lives lost reflects workers as well as expected local (civilian bystander) lives lost. The hierarchy of objectives is:



D.L. Olson, D.D. Wu, *Enterprise Risk Management Models*, Springer Texts in Business and Economics, DOI 10.1007/978-3-662-53785-5_8

**Table 8.1** Dump site data

| Alternatives | Cost (billions) | Expected lives lost | Risk | Civic improvement |
|---|---|---|---|---|
| Nome AK | 40 | 60 | Very high | Low |
| Newark NJ | 100 | 140 | Very low | Very high |
| Rock Springs WY | 60 | 40 | Low | High |
| Duquesne PA | 60 | 40 | Medium | Medium |
| Gary IN | 70 | 80 | Low | Very high |
| Yakima Flats WA | 70 | 80 | High | Medium |
| Turkey TX | 60 | 50 | High | High |
| Wells NE | 50 | 30 | Medium | Medium |
| Anaheim CA | 90 | 130 | Very high | Very low |
| Epcot Center FL | 80 | 120 | Very low | Very low |
| Duckwater NV | 80 | 70 | Medium | Low |
| Santa Cruz CA | 90 | 100 | Very high | Very low |

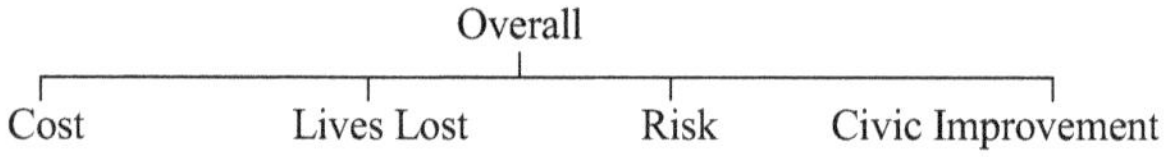

Overall

Cost | Lives Lost | Risk | Civic Improvement

The alternatives available, with measures on each criterion (including two categorical measures) are given in Table 8.1:

Models require numerical data, and it is easier to keep things straight if we make higher scores be better. So we adjust the Cost and Expected Lives Lost scores by subtracting them from the maximum, and we assign consistent scores on a 0–100 scale for the qualitative ratings given Risk and Civic Improvement, yielding Table 8.2:

Nondominated solutions can be identified by inspection. For instance, Nome AK has the lowest estimated cost, so is by definition nondominated. Similarly, Wells NE has the best expected lives lost. There is a tie for risk of catastrophe (Newark NJ and Epcot Center FL have the best ratings, with tradeoff in that Epcot Center FL has better cost and lives lost estimates while Newark NJ has better civic improvement rating, and both are nondominated). There are also is a tie for best civic improvement (Newark NJ and Gary IN), and tradeoff in that Gary IN has better cost and lives lost estimates while Newark NJ has a better risk of catastrophe rating, and again both are nondominated. There is one other nondominated solution (Rock Springs WY), which can be compared to all of the other 11 alternatives and shown to be better on at least one alternative.

**Table 8.2** Scores used

| Alternatives | Cost | Expected lives lost | Risk | Civic improvement |
|---|---|---|---|---|
| Nome AK | 60 | 80 | 0 | 25 |
| Newark NJ | 0 | 0 | 100 | 100 |
| Rock Springs WY | 40 | 100 | 80 | 80 |
| Duquesne PA | 40 | 100 | 50 | 50 |
| Gary IN | 30 | 60 | 80 | 100 |
| Yakima Flats WA | 30 | 60 | 30 | 50 |
| Turkey TX | 40 | 90 | 30 | 80 |
| Wells NE | 50 | 110 | 50 | 50 |
| Anaheim CA | 10 | 10 | 0 | 0 |
| Epcot Center FL | 20 | 20 | 100 | 0 |
| Duckwater NV | 20 | 70 | 50 | 25 |
| Santa Cruz CA | 10 | 40 | 0 | 0 |

## Multiple Criteria Models

Nondominance can also be established by a linear programming model. We create a variable for each criterion, with the decision variables weights (which we hold strictly greater than 0, and to sum to 1). The objective function is to maximize the sum-product of measure values multiplied by weights for each alternative site in turn, subject to this function being strictly greater than each sum-product of measure values time weights for each of the other sites. For the first alternative, the formulation of the linear programming model is:

$$\text{Max} \sum_{i=1}^{4} w_i y_1$$

s.t. $\sum_{i=1}^{4} w_i = 1$

For each j from 2 to 12: $\sum_{i=1}^{4} w_i y x_1 \geq \sum_{i=1}^{4} w_i y_j + 0.0001$

$$w_i \geq 0.0001$$

This model was run for each of the 12 available sites. Non-dominated alternatives (defined as at least as good on all criteria, and strictly better on at least one criterion relative to all other alternatives) are identified if this model is feasible. The reason to add the 0.0001 to some of the constraints is that strict dominance might not be identified otherwise (the model would have ties). The solution for the Newark NJ alternative was as shown in Table 8.3:

The set of weights were minimum for the criteria of Cost and Expected Lives lost, with roughly equal weights on Risk of Catastrophe and Civic Improvement. That makes sense, because Newark NJ had the best scores for Risk of Catastrophe and Civic Improvement and low scores on the other two Criteria.

Running all 12 linear programming models, six solutions were feasible, indicating that they were not dominated {Nome AK, Newark NJ, Rock Springs

**Table 8.3** MCDM LP solution for Nome AK

| | Criteria | Cost | Lives | Risk | Improve | |
|---|---|---|---|---|---|---|
| Object | Newark NJ | 0 | 0 | 100 | 100 | 99.9801 |
| Weights | | 0.0001 | 0.0001 | 0.4975 | 0.5023 | 1.0000 |
| | Nome AK | 60 | 80 | 0 | 25 | 12.5708 |
| | Rock Springs WY | 40 | 100 | 80 | 80 | 79.9980 |
| | Duquesne PA | 40 | 100 | 50 | 50 | 50.0040 |
| | Gary IN | 30 | 60 | 80 | 100 | 90.0385 |
| | Yakima Flats WA | 30 | 60 | 30 | 50 | 40.0485 |
| | Turkey TX | 40 | 90 | 30 | 80 | 55.1207 |
| | Wells NE | 50 | 110 | 50 | 50 | 50.0060 |
| | Anaheim CA | 10 | 10 | 0 | 0 | 0.0020 |
| | Epcot Center FL | 20 | 20 | 100 | 0 | 49.7567 |
| | Duckwater NV | 20 | 70 | 50 | 25 | 37.4422 |
| | Santa Cruz CA | 10 | 40 | 0 | 0 | 0.0050 |

**Table 8.4** LP solution for Duquesne PA

| | Criteria | Cost | Lives | Risk | Improve | |
|---|---|---|---|---|---|---|
| Object | Duquesne PA | 40 | 100 | 50 | 50 | 99.9840 |
| Weights | | 0.0001 | 0.9997 | 0.0001 | 0.0001 | 1.0000 |
| | Nome AK | 60 | 80 | 0 | 25 | 79.9845 |
| | Newark NJ | 0 | 0 | 100 | 100 | 0.0200 |
| | **Rock Springs WY** | **40** | **100** | **80** | **80** | **99.9900** |
| | Gary IN | 30 | 60 | 80 | 100 | 60.0030 |
| | Yakima Flats WA | 30 | 60 | 30 | 50 | 59.9930 |
| | Turkey TX | 40 | 90 | 30 | 80 | 89.9880 |
| | **Wells NE** | **50** | **110** | **50** | **50** | **109.9820** |
| | Anaheim CA | 10 | 10 | 0 | 0 | 9.9980 |
| | Epcot Center FL | 20 | 20 | 100 | 0 | 20.0060 |
| | Duckwater NV | 20 | 70 | 50 | 25 | 69.9885 |
| | Santa Cruz CA | 10 | 40 | 0 | 0 | 39.9890 |

WY, Gary IN, Wells NE and Epcot Center FL}. The corresponding weights identified are not unique (many different weight combinations might have yielded these alternatives as feasible). These weights also reflect scale (here the range for Cost was 60, and for Lives Lost was 110, while the range for the other two criteria were 100—in this case this difference is slight, but the scales do not need to be similar. The more dissimilar, the more warped are the weights.) For the other six dominated solutions, no set of weights would yield them as feasible. For instance, Table 8.4 shows the infeasible solution for Duquesne PA:

Here Rock Springs WY and Wells NE had higher functional values than Duquesne PA. This is clear by looking at criteria attainments. Rock Springs WY is equal to Duquesne PA on Cost and Lives Lost, and better on Risk and Civic Improvement.

**Table 8.5** Results using scaled weights

| Alternative | Cost | Lives | Risk | Improve | Dominated by |
|---|---|---|---|---|---|
| Nome AK | 0.9997 | 0.0001 | 0.0001 | 0.0001 | |
| Newark NJ | 0.0001 | 0.0001 | 0.4979 | 0.5019 | |
| Rock Springs WY | 0.0001 | 0.7673 | 0.0001 | 0.2325 | |
| Gary IN | 0.00001 | 0.0001 | 0.0001 | 0.9997 | |
| Wells NE | 0.0001 | 0.9997 | 0.0001 | 0.0001 | |
| Epcot Center FL | 0.0002 | 0.0001 | 0.9996 | 0.0001 | |
| Duquesne PA | | | | | Rock Springs WY<br>Wells NE |
| Yakima Flats WA | | | | | Six alternatives |
| Turkey TX | | | | | Rock Springs WY |
| Anaheim CA | | | | | All but Newark NJ |
| Duckwater NV | | | | | Five alternatives |
| Santa Cruz CA | | | | | Eight alternatives |

## Scales

The above analysis used input data with different scales. Cost ranged from 0 to 60, Lives Lost from 0 to 110, and the two subjective criteria (Risk, Civic Improvement) from 0 to 100. While they were similar, there were slightly different ranges. The resulting weights are one possible set of weights that would yield the analyzed alternative as non-dominated. If we proportioned the ranges to all be equal (divide Cost scores in Table 8.2 by 0.6, Expected Lives Lost scores by 1.1), the resulting weights would represent the implied relative importance of each criterion that would yield a non-dominated solution. The non-dominated set is the same, only weights varying. Results are given in Table 8.5.

## Stochastic Mathematical Formulation

Value-at-risk (VaR) methods are popular in financial risk management.[11] VaR models were motivated in part by several major financial disasters in the late 1980s and 1990s, to include the fall of Barings Bank and the bankruptcy of Orange County. In both instances, large amounts of capital were invested in volatile markets when traders concealed their risk exposure. VaR models allow managers to quantify their risk exposure at the portfolio level, and can be used as a benchmark to compare risk positions across different markets. Value-at-risk can be defined as the expected loss for an investment or portfolio at a given confidence level over a stated time horizon. If we define the risk exposure of the investment as $L$, we can express VaR as:

$$Prob\{L \leq VaR\} = 1 - \alpha$$

A rational investor will minimize expected losses, or the loss level at the stated probability (1 – α). This statement of risk exposure can also be used as a constraint in a chance-constrained programming model, imposing a restriction that the probability of loss greater than some stated value should be less than (1 – α).

The standard deviation or volatility of asset returns, σ, is a widely used measure of financial models such as VaR. Volatility σ represents the variation of asset returns during some time horizon in the VaR framework. This measure will be employed in our approach. Monte Carlo Simulation techniques are often applied to measure the variability of asset risk factors.[12] We will employ Monte Carlo Simulation for benchmarking our proposed method.

Stochastic models construct production frontiers that incorporate both inefficiency and stochastic error. The stochastic frontier associates extreme outliers with the stochastic error term and this has the effect of moving the frontier closer to the bulk of the producing units. As a result, the measured technical efficiency of every DMU is raised relative to the deterministic model. In some realizations, some DMUs will have a super-efficiency larger than unity.[13]

Now we consider the stochastic vendor selection model. Consider $N$ suppliers to be evaluated, each has $s$ random variables. Note that all input variables are transformed to output variables, as was done in Moskowitz et al.[14] The variables of supplier j (j=1,2...$N$) exhibit random behavior represented by $\widetilde{y}_j = \left(\widetilde{y}_{1j}, \cdots, \widetilde{y}_{sj}\right)$, where each $\widetilde{y}_{rj}$ $(r = 1, 2, \ldots, s)$ has a known probability distribution. By maximizing the expected efficiency of a vendor under evaluation subject to VaR being restricted to be no worse than some limit, the following model (1) is developed:

$$\text{Max} \sum_{i=1}^{4} w_i y_1$$

s.t. $\sum_{i=1}^{4} w_i = 1$

For each j from 2 to 12: $\text{Prob}\{\sum_{i=1}^{4} w_i y x_1 \geq \sum_{i=1}^{4} w_i y_j + 0.0001\} \geq (1\text{-}\alpha)$

$$w_i \geq 0.0001$$

Because each $\widetilde{y}_j$ is potentially a random variable, it has a distribution rather than being a constant. The objective function is now an expectation, but the expectation is the mean, so this function is still linear, using the mean rather than the constant parameter. The constraints on each location's performance being greater than or equal to all other location performances is now a nonlinear function. The weights $w_i$ are still variables to be solved for, as in the deterministic version used above.

The scalar $\alpha$ is referred to as the modeler's risk level, indicating the probability measure of the extent to which Pareto efficiency violation is admitted as most $\alpha$ proportion of the time. The $\alpha_j$ $(0 \leq \alpha_j \leq 1)$ in the constraints are predetermined scalars which stand for an allowable risk of violating the associated constraints, where $1 - \alpha_j$ indicates the probability of attaining the requirement. The higher the value of $\alpha$, the higher the modeler's risk and the lower the modeler's confidence about the 0th vendor's Pareto efficiency and vice-visa. At the $(1 - \alpha)\%$ confidence level, the 0th supplier is stochastic efficient only if the optimal objective value is equal to one.

To transform the stochastic model (1) into a deterministic DEA, Charnes and Cooper[15] employed chance constrained programming.[16] The transformation steps presented in this study follow this technique and can be considered as a special case of their stochastic DEA,[17] where both stochastic inputs and outputs are used. This yields a non-linear programming problem in the variables $w_i$, which has computational difficulties due to the objective function and the constraints, including the variance-covariance yielding quadratic expressions in constraints. We assume that $\tilde{y}_j$ follows a normal distribution N($\bar{y}_j$, $B_{jk}$), where $\bar{y}_j$ is its vector of expected value and $B_{jk}$ indicates the variance-covariance matrix of the jth alternative with the kth alternative. The development of stochastic DEA is given in Wu and Olson (2008).[18]

We adjust the data set used in the nuclear waste siting problem by making cost a stochastic variable (following an assumed normal distribution, thus requiring a variance). The mathematical programming model decision variables are the weights on each criterion, which are not stochastic. What is stochastic is the parameter on costs. Thus the adjustment is in the constraints. For each evaluated alternative $y_j$ compared to alternative $y_k$:

$$\mathrm{w}_{\mathrm{cost}}(y_{j\ cost} - \mathrm{z}^*\mathrm{SQRT}(\mathrm{Var}[y_{j\ cost}]) + w_{lives}y_{j\ lives} + w_{risk}y_{j\ risk} + w_{imp}y_{j\ imp} \geq$$
$$\mathrm{w}_{\mathrm{cost}}(y_{k\ cost} - \mathrm{zSQRT}(\mathrm{Var}[y_{k\ cost}] + 2^*\mathrm{Cov}[y_{j\ cost}, y_{k\ cost}]$$
$$+ \mathrm{Var}[y_{k\ cost}] + w_{lives}y_{k\ lives} + w_{risk}y_{k\ risk} + w_{imp}y_{k\ imp}$$

These functions need to include the covariance term for costs between alternative $y_j$ compared to alternative $y_k$.

Table 8.6 shows the stochastic cost data in billions of dollars, and the converted cost scores (also billions of dollars transformed as $100 billion minus the cost measure for that site) as in Table 8.2. The cost variances will remain as they were, as the relative scale did not change.

The variance-covariance matrix of costs is required (Table 8.7):

The degree of risk aversion used (α) is 0.95, or a z-value of 1.645 for a one-sided distribution. The adjustment affected the model by lowering the cost parameter proportional to its variance for the evaluated alternative, and inflating it for the other alternatives. Thus the stochastic model required a 0.95 assurance that the cost for the evaluated alternative be superior to each of the other 11 alternatives, a more difficult standard. The DEA models were run for each of the 12 alternatives. Only two of the six alternatives found to be nondominated with deterministic data above were still nondominated {Rock Springs WY and Wells NE}. The model results in Table 8.8 show the results for Rock Springs WY, with one set of weights {0, 0.75, 0.25, 0} yielding Rock Springs with a greater functional value than any of the other 11 alternatives. The weights yielding Wells NE as nondominated had all the weight on Lives Lost.

One of the alternatives that was nondominated with deterministic data {Nome AK} was found to be dominated with stochastic data. Table 8.9 shows the results for the original deterministic model for Nome AK.

The stochastic results are shown in Table 8.10:

**Table 8.6** Stochastic data

| Alternative | Cost measure | Mean cost | Cost variance | Expected lives lost | Risk | Civic improvement |
|---|---|---|---|---|---|---|
| S1 Nome AK | N(40,6) | 60 | 6 | 80 | 0 | 25 |
| S2 Newark NJ | N (100,20) | 0 | 20 | 0 | 100 | 100 |
| S3 Rock Springs WY | N(60,5) | 40 | 5 | 100 | 80 | 80 |
| S4 Duquesne PA | N(60,30) | 40 | 30 | 100 | 50 | 50 |
| S5 Gary IN | N(70,35) | 30 | 35 | 60 | 80 | 100 |
| S6 Yakima Flats WA | N(70,20) | 30 | 20 | 60 | 30 | 50 |
| S7 Turkey TX | N(60,10) | 40 | 10 | 90 | 30 | 80 |
| S8 Wells NE | N(50,8) | 50 | 8 | 110 | 50 | 50 |
| S9 Anaheim CA | N(90,40) | 10 | 40 | 10 | 0 | 0 |
| S10 Epcot Center FL | N(80,50) | 20 | 50 | 20 | 100 | 0 |
| S11 Duckwater NV | N(80,20) | 20 | 20 | 70 | 50 | 25 |
| S12 Santa Cruz CA | N(90,40) | 10 | 40 | 40 | 0 | 0 |

**Table 8.7** Site covariances

| | S1 | S2 | S3 | S4 | S5 | S6 | S7 | S8 | S9 | S10 | S11 | S12 |
|---|---|---|---|---|---|---|---|---|---|---|---|---|
| S1 | 6 | 2 | 4 | 2 | 2 | 3 | 3 | 3 | 2 | 1 | 3 | 2 |
| S2 | | 20 | 3 | 10 | 9 | 5 | 2 | 1 | 4 | 5 | 1 | 4 |
| S3 | | | 5 | 2 | 1 | 2 | 3 | 3 | 2 | 1 | 3 | 2 |
| S4 | | | | 30 | 10 | 8 | 2 | 2 | 6 | 5 | 1 | 4 |
| S5 | | | | | 35 | 9 | 3 | 2 | 5 | 6 | 1 | 4 |
| S6 | | | | | | 20 | 3 | 2 | 10 | 8 | 2 | 12 |
| S7 | | | | | | | 10 | 3 | 2 | 1 | 3 | 2 |
| S8 | | | | | | | | 8 | 2 | 1 | 3 | 2 |
| S9 | | | | | | | | | 40 | 5 | 1 | 12 |
| S10 | | | | | | | | | | 50 | 2 | 8 |
| S11 | | | | | | | | | | | 20 | 2 |
| S12 | | | | | | | | | | | | 40 |

Wells NE is shown to be superior to Nome AK at the last set of weights the SOLVER algorithm in EXCEL attempted. Looking at the stochastically adjusted scores for cost, Wells NE now has a superior cost value to Nome AK (the objective functional cost value is penalized downward, the constraint cost value for Wells NE and other alternatives are penalized upward to make a harder standard to meet).

**Table 8.8** Output for Stochastic Model for Rock Springs WY

| Object | Rock Springs WY | 36.322 | 100 | 80 | 80 | 94.99304 |
|---|---|---|---|---|---|---|
| Weights | | 0.0001 | 0.7499 | 0.24993 | 0.0001 | 1 |
| | Nome AK | 67.170 | 80 | 0 | 25 | 59.999 |
| | Newark NJ | 9.158 | 0 | 100 | 100 | 25.004 |
| | Duquesne PA | 50.272 | 100 | 50 | 50 | 87.494 |
| | Gary IN | 40.660 | 60 | 80 | 80 | 64.999 |
| | Yakima Flats WA | 38.858 | 60 | 30 | 30 | 52.497 |
| | Turkey TX | 47.538 | 90 | 30 | 30 | 74.994 |
| | Wells NE | 57.170 | 110 | 50 | 50 | 94.993 |
| | Anaheim CA | 21.514 | 10 | 0 | 0 | 7.501 |
| | Epcot Center FL | 32.418 | 20 | 100 | 100 | 40.004 |
| | Duckwater NV | 29.158 | 70 | 50 | 50 | 64.995 |
| | Santa Cruz CA | 21.514 | 40 | 0 | 0 | 29.997 |

**Table 8.9** Nome AK alternative results with original model

| Object | Nome AK | 60 | 80 | 0 | 25 | 64.9857 |
|---|---|---|---|---|---|---|
| Weights | | 0.7500 | 0.2498 | 0.0001 | 0.0001 | 1 |
| | Newark NJ | 0 | 0 | 100 | 100 | 0.020 |
| | Rock Springs WY | 40 | 100 | 80 | 80 | 54.994 |
| | Duquesne PA | 40 | 100 | 50 | 50 | 54.988 |
| | Gary IN | 30 | 60 | 80 | 100 | 37.505 |
| | Yakima Flats WA | 30 | 60 | 30 | 50 | 37.495 |
| | Turkey TX | 40 | 90 | 30 | 80 | 52.491 |
| | Wells NE | 50 | 110 | 50 | 50 | 64.986 |
| | Anaheim CA | 10 | 10 | 0 | 0 | 9.998 |
| | Epcot Center FL | 20 | 20 | 100 | 0 | 20.006 |
| | Duckwater NV | 20 | 70 | 50 | 25 | 32.492 |
| | Santa Cruz CA | 10 | 40 | 0 | 0 | 17.491 |

## DEA Models

DEA evaluates alternatives by seeking to maximize the ratio of efficiency of output attainments to inputs, considering the relative performance of each alternative. The mathematical programming model creates a variable for each output (outputs designated by $u_i$) and input (inputs designated by $v_j$). Each alternative $k$ has performance coefficients for each output ($y_{ik}$) and input ($x_{jk}$).

The classic Charnes, Cooper and Rhodes (CCR)[19] DEA model is:

$$Max\ efficiency_k = \frac{\sum_{i=1}^{2} u_i y_{ik}}{\sum_{j=1}^{2} v_j x_{jk}}$$

error. We must point out the main difference for implementing investment VaR in financial markets such as banking industry and our DEA VaR used for supplier selection is that the underlying asset volatility or standard deviation is typically a managerial assumption due to lack of sufficient historical data to calibrate the risk measure.

## Notes

1. Charnes, A., Cooper, W.W. and Rhodes, E. (1978). Measuring the efficiency of decision-making units, *European Journal of Operational Research* 2, 429–444.
2. Banker, R.D., Chang,H. and Lee, S.-Y. (2010). Differential impact of Korean banking system reforms on bank productivity. *Journal of Banking & Finance* 34(7), 1450–1460; Gunay, E.N.O. (2012). Risk incorporation and efficiency in emerging market banks during the global crisis: Evidence from Turkey, 2002–2009. *Emerging Markets Finance & Trade* 48(supp5), 91–102; Yang, C.-C. (2014). An enhanced DEA model for decomposition of technical efficiency in banking. *Annals of Operations Research* 214(1), 167–185.
3. Segovia-Gonzalez, M.M., Contreras, I. and Mar-Molinero, C. (2009). A DEA analysis of risk, cost, and revenues in insurance. *Journal of the Operational Research Society* 60(11), 1483–1494.
4. Ross, A. and Droge, C. (2002). An integrated benchmarking approach to distribution center performance using DEA modeling, *Journal of Operations Management* 20, 19–32; Wu, D.D. and Olson, D. (2010). Enterprise risk management: A DEA VaR approach in vendor selection. *International Journal of Production Research* 48(16), 4919–4932.
5. Ross, A. and Droge, C. (2004). An analysis of operations efficiency in large-scale distribution systems, *Journal of Operations Management* 21, 673–688.
6. Narasimhan, R., Talluri, S., Sarkis, J. and Ross, A. (2005). Efficient service location design in government services: A decision support system framework, *Journal of Operations Management* 23:2, 163–176.
7. Lahdelma, R. and Salminen, P. (2006). Stochastic multicriteria acceptability analysis using the data envelopment model, *European Journal of Operational Research* 170, 241–252; Olson, D.L. and Wu, D.D. (2011). Multiple criteria analysis for evaluation of information system risk. *Asia-Pacific Journal of Operational Research* 28(1), 25–39.
8. Moskowitz, H., Tang, J. and Lam, P. (2000). Distribution of aggregate utility using stochastic elements of additive multiattribute utility models, *Decision Sciences* 31, 327–360.
9. Wu, D. and Olson, D.L. (2008). A comparison of stochastic dominance and stochastic DEA for vendor evaluation, *International Journal of Production Research* 46:8, 2313–2327.
10. Alquier, A.M.B. and Tignol, M.H.L. (2006). Risk management in small- and medium-sized enterprises, *Production Planning & Control,* 17, 273–282.
11. Duffie, D. and Pan, J. (2001). Analytical value-at-risk with jumps and credit risk, *Finance & Stochastics* 5:2, 155–180; Jorion, P. (2007). *Value-at-risk: The New Benchmark for Controlling Market Risk*. New York: Irwin.
12. Crouhy, M., Galai, D., and Mark, R. M. (2001). *Risk Management*. New York, NY: McGraw Hill.
13. Olesen, O.B. and Petersen, N.C. (1995). Comment on assessing marginal impact of investment on the performance of organizational units, *International Journal of Production Economics* 39, 162–163; Cooper, W.W., Hemphill, H., Huang, Z., Li, S., Lelas, V., and Sullivan, D.W. (1996). Survey of mathematical programming models in air pollution management, *European Journal of Operational Research* 96, 1–35; Cooper, W.W., Deng, H., Huang,

Z.M. and Li, S.X. (2002). A one-model approach to congestion in data envelopment analysis, *Socio-Economic Planning Sciences* 36, 231–238.

14. Moskowitz et al. (2000), op. cit.
15. Charnes, A. and Cooper, W.W. (1959). Chance-constrained programming, *Management Science* 6:1, 73–79; see also Huang, Z. and Li, S.X. (2001). Co-op advertising models in manufacturer-retailer supply chains: A game theory approach, *European Journal of Operational Research* 135:3, 527–544.
16. Charnes, A., Cooper, W.W. and Symonds, G.H. (1958). Cost horizons and certainty equivalents: An approach to stochastic programming of heating oil, *Management Science* 4:3, 235–263.
17. Cooper, W.W., Park, K.S. and Yu, G. (1999). IDEA and AR-IDEA: Models for dealing with imprecise data in DEA, *Management Science* 45, 597–607.
18. Wu and Olson (2008), op cit.
19. Charnes, A., Cooper, W. and Rhodes, E. (1978), op cit.

# Data Mining Models and Enterprise Risk Management

# 9

Datamining applications to business cover a variety of fields.[1] Risk-related applications are especially strong in insurance, specifically fraud detection.[2] Fraud detection modeling includes text mining.[3] There are many financial risk management applications, with heavy interest in developing tools to support investment. Automated trading has been widely applied in practice for decades. More recent efforts have gone into sentiment analysis, mining text of investment comments to detect patterns, especially related to investment risk.[4]

There are a number of data mining tools. This includes a variety of software, some commercial (powerful and expensive) as well as open-source. Open-source classification software tools have been published.[5] There are other modeling forms as well, to include application of clustering analysis in fraud detection.[6] We will use an example dataset involving data mining of bankruptcy, a severe form of financial risk.

## Bankruptcy Data Demonstration

This data concerns 100 US firms that underwent bankruptcy.[7] All of the sample data are from the USA companies. About 400 bankrupt company names were obtained from the Compustat database, focusing on the companies that went bankrupt over the period January 2006 through December 2009. This yielded 99 firms. Using the company Ticker code list, financial data ratios over the period January 2005–December 2009 were obtained and used in prediction models of company bankruptcy. The factor collected contain total asset, book value per share, inventories, liabilities, receivables, cost of goods sold, total dividends, earnings before interest and taxes, gross profit (loss), net income (loss), operating income after depreciation, total revenue, sales, dividends per share, and total market value. To obtain non-bankrupt cases for comparison, the same financial ratios for 200 non-failed companies were gathered for the same time period. The LexisNexis database provided SEC fillings after June 2010, to identify firm survival with CIK code.



D.L. Olson, D.D. Wu, *Enterprise Risk Management Models*, Springer Texts in Business and Economics, DOI 10.1007/978-3-662-53785-5_9

**Table 9.1** Attributes in bankruptcy data

| No | Short name | Long name |
|---|---|---|
| 1 | fyear | Data year—Fiscal |
| 2 | cik | CIK number |
| 3 | at | Assets—Total |
| 4 | bkvlps | Book value per share |
| 5 | invt | Inventories—Total |
| 6 | Lt | Liabilities—Total |
| 7 | rectr | Receivables—Trade |
| 8 | cogs | Cost of goods sold |
| 9 | dvt | Dividends—Total |
| 10 | ebit | Earnings before interest and taxes |
| 11 | gp | Gross profit (Loss) |
| 12 | ni | Net income (Loss) |
| 13 | oiadp | Operating income after depreciation |
| 14 | revt | Revenue—Total |
| 15 | sale | Sales-turnover (Net) |
| 16 | dvpsx_f | Dividends per share—Ex-date—Fiscal |
| 17 | mkvalt | Market value—Total—Fiscal |
| 18 | prch_f | Price high—Annual—Fiscal |
| 19 | bankruptcy | Bankruptcy (output variable) |

The CIK code list was input to the Compustat database to obtain financial data and ratios for the period January 2005–December 2009 to match that of failed companies.

The data set consists of 1321 records with full data over 19 attributes as shown in Table 9.1. The outcome attribute is bankruptcy, which has a value of 1 if the firm went bankrupt by 2011 (697 cases), and a value of 0 if it did not (624 cases).

This is real data concerning firm bankruptcy, which could be updated by going to web sources.

## Software

R is a widely used open source software. Rattle is a GUI system for R (also open source) that makes it easy to implement R for data mining.

To install R, visit https://cran.rstudio.com/

Open a folder for R.

Select Download R for windows.

To install Rattle:

Open the R Desktop icon (32 bit or 64 bit) and enter the following command at the R prompt. R will ask for a CRAN mirror. Choose a nearby location.

- install.packages("rattle")

Enter the following two commands at the R prompt. This loads the Rattle package into the library and then starts up Rattle.

- library(rattle)
- rattle()

If the RGtk2 package has yet to be installed, there will be an error popup indicating that libatk-1.0-0.dll is missing from your computer. Click on the OK and then you will be asked if you would like to install GTK+. Click OK to do so. This then downloads and installs the appropriate GTK+ libraries for your computer. After this has finished, do exit from R and restart it so that it can find the newly installed libraries.

When running Rattle a number of other packages will be downloaded and installed as needed, with Rattle asking for the user's permission before doing so. They only need to be downloaded once.The installation has been tested to work on Microsoft Windows, 32bit and 64bit, XP, Vista and 7 with R 3.1.1, Rattle 3.1.0 and RGtk2 2.20.31. If you are missing something, you will get a message from R asking you to install a package. I read nominal data (string), and was prompted that I needed "stringr". On the R console (see Fig. 9.1), click on the "Packages" word on the top line:Give the command "Install packages" which will direct you to HTTPS CRAN mirror. Select one of the sites (like "USA(TX) [https]") and find "stringr" and click on it. Then upload that package. You may have to restart R.

Data mining practice usually utilizes a training set to build a model, which can be applied to a test set. In this case, 1178 observations (those through 2008) were used for the training set and 143 observations (2009 and 2010) held out for testing. To run a model, on the **Filename** line, click on the icon and browse for the file "bankruptcyTrain.csv". Click on the **Execute** icon on the upper left of the Rattle window. This yields Fig. 9.2:Bankrupt is a categoric variable, and R assumes that is the Target (as we want). We could delete other variables if we choose to, and redo the Execute step for the Data tab. We can **Explore**—the default is **Summary**. **Execute** yields macrodata, identify data types as well as descriptive statistics (minima, maxima, medians, means, and quartiles). R by default holds out 30 % of the training data as an intermediate test set, and thus builds models on the remaining 70 % (here 824 observations). The summary identifies the outcome of the training set (369 not bankrupt, 455 bankrupt).

We can further explore the data through correlation analysis. Figure 9.3 shows the R screen with the correlation radio button selected.**Execute** on this screen yields output over the numerical variables as shown in Fig. 9.4:

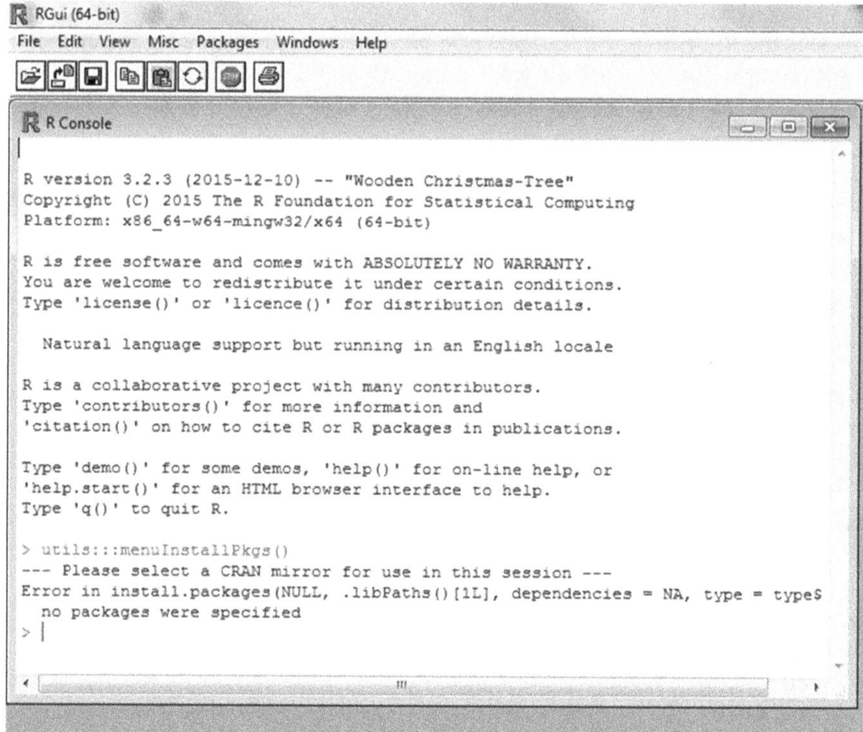


**Fig. 9.1** R console

Figure 9.4 indicates high degrees of correlation across potential independent variables, and further analysis might select some for elimination. Numerical correlation values are also provided by R. The dependent variable was alphabetical, so R didn't include it, but outside analysis indicates low correlation between bankruptcy and all independent variables—the highest in magnitude being 0.180 with cost of goods sold (cogs) and with total revenue (revt).

## Decision Tree Model

We can click on the **Model** tab and run models. Data mining for classification models have three basic tools—decision trees, logistic regression, and neural network models. To run a decision tree, select the radio button as indicated in Fig. 9.5:Note that the defaults are to require a minimum of 20 cases per rule, with a maximum number of 30 branches. These can be changed by entering desired values in the appropriate window. **Execute** yields Fig. 9.6:Rattle also provides a graphical display of this decision tree, as shown in Fig. 9.7:This model begins with the variable revt, stating that if revt is less than 78, the conclusion is that bankruptcy

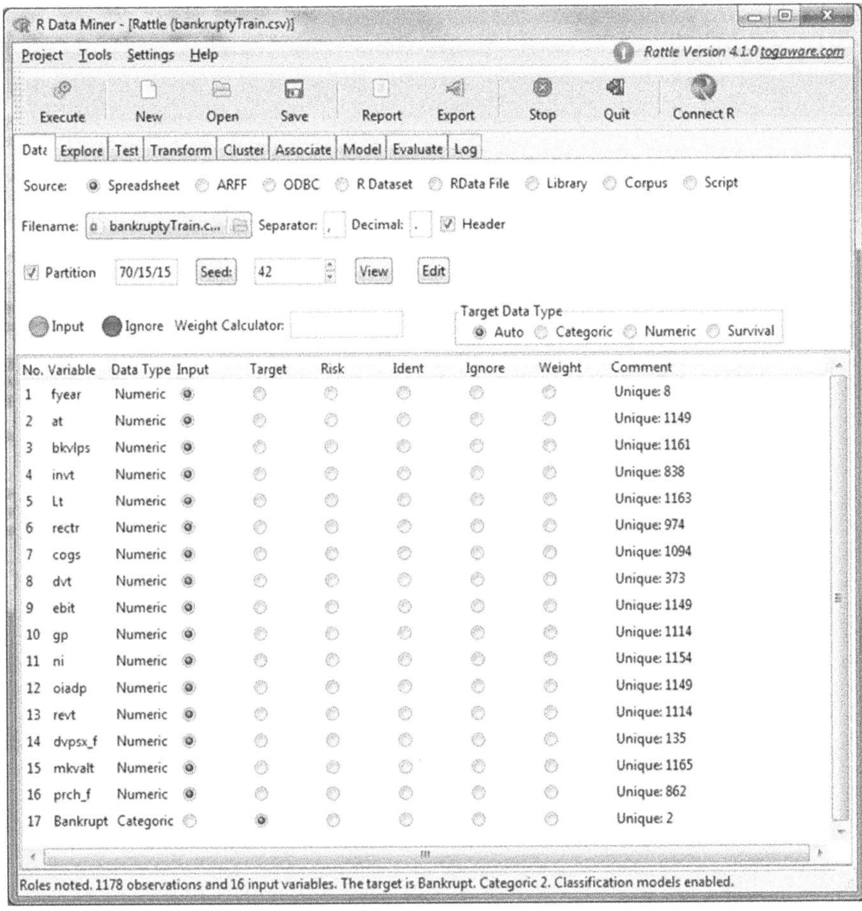


**Fig. 9.2** LoanRaw.csv data read

would not occur. This rule was based on 44 % of the training data (360 out of 824), over which 84 % of these cases were not bankrupt (count of 304 no and 56 yes).

On the other branch, the next variable to consider is dvpsx_f. If dvpsx_f was less than 0.215 (364 cases of 464, or 44 % of the total), the conclusion is bankruptcy (340 yes and 24 no, for 93 %).

If revt $\geq$ 78 and dvpsx_f $\geq$ 0.215 (100 cases), the tree branches on variable at. If at $\geq$4169.341, the conclusion is bankruptcy (based on 31 of 31 cases). If at$<$4169.341, the model branches on variable invt.

For these 69 cases, if invt $<$ 16.179 (23 cases), there is a further branch on variable at. For these 23 cases if at $<$818.4345, the conclusion is bankruptcy (based on 13 of 13 cases). If at $\geq$818.4345, the conclusion is no bankruptcy (based on 7 of 10 cases).

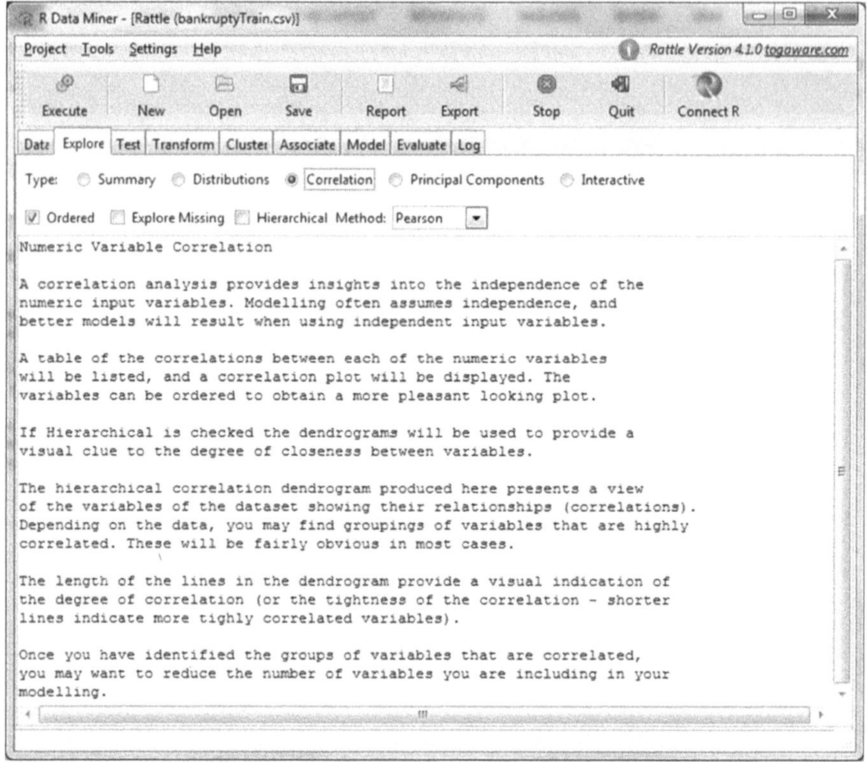


**Fig. 9.3** Selecting correlation

If invt $\geq$ 16.179 (46 cases), the model splits further on invt. If invt $<$ 74.9215, the conclusion is no bankruptcy (based on 18 of 18 cases). If invt $\geq$ 74.9215, there is further branching on variable mkvalt. For mkvalt $<$ 586.9472, the conclusion is bankruptcy based on 11 of 14 cases. If mkvalt $\geq$ 586.9472, the conclusion is no bankruptcy (based on 13 of 14 cases).

This demonstrates well how a decision tree works. It simply splits the data into bins, and uses outcome counts to determine rules. Variables are selected by various algorithms, often using entropy as a basis to select the next variable to split on (Table 9.2).This model shows overall accuracy of 164/176, or 0.932. These validation were over the same period over which the model was built, up to 2008. We now test on a more independent testing set (2009–2010) as shown in Table 9.3:Here the overall correct classification rate is 126/143, or 0.881. The model was correct in 80 of 90 cases where firms actually went bankrupt (0.889 correct). For test cases where firms survived, the model was correct 46 of 53 times (0.868 correct).

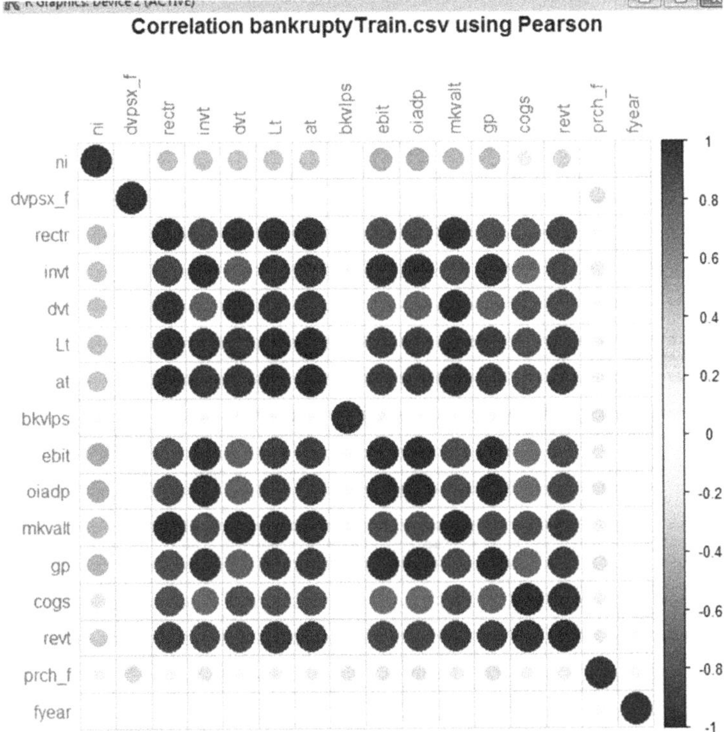


**Fig. 9.4** Correlation plot

## Logistic Regression Model

We can obtain a logistic regression model from Rattle by clicking the Linear button in Fig. 9.8, followed by the Logistic button.**Execute** yields Fig. 9.9 output:

Note that R threw out two variables (oiadp and revt), due to detected singularity. This output indicates that variables rectr and gp are highly significant. Further refinement of logistic regression might consider deleting some variables in light of correlation output. Here we are simply demonstrating running models, so we will evaluate the above model on both the validation set (Table 9.4) and the test set.This model shows overall accuracy of 158/176, or 0.898. This is slightly inferior to the decision tree model. We now test on a more independent testing set (2009–2010) as shown in Table 9.5:Here the overall correct classification rate is 111/143, or 0.776. The model was correct in 78 of 90 cases where firms actually went bankrupt (0.867 correct). For test cases where firms survived, the model was correct 33 of 53 times (0.623 correct).

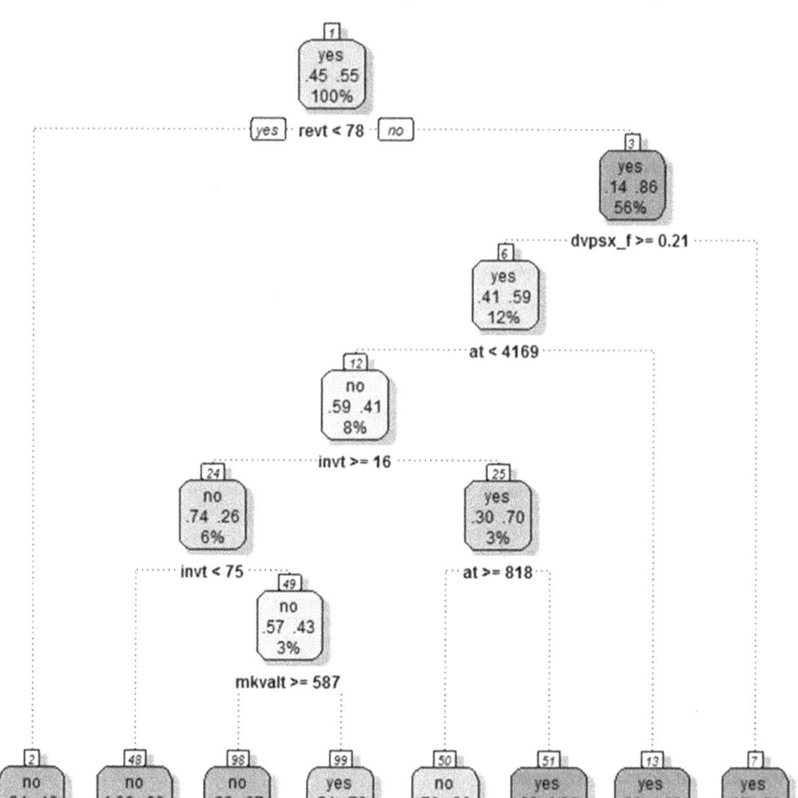


**Fig. 9.7** Rattle graphical decision tree

**Table 9.2** Coincidence matrix for validation set of decision tree model

| | Model not bankrupt | Model bankrupt | |
|---|---|---|---|
| Actual not bankrupt | 70 | 6 | 76 |
| Actual bankrupt | 6 | 94 | 100 |
| | 76 | 100 | 176 |

**Table 9.3** Coincidence matrix for test set of decision tree model

| | Model not bankrupt | Model bankrupt | |
|---|---|---|---|
| Actual not bankrupt | 80 | 10 | 90 |
| Actual bankrupt | 7 | 46 | 53 |
| | 87 | 56 | 143 |

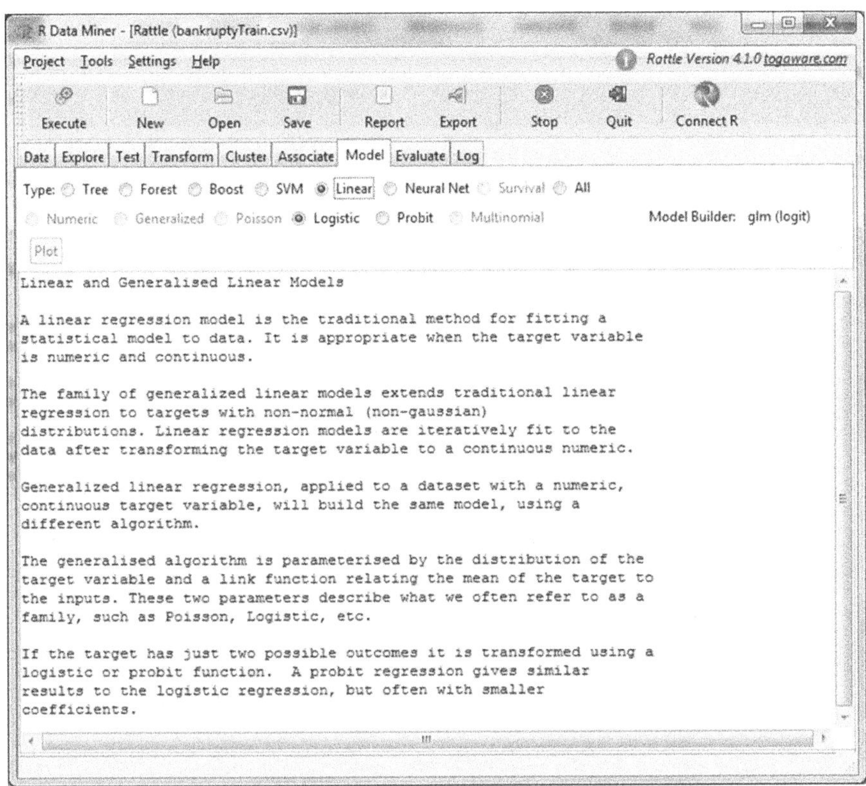


**Fig. 9.8** Selecting logistic regression

## Summary

We have demonstrated data mining on a financial risk set of data using R (Rattle) computations for the basic classification algorithms in data mining. The advent of big data has led to an environment where billions of records are possible. We have not demonstrated that scope by any means, but it has demonstrated the small-scale version of the basic algorithms. The intent is to make data mining less of a black-box exercise, thus hopefully enabling users to be more intelligent in their application of data mining.

We have demonstrated an open source software product. R is a very useful software, widely used in industry and has all of the benefits of open source software (many eyes are monitoring it, leading to fewer bugs; it is free; it is scalable). Further, the R system enables widespread data manipulation and management.

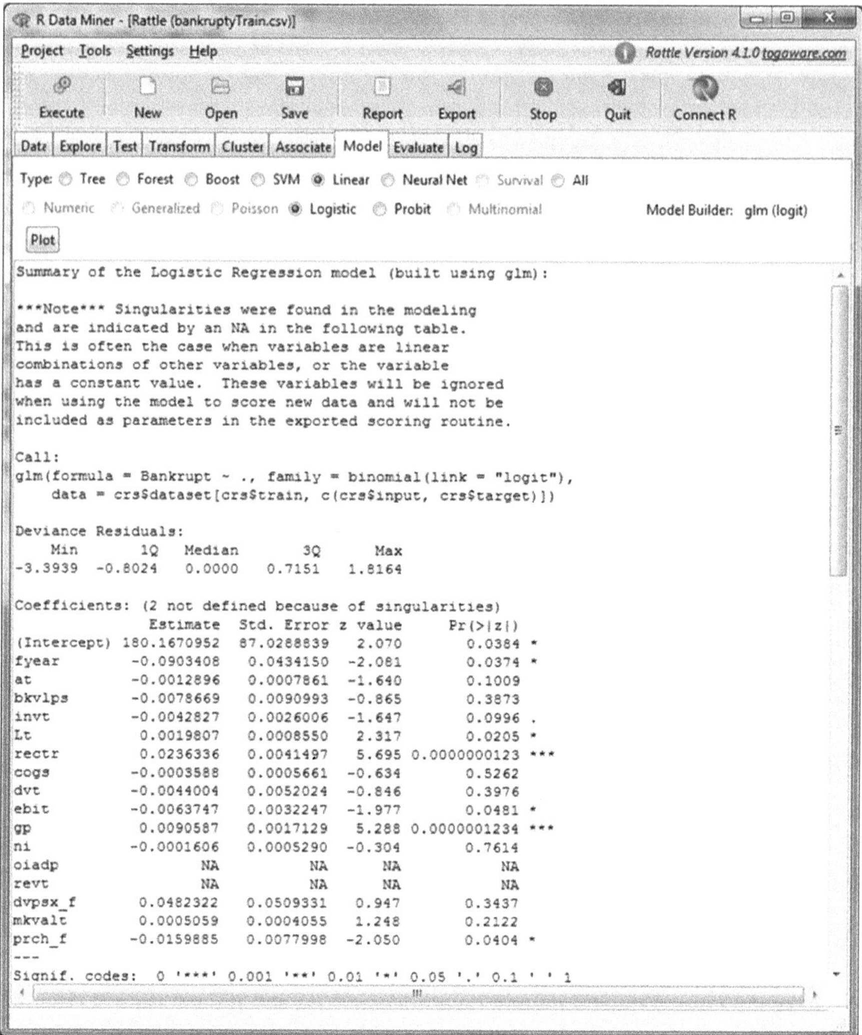


**Fig. 9.9** Logistic regression output

**Table 9.4** Coincidence matrix for validation set of logistic regression model

| | Model not bankrupt | Model bankrupt | |
|---|---|---|---|
| Actual not bankrupt | 72 | 4 | 76 |
| Actual bankrupt | 14 | 86 | 100 |
| | 86 | 90 | 176 |

**Table 9.5** Coincidence matrix for test set of logistic regression model

| | Model not bankrupt | Model bankrupt | |
|---|---|---|---|
| Actual not bankrupt | 78 | 12 | 90 |
| Actual bankrupt | 20 | 33 | 53 |
| | 98 | 45 | 143 |

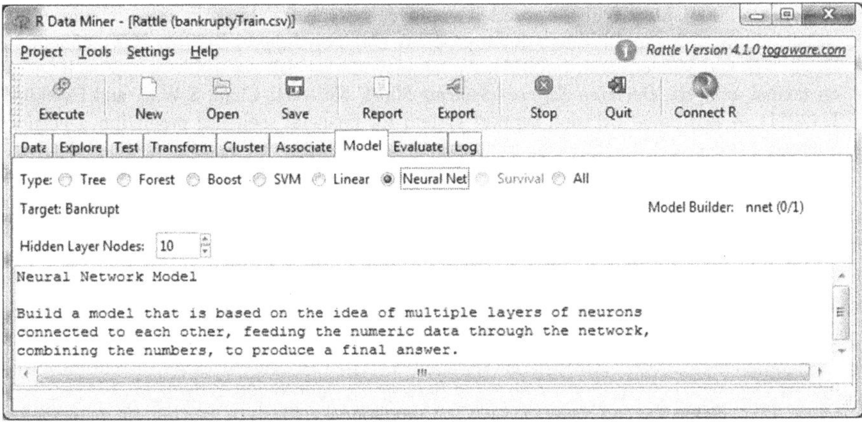


**Fig. 9.10** Selecting neural network model

**Table 9.6** Coincidence matrix for validation set of neural network model

| | Model not bankrupt | Model bankrupt | |
|---|---|---|---|
| Actual not bankrupt | 67 | 9 | 76 |
| Actual bankrupt | 11 | 89 | 100 |
| | 78 | 98 | 176 |

**Table 9.7** Coincidence matrix for test set of neural network model

| | Model not bankrupt | Model bankrupt | |
|---|---|---|---|
| Actual not bankrupt | 75 | 15 | 90 |
| Actual bankrupt | 7 | 46 | 53 |
| | 82 | 61 | 143 |

**Table 9.8** Comparative test results

| Model | Correct not bankrupt | Correct bankrupt | Overall |
|---|---|---|---|
| Decision tree | 0.889 | 0.868 | 0.889 |
| Logistic regression | 0.867 | 0.623 | 0.776 |
| Neural network | 0.833 | 0.867 | 0.846 |

## ERM and Balanced Scorecards

Beasley et al.[8] argued that balanced scorecards broaden the perspective of enterprise risk management. While many firms focus on Sarbanes-Oxley compliance, there is a need to consider strategic, market, and reputation risks as well. Balanced scorecards explicitly link risk management to strategic performance. To demonstrate this, Beasley et al. provided an example balanced scorecard for supply chain management, outlined in Table 10.1.

Other examples of balanced scorecard use have been presented as well, as tools providing measurement on a broader, strategic perspective. For instance, balanced scorecards have been applied to internal auditing in accounting[9] and to mental health governance.[10] Janssen et al.[11]applied a system dynamics model to the marketing of natural gas vehicles, considering the perspective of sixteen stakeholders ranging across automobile manufacturers and customers to the natural gas industry and government. Policy options were compared, using balanced scorecards with the following strategic categories of analysis:

- Natural gas vehicle subsidies
- Fueling station subsidies
- Compressed natural gas tax reductions
- Natural gas vehicle advertising effectiveness.

Balanced scorecards provided a systematic focus on strategic issues, allowing the analysts to examine the nonlinear responses of policy options as modeled with system dynamics. Five indicators were proposed to measure progress of market penetration:

1. Ratio of natural gas vehicles per compress natural gas fueling stations
2. Type coverages (how many different natural gas vehicle types were available)
3. Natural gas vehicle investment pay-back time
4. Sales per type
5. Subsidies par automobile

## Small Business Scorecard Analysis

This section discusses computational results on various scorecard performances currently being used in a large bank to evaluate loans to small businesses. This bank uses various ERM performance measures to validate a small business scorecard (SBB). Because scorecards have a tendency to deteriorate over time, it is appropriate to examine how well they are performing and to examine any possible changes in the scoring population. A number of statistics and analyses will be employed to determine if the scorecard is still effective.

**Table 10.1** Supply chain management balanced scorecard

| Measure | Goals | Measures |
|---|---|---|
| **Learning & growth for employees** To achieve our vision, how will we sustain our ability to change & improve? | Increase employee ownership over process | Employee survey scores |
| | Improve information flows across supply chain stages | Changes in information reports, frequencies across supply chain partners |
| | Increase employee identification of potential supply chain disruptions | Comparison of actual disruptions with reports about drivers of potential disruptions |
| | **Risk-related goals:** | |
| | Increase employee awareness of supply chain risks | Number of employees attending risk management training |
| | Increase supplier accountabilities for disruptions | Supplier contract provisions addressing risk management accountability & penalties |
| | Increase employee awareness of integration of supply chain and other enterprise risks | Number of departments participating in supply chain risk identification & assessment workshops |
| **Internal business processes** To satisfy our stakeholders and customers, where must we excel in our business processes? | Reduce waste generated across the supply chain | Pounds of scrap |
| | Shorten time from start to finish | Time from raw material purchase to product/service delivery to customer |
| | Achieve unit cost reductions | Unit costs per product/service delivered, % of target costs achieved |
| | **Risk-related goals:** | |
| | Reduce probability and impact of threats to supply chain processes | Number of employees attending risk management training |
| | Identify specific tolerances for key supply chain processes | Number of process variances exceeding specified acceptable risk tolerances |
| | Reduce number of exchanges of supply chain risks to other enterprise processes | Extent of risks realized in other functions from supply chain process risk drivers |
| **Customer satisfaction** To achieve our vision, how should we appear to our customers? | Improve product/service quality | Number of customer contact points |
| | Improve timeliness of product/service delivery | Time from customer order to delivery |
| | Improve customer perception of value | Customer scores of value |
| | **Risk-related goals:** | |
| | Reduce customer defections | Number of customers retained |
| | Monitor threats to product/service reputation | Extent of negative coverage in business press of quality |

(continued)

**Table 10.1** (continued)

| Measure | Goals | Measures |
|---|---|---|
| | Increase customer feedback | Number of completed customer surveys about delivery comparisons to other providers |
| **Financial performance** To succeed financially, how should we appear to our stakeholders? | Higher profit margins | Profit margin by supply chain partner |
| | Improved cash flows | Net cash generated over supply chain |
| | Revenue growth | Increase in number of customers & sales per customer; % annual return on supply chain assets |
| | **Risk-related goals:** | |
| | Reduce threats from price competition | Number of customer defections due to price |
| | Reduce cost overruns | Surcharges paid, holding costs incurred, overtime charges applied |
| | Reduce costs outside the supply chain from supply chain processes | Warranty claims incurred, legal costs paid, sales returns processed |

Developed from Beasley et al. (2006)

## ERM Performance Measurement

Some performance measures for enterprise risk modeling are reviewed in this section. They are used to determine the relative effectiveness of the scorecards. More details are given in our work published elsewhere.[12] There are four measures reviewed: the Divergence, Kolmogorov-Smirnov (KS) Statistic, Lorenz Curve and the Population stability index. **Divergence** is calculated as the squared difference between the mean score of good and bad accounts divided by their average variance. The dispersion of the data about the means is captured by the variances in the denominator. The divergence will be lower if the variance is high. A high divergence value indicates the score is able to differentiate between good and bad accounts. Divergence is a relative measure and should be compared to other measures. The KS Statistic is the maximum difference between the cumulative percentage of goods and cumulative percentage of bads for the population rank-ordered according to its score. A high KS value shows it is very possible that good applicants can receive high scores and bad applicants receive low scores. The maximum possible K-S statistic is unity. **Lorenz Curve** is the graph that depicts the power of a model capturing bad accounts relative to the entire population. Usually, three curves are depicted: a piecewise curve representing the perfect model which captures all the bads in the lowest scores range of the model, the random line as a point of reference indicating no predictive ability, and the curve lying between these two capturing the discriminant power of the model under evaluation. **Population stability index** measures a change in score distributions by comparing the frequencies of the corresponding scorebands, i.e., it measures the difference between two populations. In practice, one can judge there is no real change between the populations if an index value is no larger than and a definite population change if index value is greater than 0.25. An index value between 0.10 and 0.25 indicates some shift.

## Data

Data are collected from the bank's internal database. 'Bad' accounts are defined into two types: 'Bad 1' indicating Overlimit at month-end, and 'Bad 2' referring to those with 35 days since last deposit at month-end. All non-bad accounts will be classified as 'Good'. We split the population according to Credit Limit: one for Credit Limit less than or equal to $50,0000 and the other for Credit Limit between $50,000 and $100,000. Data are gathered from two time slots: observed time slot and validated time slot. Two sets (denoted as Set1 and Set2) are used in the validation. Observed time slots are from August 2002 to January 2003 for Set1 and from September 2001 to February 2002 for Set2 respectively. While this data is relative dated, the system demonstrated using this data is still in use, as the bank has found it stable, and they feel that there is a high cost in switching. Validated time slot are from February 2003 to June 2003 for Set1 and from March 2002 to July 2002 for Set2 respectively. All accounts are scored on the last business day of each month. All non-scored accounts will be excluded from the analyses.

Table 10.2 gives the bad rates summary by Line Size for both sets while Table 10.3 reports the score distribution for both sets, to include the Beacon score accounts. From Table 10.2, we can see that in both sets, although the number of Bad1 accounts is a bit less than that of Bad2 accounts, it is still a pretty balanced

**Table 10.2** Bad loan rates by loan size

| Limit | Bad loans 1 Jan. 2003 (set1) | | | Bad loans 2 Jan. 2003 (set1) | | |
|---|---|---|---|---|---|---|
| | *N* | # of bad loans | Bad rate (%) | *N* | # of bad loans | Bad rate (%) |
| ≤$50 M | 59,332 | 5022 | 8.46 | 61,067 | 1127 | 1.85 |
| $50–100 M | 6777 | 545 | 8.04 | 7000 | 69 | 0.99 |
| Total | 66,109 | 5567 | 8.42 | 68,067 | 1196 | 1.76 |
| | Bad loans 1 Feb. 2002 (set2) | | | Bad loans 2 Feb. 2002 (set2) | | |
| | *N* | # of bad loans | Bad rate (%) | *N* | # of bad loans | Bad rate (%) |
| ≤$50 M | 61,183 | 5790 | 9.46 | 63,981 | 1791 | 2.80 |
| $50–$ 100 M | 6915 | 637 | 9.21 | 7210 | 88 | 1.22 |
| Total | 68,098 | 6427 | 9.44 | 71,191 | 1879 | 2.64 |

Note: Bad 1: Overlimit; Bad 2: 35+ days since last deposit and overlimit

**Table 10.3** Score statistical summary

| Score band | Bad loans 1 Jan. 2003 (set1) | | | Bad loans 2 Jan. 2003 (set1) | | |
|---|---|---|---|---|---|---|
| | *N* | Bad | Bad rate (%) | *N* | Bad | Bad rate (%) |
| 0 | 1210 | 125 | 10.33 | 1263 | 27 | 2.14 |
| 1–500 | 152 | 58 | 38.16 | 197 | 27 | 13.70 |
| 501–550 | 418 | 117 | 27.99 | 508 | 49 | 9.65 |
| 551–600 | 1438 | 350 | 24.34 | 1593 | 109 | 6.84 |
| 601–650 | 4514 | 858 | 19.01 | 4841 | 194 | 4.01 |
| 651–700 | 11,080 | 1494 | 13.48 | 11,599 | 321 | 2.77 |
| 701–750 | 18,328 | 1540 | 8.40 | 18,799 | 312 | 1.66 |
| 751–800 | 21,083 | 888 | 4.20 | 21,356 | 149 | 0.70 |
| ≥800 | 9096 | 262 | 2.88 | 9174 | 35 | 0.38 |
| Beacon | 12,813 | 769 | 6.00 | 13,054 | 328 | 2.51 |
| Total | 80,132 | 6461 | 8.06 | 82,384 | 1551 | 1.88 |
| Score band | Bad loans 1 Feb. 2002(set2) | | | Bad loans 2 Feb. 2002(set2) | | |
| | *N* | Bad | *N* | Bad | *N* | Bad |
| 0 | 1840 | 215 | 1840 | 215 | 1840 | 215 |
| 1–500 | 231 | 92 | 231 | 92 | 231 | 92 |
| 501–550 | 646 | 189 | 646 | 189 | 646 | 189 |
| 551–600 | 2106 | 533 | 2106 | 533 | 2106 | 533 |
| 601–650 | 5348 | 1078 | 5348 | 1078 | 5348 | 1078 |
| 651–700 | 11,624 | 1641 | 11,624 | 1641 | 11,624 | 1641 |
| 701–750 | 18,392 | 1647 | 18,392 | 1647 | 18,392 | 1647 |
| 751–800 | 20,951 | 969 | 20,951 | 969 | 20,951 | 969 |
| ≥800 | 8800 | 278 | 8800 | 278 | 8800 | 278 |
| Beacon | 17,339 | 1349 | 17,339 | 1349 | 17,339 | 1349 |
| Total | 87,277 | 7991 | 87,277 | 7991 | 87,277 | 7991 |

data. The bad rates by product line size are less than 10 %. The bad rates decreased with respect to time by both product line and score band, as can be seen from both tables. For example, for accounts less than or equal to 50 M dollars, we can see from the third row of Table 10.2 that the bad rate decreased from 9.46 % and 2.80 % in Feb. 2002 to 8.46 % and 1.85 % in Jan. 2003 respectively.

## Results and Discussion

Computation is done in two steps: (1) Score Distribution and (2) Performance Validation. The first step examines the evidence of a score shift. This population consists of the four types of business line of credit (BLOC) products. The second step measures how well models can predict the bad accounts within a 5-month period. This population only contains one type of BLOC account.

## Score Distribution

Figure 10.1 depicts the population stability indices values from January 2001 to June 2003. The values of indices for the $50,000 and $100,000 segments show a steady increase with respect time. The score distribution of the data set is becoming more unlike the most current population as time spans. Yet, the indices still remain below the benchmark of 0.25 that would indicate a significant shift in the score population.

The upward trend is due to two factors: time on books of the accounts and credit balance. A book of the account refers to a record in which commercial accounts are recorded. First, as the portfolio ages, more accounts will be assigned lower values (i.e. less risky) by the variable time on books of the accounts, thus contributing to a shift in the overall score. Second, more and more accounts do not have a credit balance as time goes. As a result, more accounts will receive higher scores to indicate riskier behavior.

The shifted score distribution indicates that the population used to develop the model is different from the most recent population. As a result, the weights that had been assigned to each characteristic value might not be the ones most suitable for the current population. Therefore, we have to conduct the following performance validation computation.

## Performance

To compare the discriminate power of the SBB scorecard with the credit bureau scorecard model, we depict the Lorenz Curve for both 'Bad 1' and 'Bad 2' accounts in Figs. 10.2 and 10.3. From both Figs. 10.2 and 10.3, we can see that the SBB model still provides an effective means of discriminating the 'good' from 'bad' accounts and that the SBB scorecard captures bad accounts much more quickly than the Beacon score. Based on the 'Bad 1' accounts in January 2003, SBS capture 58 % of bad accounts, and outperforms the Beacon value of 42 %. One of the reason for Beacon model being bad in capturing bad accounts is that the credit risk of one of the owners may not necessarily be indicative of the credit risk of the business. Instead, a Credit Bureau scorecard based on the business may be more suitable.

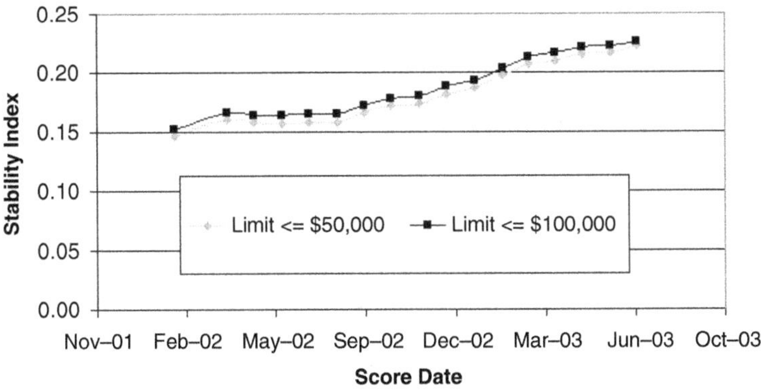


**Fig. 10.1** Population stability indices (Jan. 02–June 03)

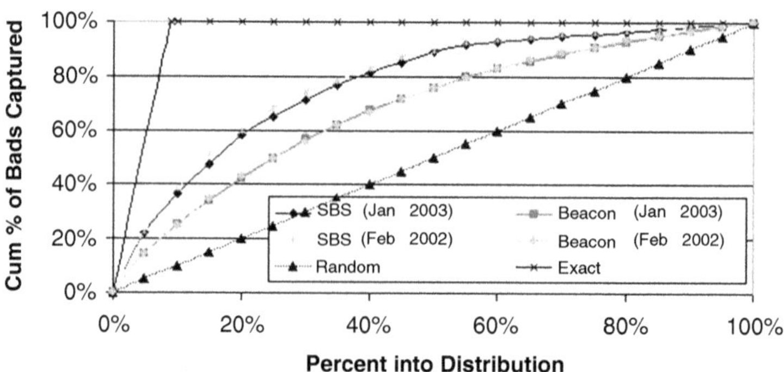


**Fig. 10.2** Lorenz curve for 'Bad 1' accounts

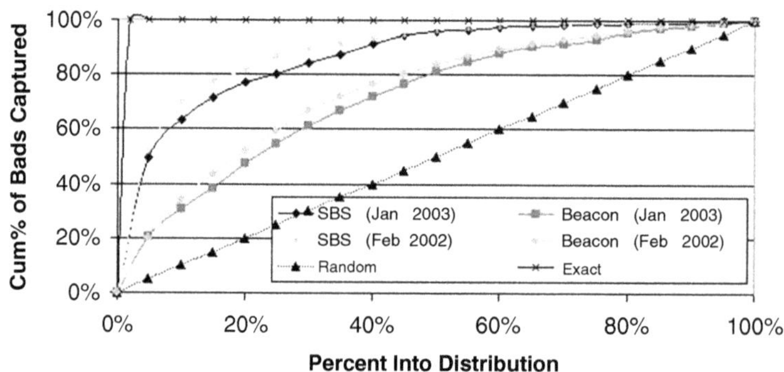


**Fig. 10.3** Lorenz curve for 'Bad 2' accounts

Table 10.4 reports various performance statistic values for both 'Bad 1' and 'Bad 2' accounts. Two main patterns are found. First, the Divergence and K-S score values produce consistent results as Lorenz Curve did. For both 'Bad 1' and 'Bad 2', the SBB scorecard performs better than the bureau score in predicting a bad account. Second, SBS based on both bad accounts possibly experience performance deterioration. Table 10.4 shows that all performance statistic based on the January 2003 data are worse than those of the February 2002 period. For example, the 'Bad 1' scorecard generates K-S statistic scores of 78 and 136, for January 2003 and February 2003 respectively. The 'Bad 2' scorecard generates K-S statistic scores of 233 and 394 for both periods.

Table 10.5 gives performance statistic values for both credit lines. i.e., accounts with Credit Limit less than or equal to \$50 M and between \$50 M and 100 M. This table shows a comparison between accounts with a limit of \$50 M and those with limits between \$50 M and 100 M. Two main patterns are found. First, the Small Business Scorecards perform well on both, and outperform the Beacon score on both segments. Second, both scorecards, especially the Small Business Scorecard,

**Table 10.4** Performance statistic for both ‘Bad 1’ and ‘Bad 2’ accounts

| Statistic | SBS (Jan. 2003) | Beacon (Jan. 2003) | SBS (Feb. 2002) | Beacon (Feb. 2002) | SBS (Jan. 2003) | Beacon (Jan. 2003) | SBS (Feb. 2002) | Beacon (Feb. 2002) |
|---|---|---|---|---|---|---|---|---|
| # Good | 60,542 | 60,542 | 51,671 | 61,671 | 66,871 | 66,871 | 69,312 | 69,312 |
| Mean good | 108.89 | 738.71 | 127.3 | 734.67 | 137.4 | 734.28 | 171.81 | 729.23 |
| Standard good | 172.74 | 60.18 | 203.26 | 63.53 | 221.22 | 62.78 | 284.21 | 66.66 |
| | ‘Bad 1’ accounts | | | | ‘Bad 2’ accounts | | | |
| # Accounts | 5567 | 5567 | 5427 | 6427 | 1196 | 1196 | 1879 | 1879 |
| Mean score | 344.9 | 693.13 | 439.63 | 685.79 | 699.82 | 678.03 | 995.65 | 663.2 |
| Standard deviation | 321.53 | 69.45 | 387.24 | 73.27 | 570.77 | 75.42 | 756.34 | 76.08 |
| Bad rate | 8.42 % | 8.42 % | 9.44 % | 9.44 % | 1.76 % | 1.76 % | 2.64 % | 2.64 % |
| Divergence | 0.836 | 0.492 | 1.02 | 0.508 | 1.688 | 0.657 | 2.079 | 0.852 |
| K-S | 78 | 726 | 136 | 716 | 233 | 726 | 394 | 707 |

**Table 10.5** Performance statistics for both credit lines

| | Credit line | Limit ≤ $50 M | | | | Limit $50–100 M | | | |
|---|---|---|---|---|---|---|---|---|---|
| | Statistic | SBS (Jan. 2003) | Beacon (Jan. 2003) | SBS (Feb. 2002) | Beacon (Feb. 2002) | SBS (Jan. 2003) | Beacon(Jan. 2003) | SBS(Feb. 2002) | Beacon (Feb. 2002) |
| Good | # Accounts | 47,682 | 47,682 | 48,539 | 48,539 | 6232 | 6232 | 6278 | 6278 |
| | Mean | 116.12 | 737.77 | 138.80 | 733.12 | 115.13 | 752.18 | 125.52 | 752.64 |
| | Standard | 177.34 | 59.12 | 213.62 | 62.52 | 161.93 | 54.61 | 174.07 | 55.86 |
| Bad | # Accounts | 4393 | 4393 | 5226 | 5226 | 545 | 545 | 637 | 637 |
| | Mean score | 347.40 | 695.10 | 461.06 | 686.03 | 345.82 | 715.80 | 398.05 | 711.95 |
| | Standard deviation | 314.69 | 65.68 | 391.94 | 71.87 | 285.01 | 68.35 | 310.59 | 62.28 |
| Performance | Bad rate | 8.44 % | 8.44 % | 9.72 % | 9.72 % | 8.04 % | 8.04 % | 9.21 % | 9.21 % |
| | Divergence | 0.820 | 0.466 | 1.042 | 0.489 | 0.991 | 0.346 | 1.172 | 0.473 |
| | K-S | 78 | 726 | 136 | 717 | 125 | 735 | 162 | 742 |

perform better on 'Bad 2' accounts. The main reason is that 'Bad 2' definition specifies a more severe degree of delinquency and the difference between the good and bad accounts is more distinct.

## Conclusions

Balanced scorecard analysis provides a means to measure multiple strategic perspectives. The basic principle is to select four diverse areas of strategic importance, and within each, to identify concrete measures that managers can use to gauge organizational performance on multiple scales. This allows consideration of multiple perspectives or stakeholders. Examples given included supply chain risk analysis, and policy analysis of natural gas vehicle adoption. This chapter focused on the example of a small bank credit situation. Computation results indicate there is evidence of a shifting score distribution utilized by the scorecard. However, the scorecard still provides an effective means to predict 'bad' accounts.

Balanced scorecards have been widely applied in general, but not specifically to enterprise risk management. This chapter demonstrates how the balanced scorecard can be applied to evaluate the risk management posture of a particular organization. The demonstration specifically is for a bank, but other organizations could measure appropriate risk elements for their circumstances. Balanced scorecards offer the flexibility to include any type of measure key to production planning and operations of any type of organization.

## Notes

1. Kaplan, R.S. and Norton, D.P. (2006). *Alignment: Using the Balanced Scorecard to Create Corporate Synergies*. Cambridge, MA: Harvard Business School Press Books.
2. Olhager, J. and Wikner, J. (2000). Production Planning and Control Tools. *Production Planning and Control* 11:3, 210–222.
3. Al-Mashari, M., Al-Mudimigh, A. and Zairi, M. (2003). Enterprise resource planning: A taxonomy of critical factors. *European Journal of Operational Research*, 146:2, 352–364.
4. Alquier, A.M.B. and Tignol, M.H.L. (2006). Risk management in small- and medium-sized enterprises. *Production Planning & Control,* 17, 273–282.
5. Kaplan and Norton (2006), op cit.
6. Elbannan, M.A. and Elbannan, M.A. (2015). Economic consequences of bank disclosure in the financial statements before and during the financial crisis: Evidence from Egypt. *Journal of Accounting, Auditing & Finance* 30(2), 181–217.
7. Schaefer, A. Cassidy, M., Marshall, K. and Rossi, J. (2006). Internal audits and executive education: A holy alliance to reduce theft and misreporting. *Employee Relations Law Journal*, *32*(1), 61–84.
8. Beasley, M. Chen, A., Nunez, K. and Wright, L. (2006). Working hand in hand: Balanced scorecards and enterprise risk management, *Strategic Finance* 87:9, 49–55.
9. Campbell, M. Adams, G.W., Campbell, D.R. and Rose, M.R. (2006). Internal audit can deliver more value, *Financial Executive* 22:1, 44–47.

2. **Information security risks are commonly considered without reference to reality**.
3. **Information security risk assessment is usually intermittent** without reference to historical data.

Internal threats are also present. Some problems arise due to turbulence in personnel, through new hires, transfers, and terminations. Most insider computer security incidents have been found to involve former employees.[2] External threats include attacks by organized criminals as well as potential threats from terrorists.[3]

## Frameworks

There are a number of best practice frameworks that have been presented to help organizations assess risks and implement controls. These include that of the international information security management standard series ISO2700x to facilitate planning, implementation and documentation of security controls.[4] In 2005 this series replaced the older ISO 17799 standards of the 1990s. The objective of the standard was to provide a model for establishing, implementing, operating, monitoring, reviewing, maintaining, and improving an information security management system. It continues reliance on the Plan-Do-Check-Act (PDCA) model of the older standard. Within the new series are:

- ISO 27001—specification for an ISMS including controls with their objectives;
- ISO 27002—code of practice with hundreds of potential control mechanisms;
- ISO 27003—guidance for implementation of an ISMS, focusing on PDCA;
- ISO 27004—standard covering ISMS measurement and metrics;
- ISO 27005—guidelines for information security risk management (ISRM);
- ISO 27006—Accreditation standards for certification and registration.

Gikas[5] compared these ISO standards with three other standards, two governmental and a third private. The Health Insurance Portability and Accountability Act (HIPAA) was enacted in 1996, requiring publication of standards for electronic exchange, privacy, and security for health information. HIPAA was intended to protect the security of individual patient health information. The Federal Information Security Management Act (FISMA) was enacted in 2002, calling upon all federal agencies to develop, document and implement programs for information systems security. The industry standard is the Payment Card Industry-Digital Security Standard (PCI-DSS), providing a general set of security requirements meant to give private organizations flexibility in implementing and customizing organization-specific security measures related to payment account data security. Table 11.1 gives PCI-DSS content:

Other frameworks address how information security can be attained. Security governance can be divided into three divisions: strategic, managerial and operational, and technical.[6] Strategic factors involved leadership and governance. These

**Table 11.1** PCI-DSS

| Principle | Requirement |
|---|---|
| Build and maintain a secure network | 1. Install and maintain a firewall to protect cardholder data<br>2. Don't use vendor-supplied default passwords and security parameters |
| Protect cardholder data | 3. Protect stored cardholder data<br>4. Encrypt cardholder data transmission over open public networks |
| Maintain a vulnerability management program | 5. Regularly update and use anti-virus software<br>6. Develop and maintain secure systems |
| Implement strong access control | 7. Restrict access to cardholder data by need-to-know<br>8. Assign unique ID to each person with computer access<br>9. Restrict physical access to cardholder data |
| Regularly monitor and test | 10. Track and monitor all access<br>11. Regularly test systems and processes |
| Maintain an information security policy | 12. To address information security |

involve sponsorship, strategy selection, IT governance, risk assessment, and measures to be used. Functions such as defining roles and responsibilities fall into this category.[7] The managerial and operational division includes organization and security policies and programs. This division includes risk management in the form of a security program, to include security culture awareness and training. Security policies manifest themselves in the form of policies, procedures, standards, guidelines, certification, and identification of best practices. The technical division includes programs for asset management, system development, and incident management, as well as plans for business continuity.

Levels of such a capability maturity model for information systems security can by[8]:

- Level 1—Security Leadership: strategy and metrics
- Level 2—Security Program: structure, resources, and skill sets needed
- Level 3—Security Policies: standards and procedures
- Level 4—Security Management: monitoring procedures, to include privacy protection
- Level 5—User Management: developing aware users and a security culture
- Level 6—Information Asset Security: meta security, protection of the network and host
- Level 7—Technology Protection & Continuity: protection of physical environment, to include continuity planning.

Information security faces many challenges, to include evolving business requirements, constant upgrades of technology, and threats from a variety of sources. Vendors and computer security firms send a steady stream of alerts about new threats arising from the Internet. Internally, new hires, transfers, and terminations may be the germination of threats from current or former employees. There also are many changes in legal requirements, especially for those organizations doing work involving the government.

## Security Process

As a means to attain information technology security, consider the following[9]:

**Establish a Mentality** To be effective, the organization members have to buy in to operating securely. This includes sensible use of passwords. Those dealing with critical information probably need to change their passwords at least every 60 days, which may be burdensome, but provides protection for highly vulnerable information. Passwords themselves should be difficult to decipher, running counter to what most of us are inclined to use. Training is essential in inculcating a security climate within the organization.

**Include Security in Business Decision Making** When software systems are developed, especially in-house, an information security manager should certify that organizational policies and procedures have been followed to protect organizational systems and data. When pricing products, required funding for security measures need to be included in business cases.

**Establish and Continuously Assess the Network** Security audits need to be conducted using testable metrics. These audits should identify lost productivity due to security failures, to include subsequent user awareness training.

Automation can be applied in many cases to accomplish essential risk compliance and assessment tasks. This can include vulnerability testing, as well as incident management and response. The benefits can include better use of information, lower cost of compliance, and more complete compliance with regulations such as Sarbanes-Oxley and HIPAA.

Table 11.2 provides a security process cycle within this framework:

This cycle emphasizes the ability to automate within an enterprise information system context. A means to aid in assessing vulnerabilities is provided by the risk matrices we discussed in Chap. 2. Cyber-crime includes ransom-ware (where consumer computers are frozen until a ransom is paid), cyber blackmail (holding banks at ransom with threat to publish client data), on-line banking, Trojan horses, phishing, and denial of service, spying (governmental or commercial), as well as mass hacking for political or ideological reasons. Table 11.3 provides a risk matrix for this case[11]:

This matrix could be implemented by assigning responsibility for risk to the executive board for Red categories, to heads of division for Yellow, and to line managers for Green. Each of these responsibility levels could determine the extra

**Table 11.2** Tracy's security process cycle[10]

| Process | IT impact | Function |
|---|---|---|
| Inventory | Assets available | Access assets in hardware and software |
| Assess | Vulnerabilities | Automatically check systems for violations of risk policies based on regulatory and commercially accepted standards |
| Notify | Who needs to know? | Automatically alert those responsible for patch management, compliance |
| Remediate | Action needed | Automate security remediation by leveraging help desks, patch databases, configuration management tools |
| Validate | Did corrective actions work? | Automatically confirm that remediation is complete, record compliance and confirm compliance with risk posture policies |
| Report | Can you get information needed? | Give management views of enterprise IT risk and compliance, generate |

**Table 11.3** Risk tolerance matrix for cyber crime

| | Negligible impact | Low impact | Significant impact | Major impact | Very severe impact |
|---|---|---|---|---|---|
| Almost certain | Green | Yellow | Red | Red | Red |
| Likely probability | Green | Yellow | Red | Red | Red |
| Possible probability | Green | Green | Yellow | Red | Red |
| Unlikely probability | Green | Green | Yellow | Red | Red |
| Rare probability | Green | Green | Green | Yellow | Red |

mitigation measures suggested by their information technology experts to lower residual risk.

## Best Practices for Information System Security

Nine best practices to protect against information system security threats can include[12]:

1. **Firewalls**—hardware or software, which block unallowed traffic. Firewalls do not protect against malicious traffic moving through legitimate communication channels. About 70 % of security incidents have been reported to occur inside fire walls.
2. **Software updates**—application vulnerabilities are corrected by patches issued by the software source when detected. Not adopting patches has led to vulnerabilities that are commonly exploited by hackers.

3. **Anti-virus, worm and Trojan software**—should be installed on all machines. Management policies to reduce virus vulnerability include limiting shareware and Internet use, as well as user training and heightened awareness through education can supplement software protection.
4. **Password policy**—users face a constant tradeoff between sound password structure and workability (the ability to remember). But sound password use is needed to control access to authorized users. Human engineering in the form of naïve acquisition of passwords by intruders continues to be a problem.
5. **Physical security**—including disaster recovering planning and physical protection in the form of locks to control access to critical system equipment. Trash management also is important, as well as identification procedures.
6. **Policy and training**—because many information system security risks arise due to unawareness, a program of enlightenment can be very beneficial in controlling these risks. The other side of the coin is policy, the adoption of sound procedures governing the use of hardware, e-mail, and the Internet. Policy and training thus work together to accomplish a more secure system operating environment.
7. **Secure remote connections**—ubiquitous computing creates the opportunity to vastly expand mobile computing connections, and thus make workers much more productive. In order to gain these advantages, good encryption techniques are required as well as sound authentication procedures.
8. **Server lock down**—limiting server exposure is a basic principle. Those servers linking to the Internet need to be protected against intrusion.
9. **Intrusion detection**—systems are available to monitor network traffic to seek malicious bit patterns.

## Supply Chain IT Risks

Information technology makes supply chains work through the communication needed to coordinate activities across organizations, often around the world.[13] These benefits require openness of systems across organizations. While techniques have been devised to provide the required level of security that enables us to do our banking on-line, and for global supply chains to exchange information expeditiously with confidence in the security of doing so, this only happens because of the ability of information systems staff to make data and information exchange secure.

IT support to supply chains involves a number of operational forms, to include vendor management inventory (VMI), collaborative planning forecasting and replenishment (CPFR), and others. These forms include varying levels of information system linkage across supply chain members, which have been heavily studied.[14]

Within supply chains, IT security incidents can arise from within the organization, within the supply chain network, or in the overall environment.[15] Within each threat origin, points of vulnerability can be identified and risk mitigation strategies customized. The greatest threat is loss of confidentiality. An example would be a case where a supplier lost their account when a Wal-Mart invoice was unintentionally sent to Costco with a lower price for items carried by both retailers. Supply chains require data integrity, as systems like MRP and ERP don't function without accurate data. Inventory information is notoriously difficult to maintain accurately.

## Value Analysis in Information Systems Security

The value analysis procedure has been used to sort objectives related to information systems security.[16] That process involved three steps, which they described as:

1. Interviews to elicit individual values.
2. Converting individual values and statements into a common format, generally in the form of object and preference. This step included clustering objectives into groups of two levels.
3. Classifying objectives as either fundamental to the decision context or as a means to achieve fundamental objectives.

Once the initial hierarchy was developed, it was validated by review with each of the seven experts involved. Sub-objectives were then classified as essential, useful but not essential, or not necessary for the given decision context. Hierarchy clustering was also reviewed.

We will apply that hierarchy with the SMART procedure (also outlined earlier) to a hypothetical decision involving selection of an enterprise information (EIS, or ERP) system. Tradeoffs among alternative forms of ERP have been reviewed in depth.[17] The SMART method has been suggested for selecting among alternative forms of ERP.[18]

## Tradeoffs in ERP Outsourcing

Bryson and Sullivan cited specific reasons that a particular ASP might be attractive as a source for ERP.[9] These included the opportunity to use a well-known company as a reference, opening new lines of business, and opportunities to gain market-share in particular industries. Some organizations may also view ASPs as a way to aid cash flow in periods when they are financially weak and desperate for business. In many cases, cost rise precipitously after the outsourcing firm has become committed to the relationship. One explanation given was the lack of analytical models and tools to evaluate alternatives.

ASPs become risky from both success, or conversely, bankruptcy. ASP sites might be attacked and vandalized, or destroyed by natural disaster. Each organization must balance these factors and make their own decision.[19]

## ERP System Risk Assessment

The ideal theoretical approach is a rigorous cost/benefit study, in net present terms. Methods supporting this positivist view include cost/benefit analysis, applying net present value, calculating internal rate of return or payback. Many academics as well as consulting practitioners take the position that this is crucial. However, nobody really has a strong grasp on predicting the future in a dynamic environment such as ERP, and practically, complete analysis in economic terms is often not applied.

The Gartner Group consistently reports that IS/IT projects significantly exceed their time (and cost) estimates. Thus, while almost half of the surveyed firms reported expected implementation expense to be less than $5 million, we consider that figure to still be representative of the minimum scope required. However, recent trends on the part of vendors to reduce implementation time probably have reduced ERP installation cost. In the U.S., vendors seem to take the biggest chunk of the average implementation. Consultants also take a big portion. These proportions are reversed in Sweden. The internal implementation team accounts for an additional 14 % (12 % in Sweden). These proportions are roughly reversed in Sweden with training.

Total life cycle costs are needed for evaluation of ERP systems, which have long-range impacts on organizations. Unfortunately, this makes it necessary to estimate costs that are difficult to pin down. Total costs can include:

- Software upgrades over time, to include memory and disk space requirements
- Integration, implementation, testing, and maintenance
- Providing users with individual levels of functionality, technical support and service
- Servers
- Disaster recovery and business continuance program
- Staffing.

## Qualitative Factors

While cost is clearly an important matter, there are other factors important in selection of ERP that are difficult to fit into a total cost framework. A survey of European firms in mid-1998 was conducted with the intent of measuring ERP penetration by market, including questions about criteria for supplier selection.[20] The criteria reportedly used are given in the first column of Table 11.4, in order of ranking. Product functionality and quality were the criteria most often reported to be important. Column 2 gives related factors from another framework for evaluating ASPs, while column 3 gives more specifics in that framework.[21]

While these two frameworks don't match entirely, there is a lot of overlap.

**Table 11.4** Selection evaluation factors

| ERP supplier selection (Van Everdingen et al.) | ASP evaluation (Ekanayaka et al.) | Ekanayaka et al. subelements |
|---|---|---|
| 1. Product functionality | Customer service | 1. Help desk & training |
| | | 2. Support for account administration |
| 2. Product quality | Reliability, scalability | |
| 3. Implementation speed | Availability | |
| 4. Interface with other systems | Integration | 1. Ability to share data between applications |
| 5. Price | Pricing | 1. Effect on total cost structure |
| | | 2. Hidden costs & charges |
| | | 3. ROI |
| 6. Market leadership | | |
| 7. Corporate image | | |
| 8. International orientation | | |
| | Security | Physical security of facilities |
| | | Security of data and applications |
| | | Back-up and restore procedures |
| | | Disaster recovery plan |
| | Service level monitoring & management | 1. Clearly defined performance metrics and measurement |
| | | 2. Defined procedures for opening and closing accounts |
| | | 3. Flexibility in service offerings, pricing, contract length |

## Multiple Criteria Analysis

An example is extracted here from the literature[22] to show the application of multiple criteria analysis technique in managing IT risks. The data in the example are altered to fit our analysis scope. The multiple criteria analysis was found useful when used together with cost-benefit analysis, which seeks to identify accurate measures of benefits and costs in monetary terms, and uses the ratio benefits/costs (the term benefit-cost ratio seems more appropriate, and is sometimes used, but most people refer to cost-benefit analysis). Because ERP projects involve long time frames (for benefits if not for costs as well), considering the net present value of benefits and costs is important.

Recognition that real life decisions involve high levels of uncertainty is reflected in the development of fuzzy multiattribute models. The basic multiattribute model is to maximize value as a function of importance and performance:

$$value_j = \sum_{i=1}^{K} w_i \times u(x_{ij}) \quad (1)$$

where $w_i$ is the weight of attribute $i$, $K$ is the number of attributes, and $u(x_{ij})$ is the score of alternative $x_j$ on attribute $i$.

Multiple criteria analysis considers benefits on a variety of scales without directly converting them to some common scale such as dollars. The method (there are many variants of multiple criteria analysis) is not at all perfect. But it does provide a way to demonstrate to decision makers the relative positive and negative features of alternatives, and gives a way to quantify the preferences of decision makers.

We will consider an analysis of six alternative forms of ERP: from an Australian vendor, the Australian vendor system customized to provide functionality unique to the organization, an SAP system, a Chinese vendor system, a best-of-breed system, and a South Korean ASP. We will make a leap to assume that complete total life cycle costs have been estimated for each option as given in Table 11.5.

The greatest software cost is expected to be for the best-of-breed option, while the ASP would have a major advantage. The best-of-breed option is expected to have the highest consulting cost, with ASP again having a relative advantage. Hardware is the same for the four mainline vendor options, with the ASP option saving a great deal. Implementation is expected to be highest for the customized system, with ASP having an advantage. Training is lowest for the customized system, while the best-of-breed system the highest.

But there are other important factors as well. This total cost estimate assumes that everything will go as planned, and may not consider other qualitative aspects. Multiple criteria analysis provides the ability to incorporate other factors.

Perhaps the easiest application of multiple criteria analysis is the simple multiattribute rating theory (SMART). SMART provides decision makers with a means to identify the relative importance of criteria in terms of weights, and measures the relative performance of each alternative on each criterion in terms of scores. In this application, we will include criteria of seven factors: Customer service; Reliability and scalability, Availability, Integration; Financial factors;

**Table 11.5** Total life cycle costs for each option ($ million)

| | Australian vendor | Australian vendor customized | SAP | Chinese vendor | B-of-B | South Korean ASP |
|---|---|---|---|---|---|---|
| Software | 15 | 13 | 12 | 2 | 16 | 3 |
| Consultants | 6 | 8 | 9 | 2 | 12 | 1 |
| Hardware | 6 | 6 | 6 | 4 | 6 | 0 |
| Implement | 5 | 10 | 6 | 4 | 9 | 2 |
| Train | 8 | 2 | 9 | 3 | 11 | 8 |
| Total Cost | 40 | 39 | 42 | 15 | 54 | 14 |

**Table 11.6** Relative scores by criteria for each option in example

| | Australian vendor | Australian vendor customized | SAP | Chinese vendor | B-of-B | South Korean ASP |
|---|---|---|---|---|---|---|
| Customer service | 0.6 | **1** | 0.9 | 0.5 | 0.7 | 0.3 |
| Reliability, Availability, Scalability | **1** | 0.8 | 0.9 | 0.5 | 0.4 | **0** |
| Integration | 0.8 | 0.9 | **1** | 0.6 | 0.3 | 0.3 |
| Cost | 0.6 | 0.7 | 0.5 | 0.9 | 0.2 | **1** |
| Security | **1** | 0.9 | 0.7 | 0.8 | 0.6 | **0** |
| Service level | 0.8 | 0.7 | **1** | 0.6 | 0.2 | **1** |
| Image | 0.9 | 0.7 | 0.8 | 0.5 | **1** | 0.2 |

The bold values are the extremes (zeros and ones)

Security; and Service level monitoring & management.[14] The relative importance is given by the order, following the second column of Table 11.4:

## Scores

Scores in SMART can be used to convert performances (subjective or objective) to a zero-one scale, where zero represents the worst acceptable performance level in the mind of the decision maker, and one represents the ideal, or possibly the best performance desired. Note that these ratings are subjective, a function of individual preference. Scores for the criteria given in the value analysis example could be as in Table 11.6:

The best imaginable customer service level would be provided by the customizing the Australian vendor option. The South Korean ASP option is considered suspect on this factor, but not the worst imaginable. The Australian vendor system without customization is expected to be the most reliable, while the South Korean ASP options the worst. The SAP option is rated the easiest to integrate. The South Korean ASP and best-of-breed systems are rated low on this factor, but not the worst imaginable. Costs reflect Table 11.4, converting dollar estimates into value scores on the 0–1 scale. The South Korean ASP option has the best imaginable cost. The Australian vendor system without customization is rated as the best possible with respect to security issues, while the South Korean ASP is rated the worst possible. Service level ratings are high for the SAP system and the ASP, while the best-of-breed system is rated low on this factor. The highest image score is for the best-of-breed system, and the lowest for the South Korean ASP option.

**Table 11.7** Worst and best measures by criteria

| Criteria | Worst measure | Best measure |
|---|---|---|
| Customer service | 0.3—South Korean ASP | 1—Australian vendor |
| Reliability, Availability, Scalability | 0—South Korean ASP | 1—Australian vendor customized |
| Integration | 0.3—Best-of-Breed & South Korean ASP | 1—SAP |
| Cost | 0.2—Best-of-breed | 1—ASP |
| Security | 0—South Korean ASP | 1—Australian vendor |
| Service level | 0.2—Best-of-Breed | 1—SAP & ASP |
| Image | 0.2—South Korean ASP | 1—Best-of-Breed |

**Table 11.8** Weight estimation from perspective of most important criterion

| Criteria | Worst measure | Best measure | Assigned value |
|---|---|---|---|
| 1-Customer service | 0 | 1 | 100 |
| 2-Reliability, Availability, Scalability | 0 | 1 | 80 |
| 3-Integration | 0 | 1 | 50 |
| 4-Cost | 0 | 1 | 20 |
| 5-Security | 0 | 1 | 10 |
| 6-Service level | 0 | 1 | 5 |
| 7-Image | 0 | 1 | 3 |

## Weights

The next phase of the analysis ties these ratings together into an overall value function by obtaining the relative weight of each criterion. In order to give the decision maker a reference about what exactly is being compared, the relative range between best and worst on each scale for each criterion should be explained. There are many methods to determine these weights. In SMART, the process begins with rank-ordering the four criteria. A possible ranking for a specific decision maker might be as given in Table 11.7.

Swing weighting could be used to identify weights. Here, the scoring was used to reflect 1 as the best possible and 0 as the worst imaginable. Thus the relative rank ordering reflects a common scale, and can be used directly in the order given. To obtain relative criterion weights, the first step is to rank-order criteria by importance. Two estimates of weights can be obtained. The first assigns the least important criterion ten points, and assesses the relative importance of each of the other criteria on that basis. This process (including rank-ordering and assigning relative values based upon moving from worst measure to best measure based on most important criterion) is demonstrated in Table 11.8.

The total of the assigned values is 268. One estimate of relative weights is obtained by dividing each assigned value by 268. Before we do that, we obtain a second estimate from the perspective of the least important criterion, which is assigned a value of 10 as in Table 11.9.

**Table 11.9** Weight estimation from perspective of least important criterion

| Criteria | Worst measure | Best measure | Assigned value |
|---|---|---|---|
| 7-Image | 0 | 1 | 10 |
| 6-Service level | 0 | 1 | 20 |
| 5-Security | 0 | 1 | 30 |
| 4-Cost | 0 | 1 | 60 |
| 3-Integration | 0 | 1 | 150 |
| 2-Reliability, Availability, Scalability | 0 | 1 | 250 |
| 1-Customer service | 0 | 1 | 300 |

**Table 11.10** Criterion weight development

| Criteria | Based on best | | Based on worst | | Compromise |
|---|---|---|---|---|---|
| 1-Customer service | 100/268 | 0.373 | 300/820 | 0.366 | 0.37 |
| 2-RAS | 80/268 | 0.299 | 250/820 | 0.305 | 0.30 |
| 3-Integration | 50/268 | 0.187 | 150/820 | 0.183 | 0.19 |
| 4-Cost | 20/268 | 0.075 | 60/820 | 0.073 | 0.07 |
| 5-Security | 10/268 | 0.037 | 30/820 | 0.037 | 0.04 |
| 6-Service level | 5/268 | 0.019 | 20/820 | 0.024 | 0.02 |
| 7-Image | 3/268 | 0.011 | 10/820 | 0.012 | 0.01 |

These add up to 820. The two weight estimates are now as shown in Table 11.10.

The last criterion can be used to make sure that the sum of compromise weights adds up to 1.00.

## Value Score

The next step of the SMART method is to obtain value scores for each alternative by multiplying each score on each criterion for an alternative by that criterion's weight, and adding these products by alternative. Table 11.11 shows this calculation.

In this example, the ASP turned out to be quite unattractive, even though it had the best cost and the best service level. The cost advantage was outweighed by this option's poor ratings on customer service levels expected, reliability, availability, and scalability, and security, two of which were the highest rated criteria. The value score indicates that the Australian vendor customized system would be best, followed by the SAP system and the non-customized Australian vendor system. The final ranking results reveal that adopting new technology such as ASP sometimes includes great potential risk. Multiple Criteria analysis helps focus on the tradeoffs of these potential risks.

**Table 11.11** Value score calculation

| Criteria | Wgt | Australian vendor | Australian vendor customized | SAP | Chinese vendor | Best-of-B | South Korean ASP |
|---|---|---|---|---|---|---|---|
| Customer service | 0.37 | × 0.6 = 0.222 | × 1.0 = 0.370 | × 0.9 = 0.333 | × 0.5 = 0.185 | × 0.7 = 0.259 | × 0.3 = 0.111 |
| Reliability, Availability, Scalability | 0.30 | × 1.0 = 0.300 | × 0.8 = 0.240 | × 0.9 = 0.270 | × 0.5 = 0.150 | × 0.4 = 0.120 | × 0 = 0.000 |
| Integration | 0.19 | × 0.8 = 0.152 | × 0.9 = 0.171 | × 1.0 = 0.190 | × 0.6 = 0.114 | × 0.3 = 0.057 | × 0.3 = 0.057 |
| Cost | 0.07 | × 0.6 = 0.042 | × 0.7 = 0.049 | × 0.5 = 0.035 | × 0.9 = 0.063 | × 0.2 = 0.014 | × 1.0 = 0.070 |
| Security | 0.04 | × 1.0 = 0.040 | × 0.9 = 0.036 | × 0.7 = 0.028 | × 0.8 = 0.032 | × 0.6 = 0.024 | × 0 = 0.000 |
| Service level | 0.02 | × 0.8 = 0.016 | × 0.7 = 0.014 | × 0.1 = 0.002 | × 0.6 = 0.012 | × 0.2 = 0.004 | × 1.0 = 0.020 |
| Image | 0.01 | × 0.9 = 0.009 | × 0.7 = 0.007 | × 0.8 = 0.008 | × 0.5 = 0.005 | × 1.0 = 0.010 | × 0.2 = 0.002 |
| Totals | | 0.781 | 0.887 | 0.866 | 0.561 | 0.488 | 0.260 |

## Conclusion

Information systems security is critically important to organizations, private and public. We need the Internet to contact the world, and have benefited personally and economically from using the Web. But there have been many risks that have been identified in the open Internet environment.

A number of frameworks have been proposed. Some appear in the form of standards, such as from the International Standards Organization. That set of standards provides guidance in the macro-management of information systems security. Frameworks can provide guidance in developing processes to attain IS security, to include a Security Process Cycle and a list of best practices.

Supply chains are an especially important economic use of the Internet, and involve a special set of risks. While there are many inherent risks in electronic data interchange (needed to efficiently manage supply chains), methods have been developed to make this a secure activity in well-managed supply chains.

One way that many organizations deal with information systems is to outsource, hiring experts with strong software to do their information processing. This can be a very cost-effective means, especially for those organizations who feel that their core competencies do not include information technology (or at least all aspects of IT).

To more thoroughly evaluate information systems security, we suggest value analysis, implemented through SMART. Value analysis provides a valuable means of identifying factors of general importance. Each particular decision would be able to filter this rather long list down to those issues of importance in a particular context. Here we suggest value analysis as a means to focus on the impact of information systems security factors on alternative forms of enterprise information systems. We then demonstrated how the process, combined with SMART analysis, can be used to identify the relative importance of factors, and provide a framework to more thoroughly analyze tradeoffs among alternatives.

## Notes

1. Webb, J., Ahmad, A., Maynard, S.B. and Shanks, G. (2014). A situation awareness model for information security risk management. *Computers & Security* 44, 1–15.
2. Tracy, R.P. (2007). IT security management and business process automation: Challenges, approaches, and rewards, *Information Systems Security* 16, 114–122.
3. Porter, D. (2008). Business resilience, *RMA Journal* 90:6, 60–64.
4. Mijnhardt, F., Baars, T. and Spruit, M. (2016). Organizational characteristics influencing SME information security maturity. *Journal of Computer Information Systems* 56(2), 106–115.
5. Gikas, C. (2010). A general comparison of FISMA, HIPAA, ISO 27000 and PCI-DSS standards. *Information Security Journal: A Global Perspective* 19(3), 132–141.
6. Da Veiga, A. and Eloff, J.H.P. (2007). An information security governance framework, *Information Systems Management* 24, 361–372.

7. Tudor, J.K. (2000). *Information Security Architecture: An Integrated Approach to Security in an Organization*. Boca Raton, FL: Auerbach.
8. McCarthy, M.P. and Campbell, S. (2001). *Security Transformation*. New York: McGraw-Hill.
9. Tracy (2007), op cit.
10. Ibid.
11. VandePutte, D. and Verhelst, M. (2013). Cyber crime: Can a standard risk analysis help in the challenges facing business continuity managers? *Journal of Business Continuity & Emergency Planning* 7(2), 126–137.
12. Keller, S., Powell, A., Horstmann, B., Predmore, C. and Crawford, M. (2005). Information security threats and practices in small businesses, *Information Systems Management* 22, 7–19.
13. Faisal, M.N., Banwet, D.K. and Shankar, R. (2007). Information risks management in supply chains: An assessment and mitigation framework, *Journal of Enterprise Information Management* 20:6, 677–699.
14. Cigolini, R. and Rossi, T. (2006). A note on supply risk and inventory outsourcing, *Production Planning and Control* 17:4, 424–437.
15. Smith, G.E., Watson, K.J., Baker, W.H. and Pokorski, J.A. II (2007). A critical balance: Collaboration and security in the IT-enabled supply chain, *International Journal of Production Research* 45:11, 2595–2613.
16. Dhillon, G. and Torkzadeh, G. (2006). Value-focused assessment of information system security in organizations, *Information Systems Journal* 16, 293–314.
17. Olson, D.L. (2004). *Managerial Issues in Enterprise Resource Planning Systems*. New York: McGraw-Hill/Irwin.
18. Olson, D.L. (2007). Evaluation of ERP outsourcing. *Computers & Operations Research* 34, 3715–3724.
19. Olson, D.L. (1996). *Decision Aids for Selection Problems*. New York: Springer.
20. Van Everdingen, Y., van Hellegersberg, J. and Waarts, E. (2000). ERP adoption by European midsize companies. *Communications of the ACM* 43(4), 27–31.
21. Ekanayaka, Y., Currie, W.L. and Seltsikas, P. (2003). Evaluating application service providers. *Benchmarking: An International Journal* 10(4), 343–354.
22. Olson, D.L. (2007). Evaluation of ERP outsourcing. *Computers & Operations Research* 34, 3715–3724.

# Enterprise Risk Management in Projects 12

Project management inherently involves high levels of risk, because projects by definition are being done for the first time. There are a number of classical project domain types, each with their own characteristics. For instance, construction projects focus on inanimate objects, such as materials that are transformed into some purposeful object. There are people involved, although as time passes, more and more work is done by machinery, with diminishing human control. Thus construction projects are among the more predictable project domains. Government projects often involve construction, but extend beyond that to processes, such as the generation of nuclear material, or more recently, the processing of nuclear wastes. Government projects involve high levels of bureaucracy, and the only aspect increasing predictability is that overlapping bureaucratic involvement of many agencies almost ensures long time frames with high levels of change. There is a very wide spectrum of governmental projects. They also should include civil works, which drive most construction projects. A third project domain is information system project management, focusing on the development of software tools to do whatever humans want. This field, like construction and governmental projects, has been widely studied. It is found to involve higher levels of uncertainty than construction projects, because software programming is a precise activity, and getting a computer code to work without bugs is a precise activity.

Seyedhoseini et al.[1] reviewed risk management processes within projects, using the contexts of general project management, civil engineering, software engineering, and public application. Those authors looked at sixteen risk management processes published over the period 1990–2005, spread fairly evenly over their four context areas, identifying methodologies. These contexts all involve basic project management, but we argue that each context is quite different. Project management in civil engineering is usually easier to manage, as the uncertain elements involve natural science (geology, weather). However, there are many different types of risk involved in any project, to include political aspects[2] and financial aspects.[3] While these sources provide more than enough uncertainty for project managers, there is a much more difficult task facing software engineering project managers.[4] We argue that this is because people are more fundamental to the software engineering production process, in the form of



D.L. Olson, D.D. Wu, *Enterprise Risk Management Models*, Springer Texts in Business and Economics, DOI 10.1007/978-3-662-53785-5_12

developing systems, programming them, and testing them, each activity involving high degrees of uncertainty.[5] Public application projects are also unique unto themselves, with high levels of bureaucratic process that take very long periods of time as the wheels of bureaucracy grind slowly and thoroughly. Slowly enough that political support often shifts before a project is completed, and thoroughly enough that opposition of the "not-in-my-backyard" is almost inevitably uncovered prior to project completion.

## Project Management Risk

The Project Management Institute views risk as general to projects, and through the Project Management Body of Knowledge (PMBOK)[6], which develops standards, policies and guidelines for project management. It focuses on tools and techniques related to project management skills and capabilities. Project management responsibilities include achieving cost, schedule performance objectives. Risk management is a major element of PMBOK, with major categories of:

- planning,
- risk identification,
- quantitative risk analysis,
- quantitative risk analysis,
- risk response planning, and
- risk monitoring and control.

The Project Risk Analysis and Management (PRAM) Guide in the United Kingdom is very similar in approach,[7] and fits the description of a typical risk management program from other sources. Each of these categories applies to all projects to some degree, although the level of uncertainty can make variants of tools applied appropriate. A number of recent papers have proposed risk assessment methodologies in construction, based on an iterative process of risk identification, risk analysis and evaluation, risk response development, and administration.[8] The key is to keep systematic records over time to record risk experiences, with systematic updating.[9]

### Risk Management Planning

As with any process, inputs need to be gathered to organize development of a cohesive plan. Things such as the project purpose and stakeholders need to be identified, followed by identification of tasks to be accomplished. This applies to every kind of project. These tasks are cohesive activities, usually accomplished by a specific individual or group, and for each task estimation of duration and resources required, as well as immediate predecessor activities is needed. This is the input needed for critical path analysis, to be demonstrated in this chapter. That quantitative approach deals with risk in the form of probability distributions for durations (demonstrated in this chapter through simulation).

But there are other risk aspects that need to be considered. It is important to consider the organization's attitude toward risk, and qualitatively identify things that can go wrong. Risk attitude depends upon stakeholders. Identification of what might go wrong and stakeholder preference for dealing with them can affect project management team roles and responsibilities.

Risk management planning concludes with a risk management plan. This plan should define methodologies for dealing with project risks. Such methodologies can include training internal staff, outsourcing activities that other organizations are better equipped to deal with, or insurance in various forms. Ultimately, every organization has to decide which risks they are competent to manage internally (core competencies), and which risks they should offload (at some expected cost).

## Risk Identification

Once the risk management plan is developed, it can naturally lead to the next step, risk identification. The process of risk identification identifies major potential sources of risk for the specific project. The risk management plan identifies tasks with their risks, as well as project team roles and responsibilities. Historical experience should provide guides (usually implemented in the form of checklists) to things that can go wrong, as well as the organization's ability to cope with them.

Specific types of risk can be viewed as arising in various ways. A classical view is the triumvirate of quality, time, and budget. Software projects are often said to allow any two of the three—you can get code functioning as intended on time, but it usually involves more cost than expected; you can get functional code within budget as long as you are patient; you can get code on time and within budget as long as you don't expect it to work as designed. This software engineering project view often generalizes to other projects, but with some different tendencies. In construction, there is less duration variance, although unexpected delays from geology or the weather commonly create challenges for project managers. If weather delays are encountered, the tradeoff is usually whether to wait for better weather, or to pay more overtime or extra resources. If geological elements are creating difficulties, more time and money is usually required. The functionality of the project is usually not degraded. Governmental projects may involve emergency response, where time is not something that can be sacrificed. The tradeoff is between quality of response and cost. Usually emergency response teams do the best they can within available resources, and public outcry almost always criticizes the insufficiency of the effort.

There are a number of techniques that can be used to identify risks. Some qualitative approaches include interviews of experts or stakeholders, supplemented by techniques such as brainstorming, the nominal group technique, the Delphi method, or SWOT analysis (strengths, weaknesses, opportunities, and threats). Each of these methods are relatively easy to implement, and the quality of output depends on the participation of a diverse group of stakeholders. Historical data can also be used if the organization has experience with past projects similar to the current activity. This works well if past experiences are well-documented and retrieved efficiently.

The outputs from risk identification is a more complete list of risks expected in the project, as well as possible responses along with their expected costs. This results in a set of responses that can be reviewed as events develop, allowing project managers to more intelligently select appropriate responses. While success can never be guaranteed, it is expected that organizational project performance will improve.

## Qualitative Risk Analysis

After a more precise estimation of project element risk is identified, the relative probabilities and risk consequences can be addressed. Initial estimations usually require reliance on subjective expert opinion. Historical records enable more precision, but one project element of importance is that projects by definition almost always involve new situations and activities. Experts have to judge the applicability of historical records to current challenges.

A qualitative risk analysis can be used to rank overall risks to the organization. A priority system can be used to identify those risks that are most critical, and thus require the greatest degree of managerial attention. In critical path analysis terms, critical path activities would seem to call for the greatest managerial attention. Behaviorally, humans tend to work hardest when the boss is watching. However, the fallacy of this approach is that other activities that are not watched may become critical too if they delay too far beyond their expected duration.

Qualitative risk analysis can provide a valuable screening to cancel projects that are just too risky for an organization. It also can affect project organization, with more skilled personnel assigned to tasks that call for more careful management. It also can be a guide to look for means to offload risk, either through subcontracting, outsourcing, or insurance.

## Quantitative Risk Analysis

We will present more formal quantitative tools in the following sections. Quantitative analysis requires data. The critical path method calls for a specific duration estimate, which we will demonstrate. Simulation is less restrictive, calling for probability distributions. But this is often more difficult for humans to estimate, and usually only works when there is some sort of historical data available with which to estimate probability distributions.

Quantitative risk analysis, as will be demonstrated, can be used to estimate probabilities of project completion times, as well as other items of interest that can be included in what is essentially a spreadsheet model. These examples focus on time. It is also possible to include cost probabilities.

## Risk Response Planning

Once risk analysis (qualitative, quantitative, or both) is conducted, project managers are hopefully in a more educated position to make plans and decisions to respond to events. Risk response planning is this process of developing options and reducing threats if possible. The severity of risks as well as cost, time, and impact on project output (quality) should be considered.

A broad categorization of risk treatment strategies include:

- Risk avoidance (adopting alternatives that do not include the risk at issue)
- Risk probability reduction (act to reduce the probability of adverse event occurance)
- Risk impact reduction (act to reduce the severity of the risk)
- Risk transfer (outsourcing)
- Risk transfer (insurance)
- Add buffers to the project schedule

The process of project risk management is for project decision makers to tradeoff the costs of each risk avoidance strategy in light of organizational goals. The key to success is for organizations to adopt those risks internally where they have competency in dealing with the risk at issue, and to pay some price to offload those risks outside of their core competencies.

The output of risk response planning can be a prioritized list of risks with potential responses. It also can include assignment of specific individual responsibilities for monitoring events and triggering planned responses.

### Risk Monitoring and Control

This category of activity is implementation of all prior categories. Accounting is the first line of measurement of cost activity. Operational project management personnel also need to keep on top of time and quality performance as the project proceeds. When adverse events are identified, corrective action (either adoption of contingency plans, or development of alternative actions) need to be applied. In the long run, it is important to document projects, both in terms of specific time and cost experiences, as well a qualitative case data to enable the organization to do better on future projects.

## Project Management Tools

A variety of risk management implementation tools have been applied. We referred to PMBOK earlier, which is intended to provide a process model to generic risk management projects. There are other process models, to include the Software Engineering Institute's capability maturity model (CMM). The five levels of the CMMI are shown in Table 12.1.

The CMM level 1 covers software engineering organizations that do nothing. The other four levels involve distinctly different process areas, leading to better control over software development. It should be noted that attaining each level involves an organizational cost in added bureaucracy, which requires a business decision on the part of each organization. However, there is a great deal of research that indicates that

**Table 12.1** Capability maturity model for software engineering processes

| Level | Features | Key processes |
|---|---|---|
| 1 Initial | Chaos | Survival |
| 2 Repeatable | Individual control | Software configuration management<br>Software quality assurance<br>Software subcontract management<br>Software project tracking & oversight<br>Software project planning<br>Requirements management |
| 3 Defined | Institutionalized process | Peer reviews<br>Intergroup coordination<br>Software product engineering<br>Integrated software management<br>Training program<br>Organization process definition<br>Organization process focus |
| 4 Managed | Process measured | Quality management<br>Process measurement and analysis |
| 5 Optimizing | Feedback for improvement | Process change management<br>Technology innovation<br>Defect prevention |

Source: Olson (2004)

in the long run, software quality is improved dramatically by moving from any level to the next higher level, and that overall development cost and development time are improved. This is a clear example of risk management—paying the price of more formality to yield reduced risk in terms of product output. Other process risk management models in software engineering include Boehm's spiral model,[10] which provides iterative risk analysis throughout the phases of the software development.

Bannerman[11] categorized software project risk management into the three areas of process models (reviewed above), analystical frameworks (based on some dimension such as risk source, the project life cycle, or model elements), and checklists. Checklists are often found as the means to implement risk management, with evidence of positive value.[12] Checklists can be (and have been) applied in any type of project. To work well, the project must repeat a domain, as each type of project faces its own list of specific risks. The value of a checklist of course improves with the depth of experience upon which it is based.

## Simulation Models of Project Management Risk

We will focus on demonstrating quantitative tools to project risk management. We will demonstrate how simulation can be used to evaluate the time aspect of project management risk. The models are based on critical path, which can be modeled in Excel, enabling the use of distributions through Crystal Ball simulation. We begin with a basic software engineering project using a traditional waterfall model. Figure 12.1 gives a schematic of the activities and their precedence relationships.

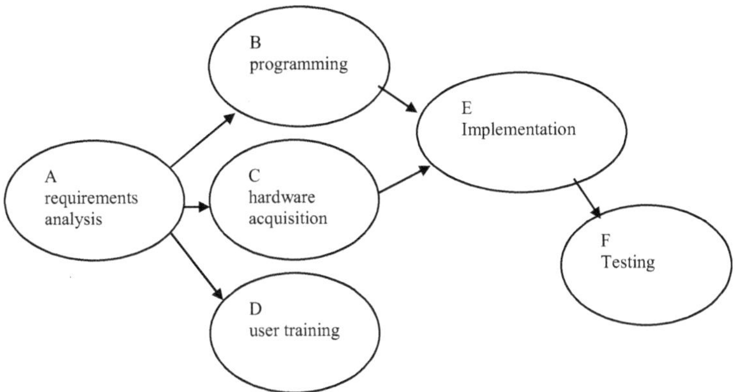


**Fig. 12.1** Network for software installation example

**Table 12.2** Software installation input data

| Activity | Duration | Distribution | Predecessors |
|---|---|---|---|
| A Requirements analysis | 3 weeks | Normal (3,0.3) | None |
| B Programming | 7 weeks | Lognormal (7,1) | A |
| C Hardware acquisition | 3 weeks | Normal (3,0.5) | A |
| D User training | 12 weeks | Constant | A |
| E Implementation | 5 weeks | Exponential (5) | B,C |
| F Testing | 1 week | Exponential (1) | E |

Table 12.2 gives the input information, along with distributions assumed for each activity. These distributions should be based on historical data if possible, subjective expert judgment if historical data is not available.

Figure 12.2 gives the Microsoft Project output for this model.

The Excel model based on critical path analysis is given in Table 12.3.

Some modeling adjustments were needed. For all distributions, durations in weeks were rounded up in the Duration column of Table 12.1. For normal distributions, a minimum of 0 was imposed. Note that the lognormal distribution in Crystal Ball requires a shape parameter (constrained to be less than the mean). Here the shape parameter is 5, the mean 7, and standard deviation 1. Also note that the exponential distribution's mean is inverted, so for E Implementation, 5 weeks becomes 0.2. Figure 12.3 gives the simulation results (based on 1000 replications).

The average for this data was 18.62 weeks, compared to the critical path analysis 16 weeks (which was based on assumed duration certainty). There was a minimum of 15 weeks (0.236 probability) and a maximum of 58 weeks. There was a 0.490 probability of exceeding 16 weeks.

There are other simulation systems used for project management. Process simulation allows contingent sequences of activities, as used in the Project Assessment by Simulation Technique (PAST).[13]

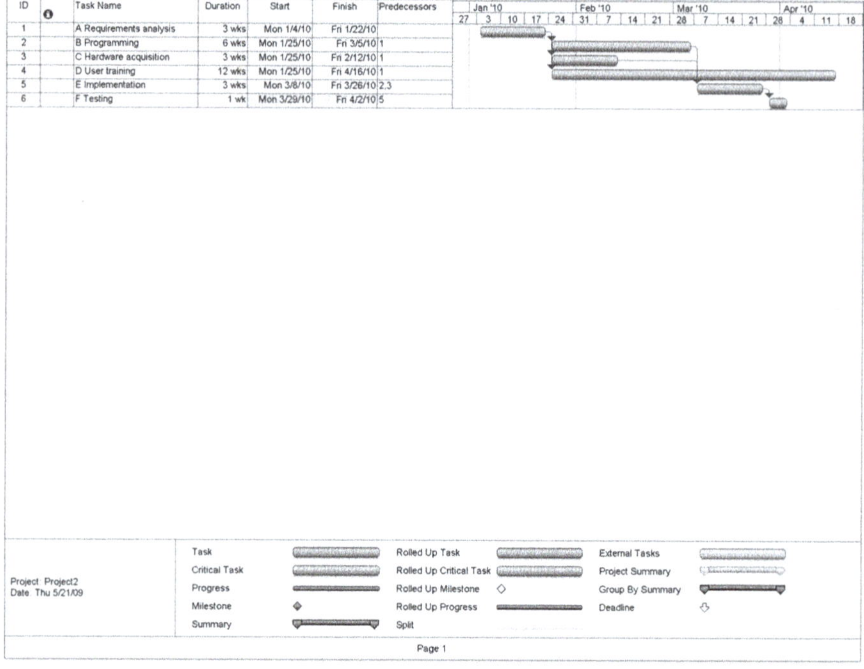


**Fig. 12.2** Microsoft Project model output

**Table 12.3** Crystal Ball model of software installation project. ©Oracle. Used with permission

| Activity | Distribution | Duration | Start | Finish |
|---|---|---|---|---|
| A Requirements analysis | =CB.Normal(3,0.3) | =INT(MAX(0,B2)+0.99) | =0 | =D2+C2 |
| B Programming | =CB.Lognormal(5,7,1) | =INT(B3+0.99) | =E2 | =D3+C3 |
| C Hardware acquisition | =CB.Normal(3,5) | =INT(MAX(0,C2)+0.99) | =E2 | =D4+C4 |
| D User training | 12 | =B5 | =E2 | =D5+C5 |
| E Implementation | =CB.Exponential(0.2) | =INT(B6+0.99) | =MAX(E3,E4) | =D6+C6 |
| F Testing | =CB.Exponential(1) | =INT(B7+0.99) | =E6 | =D7+C7 |
| | | | | |
| | | | | =MAX(E2:E7) |

Color shades emphasize key points in the prose

## Governmental Project

We assume a very long term project to dispose of nuclear waste, with activities, durations and predecessor relationships given in Table 12.4.

Table 12.5 gives the Excel (Crystal Ball) model for this scheduling project. Normal distributions were used for project manager controllable activities, and lognormal distributions used for activities beyond project manager control Figs. 12.4, 12.5, and 12.6.

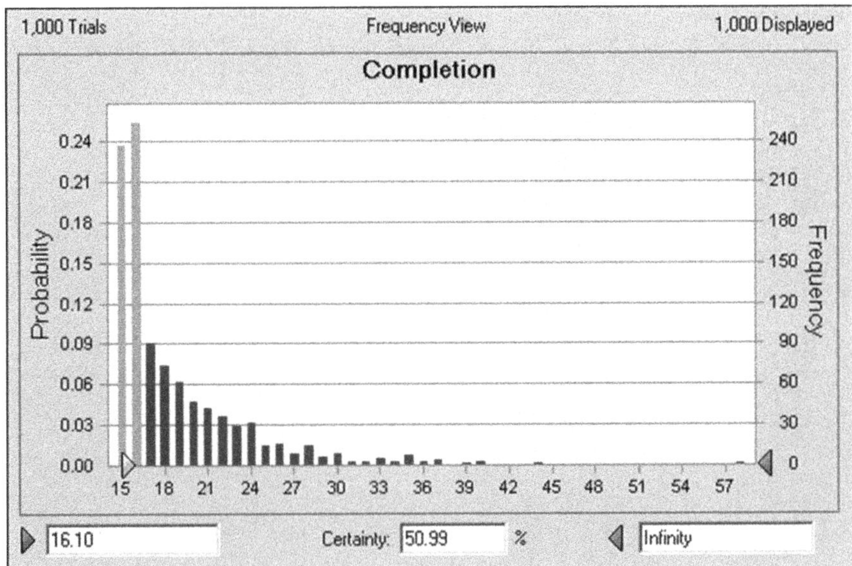


**Fig. 12.3** Simulated software installation completion time. ©Oracle. Used with permission

**Table 12.4** Nuclear waste disposal project

| Activity | Duration | Distribution | Predecessors |
|---|---|---|---|
| A Decision staffed | 60 weeks | | None |
| B EIS | 70 weeks | | A |
| C Licensing study | 60 weeks | | A |
| D NRC | 30 weeks | | A |
| E Conceptual design | 36 weeks | | A |
| F Regulation compliance | 70 weeks | | E |
| G Site selection | 40 weeks | | A |
| H Construction permit | 0 | constant | D,F,G |
| I Construction | 100 weeks | | H |
| J Procurement | 70 weeks | | F SS, I SS + 5weeks |
| K Install equipment | 72 weeks | | I |
| L Operating permit | 0 | | K |
| M Cold start test | 16 weeks | | K |
| N Readiness test | 36 weeks | | M |
| O Hot test | 16 weeks | | N |
| P Begin conversion | 0 | | L,O |

Minimum completion time based on 1000 replications was 280 months, and maximum 391 months. The mean was 332 months, with a standard deviation of 16 months. The distribution of completion times appears close to normal. Table 12.6 gives the probabilities of completion in 10-month intervals:

**Table 12.5** Model for governmental project

| | A | B | C | D | E |
|---|---|---|---|---|---|
| 1 | Activity | Duration | | Start | End |
| 2 | A Decision staffed | =INT(CB.Normal (60,5)) | None | 0 | =D2 + B2 |
| 3 | B EIS | =INT(CB. Lognormal(70,10)) | A | =E2 | =D3 + B3 |
| 4 | C Licensing study | =INT(CB. Lognormal(60,10)) | A | =E2 | =D4 + B4 |
| 5 | D NRC | =INT(CB. Lognormal(30,5)) | A | =E2 | =D5 + B5 |
| 6 | E Conceptual design | =INT(CB.Normal (36,6)) | A | =E2 | =D6 + B6 |
| 7 | F Regulation compliance | =INT(CB.Normal (70,10)) | E | =E6 | =D7 + B7 |
| 8 | G Site selection | =INT(CB.Normal (40,5)) | A | =E2 | =D8 + B8 |
| 9 | H Construction permit | =0 | D,F,G | =MAX(D5, D7,D8) | =D9 + B9 |
| 10 | I Construction | =INT(CB. Lognormal (100,10)) | H | =D9 | =D10 + B10 |
| 11 | J Procurement | =INT(CB.Normal (70,5)) | F SS, I SS + 5weeks | =MAX(D7, D10 + 5) | =D11 + B11 |
| 12 | K Install equipment | =INT(CB.Normal (72,5)) | I | =E10 | =D12 + B12 |
| 13 | L Operating permit | =0 | K | =E12 | =D13 + B13 |
| 14 | M Cold start test | =INT(CB. Lognormal(16,6)) | K | =E12 | =D14 + B14 |
| 15 | N Readiness test | =INT(CB. Lognormal(36,6)) | M | =E14 | =D15 + B15 |
| 16 | O Hot test | =INT(CB. Lognormal(16,6)) | N | =E15 | =D16 + B16 |

## Conclusions

We have argued that there are a number of distinct project types, to include more predictable projects such as those encountered in civil engineering, highly unpredictable projects such as encountered in software engineering, and projects involving massive undertakings or emergency response typically faced by government bureaucracies. There are many other types of projects, of course. For instance, we did not discuss military procurement projects, which are extremely important unto themselves. This type of project is a specific kind of governmental project, but here

Decision staffed
EIS
Licensing study
NRC
Conceptual design
Site selection
Regulation compliance
Construction permit
Construction
Procurement
Install equipment
Cold start test
Operating permit
Readiness test
Hot test
Begin conversio

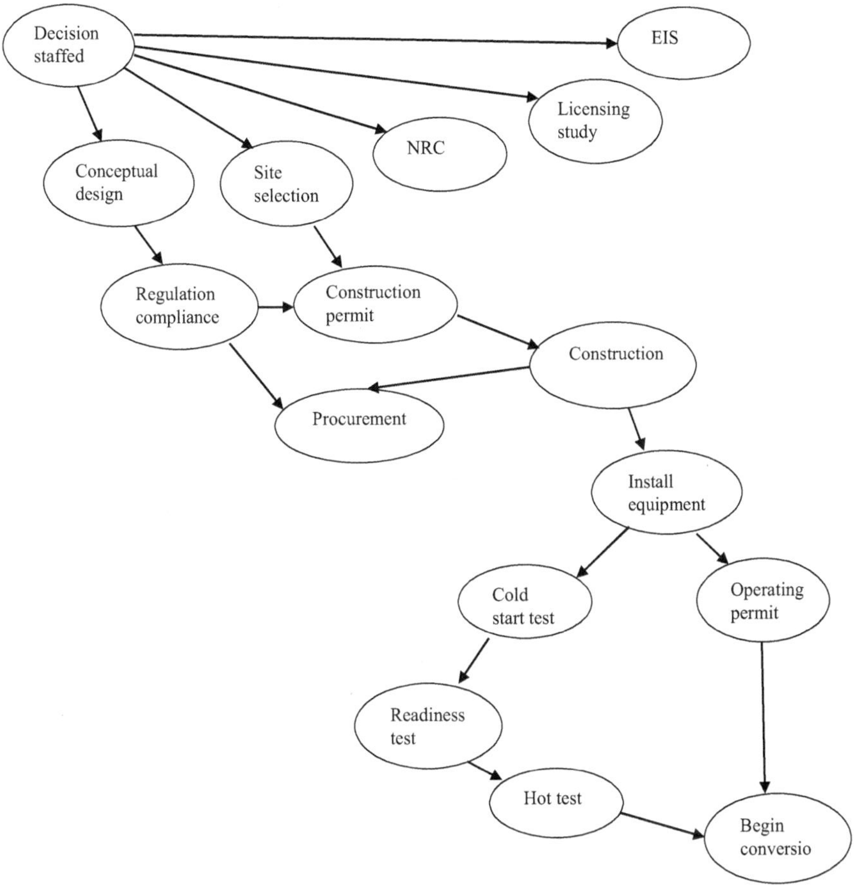

**Fig. 12.4** Network for governmental project

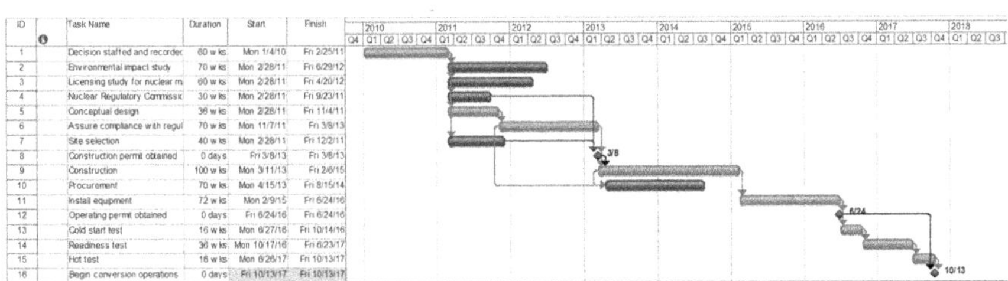

ID
Task Name
Duration
Start
Finish
1 Decision staffed and recordec 60 w ks Mon 1/4/10 Fri 2/25/11
2 Environmental impact study 70 w ks Mon 2/28/11 Fri 6/29/12
3 Licensing study for nuclear m 60 w ks Mon 2/28/11 Fri 4/20/12
4 Nuclear Regulatory Commissic 30 w ks Mon 2/28/11 Fri 9/23/11
5 Conceptual design 36 w ks Mon 2/28/11 Fri 11/4/11
6 Assure compliance with regul 70 w ks Mon 11/7/11 Fri 3/8/13
7 Site selection 40 w ks Mon 2/28/11 Fri 12/2/11
8 Construction permit obtained 0 days Fri 3/8/13 Fri 3/8/13
9 Construction 100 w ks Mon 3/11/13 Fri 2/6/15
10 Procurement 70 w ks Mon 4/15/13 Fri 8/15/14
11 Install equipment 72 w ks Mon 2/9/15 Fri 6/24/16
12 Operating permit obtained 0 days Fri 6/24/16 Fri 6/24/16
13 Cold start test 16 w ks Mon 6/27/16 Fri 10/14/16
14 Readiness test 36 w ks Mon 10/17/16 Fri 6/23/17
15 Hot test 16 w ks Mon 6/26/17 Fri 10/13/17
16 Begin conversion operations 0 days Fri 10/13/17 Fri 10/13/17
2010 2011 2012 2013 2014 2015 2016 2017 2018
3/8
6/24
10/13

**Fig. 12.5** Gantt chart for governmental project

we focused more on emergency management (which military operations is closer to).

We also presented a framework for project risk analysis, based on PMBOK. This included a number of qualitative elements which can be extremely valuable in

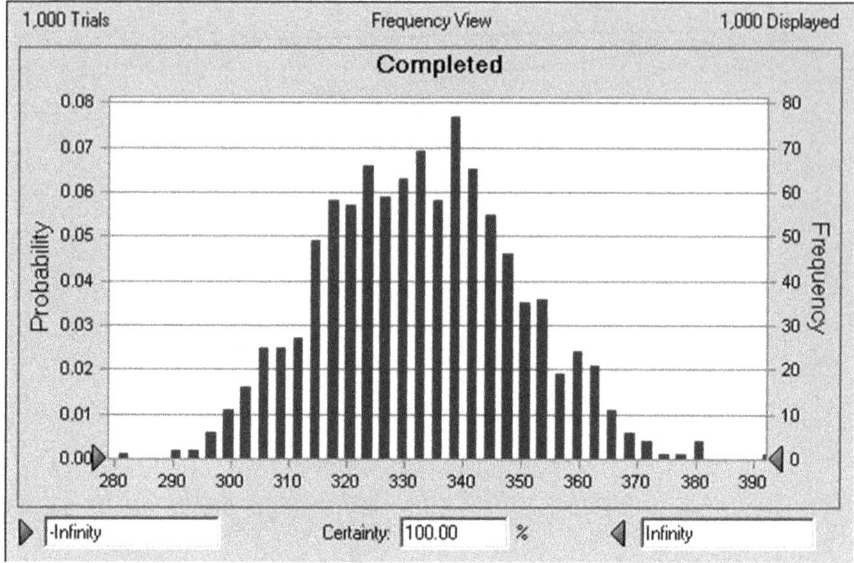


**Fig. 12.6** Histogram of governmental project completion time in months. ©Oracle. Used with permission

**Table 12.6** Probability of Completion

| Months | Probability |
|---|---|
| 310 | 0.912 |
| 320 | 0.759 |
| 330 | 0.550 |
| 340 | 0.329 |
| 350 | 0.153 |
| 360 | 0.057 |
| 370 | 0.011 |
| 380 | 0.005 |

project management. But they are less concrete, and therefore we found it easier to focus on quantitative tools. We want to point out that qualitative tools are also very important.

The qualitative tools presented start with the deterministic critical path method, which assumes no risk in duration nor in resource availability. We present simulation as a very useful means to quantify project duration risk. Simulation allows any kind of assumption, and could also incorporate some aspects of resource availability risk through spreadsheet models.

While the ability to assess the relative probability of risk is valuable, the element of subjectivity should always be kept in mind. A simulation model can assign a probability of any degree of precision imaginable, but such probabilities are only as accurate as the model inputs. These probabilities should be viewed as subject to a great deal of error. However, they provide project managers with initial tools for identification of the degree of risk associated with various project tasks.

## Notes

1. Seyedhoseini, S.M., Noori S. and AliHatefi, M. 2008, Chapter 6: Two Polar Concept of Project Risk Management, in D. L. Olson and D. Wu, eds., New Frontiers in Enterprise Risk Management. Berlin: Springer, 77–106.
2. Skorupka, D. (2008). Identification and initial risk assessment of construction projects in Poland, *Journal of Management in Engineering* 24:3, 120–127.
3. Kong, D., Tiong, R.L.K., Cheah, C.Y.J., Permana, A. and Ehrlich, M. (2008). Assessment of credit risk in project finance, *Journal of Construction Engineering and Management* 134:11, 876–884.
4. Chua, A.Y.K. (2009). Exhuming IT projects from their graves: An analysis of eight failure cases and their risk factors, *Journal of Computer Information Systems* 49:3, 31–39.
5. Olson, D.L. (2004), *Introduction to Information Systems Project Management*, 2nd ed. NY: McGraw-Hill/Irwin.
6. Project Management Institute (2013), *A Guide to the Project Management Body of Knowledge, 5th ed.*Newtown Square, PA: Project Management Institute.
7. Chapman, C. (2006). *International Journal of Project Management* 24(4), 303–313.
8. Schatteman, D., Herroelen, W., Van de Vonder, S. and Boone, A. (2008). Methodology for integrated risk management and proactive scheduling of construction projects, *Journal of Construction Engineering and Management* 134:11, 885–893.
9. Choi, H.-H. and Mahadevan, S. (2008). Construction project risk assessment using existing database and project-specific information, *Journal of Construction Engineering and Management* 134:11, 894–903.
10. Boehm, B. (1988). *Software Risk Management*. Washington, DC: IEEE Computer Society Press.
11. Bannerman, P.L. (2008). Risk and risk management in software projects: A reassessment, *The Journal of Systems and Software* 81:12, 2118 2133.
12. Keil, M., Li, L., Mathiassen, L. and Zheng, G. (2008). The influence of checklists and roles on software practitioner risk perception and decision-making, *The Journal of Systems and Software* 81:6, 908–919.
13. Cates, G.R. and Mollaghasemi, M. (2007). The Project Assessment by Simulation Technique, *Engineering Management Journal* 19:4, 3–10.

# 13 Natural Disaster Risk Management

We have considered business operational risks in the contexts of supply chains, information systems, and project management. By definition, natural disasters are surprises, and cause inconvenience and damage. Some things we do to ourselves, such as revolutions, terrorist attacks, and wars. Some things nature does to us, to include hurricanes, tornados, volcanic eruptions, and tsunamis. Some disasters are caused by combinations of human and natural causes. We dam rivers to control floods, to irrigate, to generate power, and for recreation, but dams have burst causing immense flooding. We have developed low-pollution, low-cost (at the time) electricity through nuclear power. Yet with plant failure, new protective systems have made the price very high, and we have not figured out how to acceptably dispose of the waste. While natural disasters come as surprises, we can be prepared. This chapter addresses natural domain risks in the form of disaster management.

## Emergency Management

Natural disaster management is the domain of government, fulfilling its responsibility to protect the general welfare. Local, State and Federal agencies in the United States are responsible for responding to natural and man-made disasters. This is coordinated at the Federal level through the Federal Emergency Management Agency (FEMA). While FEMA has done much good, it is almost inevitable that more is expected of them than they deliver in some cases, such as hurricane recovery. In 2006 Hurricane Katrina provided one of the greatest tests of the emergency management system in the U.S.:

1. Communications outages disrupted the ability to locate people
2. Reliable transportation was disrupted or at least restricted
3. Electrical power was disrupted, cutting off computers
4. Multiple facilities were destroyed or damaged



D.L. Olson, D.D. Wu, *Enterprise Risk Management Models*, Springer Texts in Business and Economics, DOI 10.1007/978-3-662-53785-5_13

5. Some bank branches and ATMs were flooded for weeks
6. Mail was disrupted up to months.

Disasters are abrupt and calamitous events causing great damage, loss of lives, and destruction. Emergency management is accomplished in every country to some degree. Disasters occur throughout the world, in every form of natural, man-made, and combination of disaster. Disasters by definition are unexpected, and tax the ability of governments and other agencies to cope. A number of intelligence cycles have been promulgated, but all are based on the idea of:

1. Identification of what is not known;
2. Collection—gathering information related to what is not known;
3. Production—answering management questions;
4. Dissemination—getting the answers to the right people.[1]

Information technology has been developing at a very rapid pace, creating a dynamic of its own. Many technical systems have been designed to gather, process, distribute, and analyze information in emergencies. These systems include communications and data. Tools to aid emergency planners communicate include telephones, whiteboards, and the Internet. Tools to aid in dealing with data include database systems (for efficient data organization, storage, and retrieval), data mining tools (to explore large databases), models to deal with specific problems, and combination of these resources into decision support systems to assist humans in reaching decisions quickly or expert systems to make decisions rapidly based on human expertise. The role of information technology in disaster management to include the functions of:[2]

- **Information Extraction**—gathering data from a variety of sources and storing them in efficient databases.
- **Information Retrieval**—efficiently searching and locating key information during crises.
- **Information Filtering**—focusing of pertinent data in a responsive manner.
- **Data Mining**—extract patterns and trends.
- **Decision Support**—analyze data through models to make better decisions.

## Emergency Management Support Systems

A number of software products have been marketed to support emergency management. These are often various forms of a decision support system. The Department of Homeland Security in the U.S. developed a National Incident Management System. A similar system used in Europe is the Global Emergency Management Information Network Initiative.[3] While many systems are available, there are many challenges due to unreliable inputs at one end of the spectrum, and overwhelmingly massive data content at the other extreme.

Systems in place for emergency management include the U.S. National Disaster Medical System (NDMS), providing virtual centers designed as a focal point for information processing, response planning, and inter-agency coordination. NDMS is a federally coordinated system augmenting disaster medical care. Its purpose is to supplement an integrated National medical response capacity to assist State and local authorities in dealing with medical impacts of major peacetime disasters, as well as supporting military and Veterans Affairs medical systems in casualty care. EMSS has also been implemented in Europe.[4] Intelligent emergency management systems are appearing as well.[5]

An example decision support system directed at aiding emergency response is the Critical Infrastructure Protection Decision Support System (CIPDSS).[6] CIPDSS was developed by Los Alamos, Sandia, and Argonne National Laboratories sponsored by the Department of Homeland Security in the U.S. The system includes a range of applications to organize and present information, as well as system dynamics simulation modeling of critical infrastructure sectors, such as water, public health, emergency services, telecom, energy, and transportation. Primary goals are:

1. To develop, implement, and evolve a rational approach to prioritize CIP strategies and resource allocations through modeling, simulation, and analyses to assess vulnerabilities, consequences, and risks;
2. To propose and evaluate protection, mitigation, response, and recovery strategies and options;
3. To provide real-time support to decision makers during crises and emergencies.

A key focus it to aid decision makers by enabling them to understand the consequences of policy and investment options prior to action. Decision support systems provide tools to examine trade-offs between the benefits of risk reduction and the costs of protection action. Factors considered include threat information, vulnerability assessments, and disruptive consequences. Modeling includes system dynamics, simulation, and other forms of risk analysis. The system also includes multi-attribute utility functions based upon interviews with infrastructure decision makers. CIPDSS thus serves as an example of what can be done in the way of an emergency management support system.

Other systems in place for emergency management include the U.S. National Disaster Medical System (NDMS), providing virtual centers designed as a focal point for information processing, response planning, and inter-agency coordination. Systems have been developed for forecasting earthquake impact[7] or the time and size of bioterrorism attacks. This demonstrates the need for DSS support not only during emergencies, but also in the planning stage.

## Example Disaster Management System

Sahana is foundation offering a suite of free open-source web-based disaster management system software for disaster response.[8] The primary aim of the system is to alleviate human suffering and help save lives through efficient use of information technology. Sahana Eden is a humanitarian platform customizable to integrate with local systems for planning or coping with crises. Vesuvius is a disaster preparedness and response software providing support to family reunification as well as hospital triage. Mayon provides emergency planning agencies with tools to plan preparedness, response, recovery, and mitigation. Sahana can bring together government, emergency management, non-government organizations, volunteers and victims to disaster response. It is intended to empower victims, responders, and volunteers to more efficiently utilize their efforts, while protecting victim data privacy.

Sahana is a free open-source software system initially built by Sri Lankan volunteers after the 2004 Asian tsunami.[9] It has the following main applications:

1. Missing persons registry—bulletin board of missing and found persons, and information of who is seeking individuals.
2. Organization registry—a tool to coordinate and balance distribution of relief organization to affected areas.
3. Request/Pledge management system—log of incoming requests for support, tracking relief provided and linking donors to relief requirements.
4. Shelter registry—tool to track location and numbers of victims by temporary location.
5. Volunteer coordination—tool to coordinate contact information, skills and assignments of volunteers and responders
6. Inventory management—tool to track location, quantities, and expiration dates of supplies
7. Situation awareness—a geographic information system showing current status.

Sahana has been successfully deployed in many disasters including after the tsunami as shown in Table 13.1:

The Sahana system uses plug-in architecture, which allows third party groups easy access to system components, while simplifying overall integration. The system does not need to be installed, but can be run as a portable application from a USB drive (using a USB flash drive). The system can be translated into any language. Granular security is provided through an access control system. The user interface can be viewed through a number of devices, to include a PDA.

**Table 13.1** Sahana deployments[10]

| Location | Year | Event | Details |
|---|---|---|---|
| Sri Lanka | 2005 | Tsunami | Deployed for the Government of Sri Lanka |
| Pakistan | 2005 | Earthquake | Deployed for the Government of Pakistan |
| The Philippines | 2006 | Mudslide | Southern Leyte |
| Indonesia | 2006 | Earthquake | Yogjarkata |
| New York City | 2007–2008 | Hurricanes | Coastal storm planning |
| Peru | 2007 | Earthquake | Ica |
| China | 2008 | Earthquake | Chendu-Shizuan province |
| Myanmar | 2008 | Cyclone | Monsoon disaster planning |
| Haiti | 2010 | Earthquake | Disaster planning |

## Disaster Management Criteria

We review criteria sets used by two disaster management applications involving multiple criteria. The first involved the engineering decision of protecting buildings from earthquake damage.[11] This of course is a more technical decision than what we described in the banking industry, but the point is that risks appear in almost every walk of life. Here the decision was to design buildings to be as secure as possible. Earthquakes are common. Building codes in the past have been insufficient. Building design retrofit alternatives have been developed to modify performance in terms of stiffness, strength, and ductility. Criteria that could be applied to seismic risk management are given in Table 13.2:

Their model would enable building designers to score alternatives on each of these eight risks and to express decision maker preferences.

The US Water Resource Council[13] has a comprehensive set of 20 performance criteria for infrastructure policies and investments given in Table 13.3:

A generic multiple criteria model was developed within this list[14] with the criteria of:

- Protection from coastal inundation
- Protection of public infrastructure systems
- Protection against storm surges and flooding
- Protection of wetlands and environment
- Protection of recreational activities

This model was to be used for specific coastal protection evaluations, with normal options of building different types of revetments, seawalls, or nourishing beaches or dunes. The evaluation they provided included evaluation under different scenarios

risk response if they retained complete control over the project than if they transferred through insurance or subcontract.

The score matrix given in Table 13.4 provides a tabular expression of relative value of each of the alternatives over each of the selected criteria. It can be used to identify tradeoffs among these alternatives.

## Weights

The next phase of the analysis ties these ratings together into an overall value function by obtaining the relative weight of each criterion. In order to give the decision maker a reference about what exactly is being compared, the relative range between best and worst on each scale for each criterion should be explained. There are many methods to determine these weights. In SMART, the process begins with rank-ordering the three criteria. A possible ranking for a specific decision maker might be as given in Table 13.5.

Swing weighting could be used to identify weights.[16] Here, the scoring was used to reflect 1 as the best possible and 0 as the worst imaginable. Thus the relative rank ordering reflects a common scale, and can be used directly in the order given. To obtain relative criterion weights, the first step is to rank-order criteria by importance, indicated by the order of Criteria in Table 13.6. Estimates of weights can be obtained by assigning 100 points to moving from the worst measure to the best measure on the most important criterion (here oil availability). Then each of the other criteria are assessed in a similar comparative manner in order, assuring that more important criteria get at least as much weight as other criteria down the

**Table 13.5** Worst and best measures by criteria

| Criteria | Worst measure | Best measure |
|---|---|---|
| Oil availability | Oil embargo | Successful project—in-house |
| Exploration/production | No project | Successful project—in-house |
| Environment/regulatory | Oil spills | No project |
| Reputation | Oil spills | No project |
| Transportation | Oil spills | No project |
| Geopolitical | War in drilling area | No project |

**Table 13.6** Weight estimation from perspective of most important criterion

| Criteria | Assigned value | Weight |
|---|---|---|
| 1 Oil availability | 100 | 0.282 |
| 2 Exploration/production | 90 | 0.254 |
| 3 Environment/regulatory | 70 | 0.197 |
| 4 Reputation | 60 | 0.169 |
| 5 Transportation | 20 | 0.056 |
| 6 Geopolitical | 15 | 0.042 |
| Total | 355 | 1.000 |

**Table 13.7** Value score calculations

| Criteria | Weight | Accept | Terminate | Transfer |
|---|---|---|---|---|
| 1 Oil availability | 0.282 | ×0.9 = 0.254 | ×0.2 = 0.051 | ×0.6 = 0.152 |
| 2 Exploration/production | 0.254 | ×0.8 = 0.203 | ×0.2 = 0.051 | ×0.5 = 0.127 |
| 3 Environment/regulatory | 0.197 | ×0.1 = 0.020 | ×1.0 = 0.197 | ×0.6 = 0.118 |
| 4 Reputation | 0.169 | ×0.2 = 0.034 | ×1.0 = 0.169 | ×0.5 = 0.084 |
| 5 Transportation | 0.056 | ×0.2 = 0.011 | ×1.0 = 0.056 | ×0.9 = 0.051 |
| 6 Geopolitical | 0.042 | ×0.3 = 0.013 | ×1.0 = 0.042 | ×0.4 = 0.017 |
| **Totals** | | **0.534** | **0.566** | **0.549** |

ordinal list. Here we might assign moving from the worst measure on Exploration/production 80 points compared to Oil availability's 100. For purposes of demonstration, assume the assigned values given in Table 13.6:

The total of the assigned values is 355. An estimate of relative weights is obtained by dividing each assigned value by 355.

### Value score

The next step of the SMART method is to obtain value scores for each alternative by multiplying each score on each criterion for an alternative by that criterion's weight, and adding these products by alternative. Table 13.7 shows this calculation:

In this example, the terminate was ranked first, followed by the option of transferring (outsourcing), followed by accepting risk. However, these are all quite close, implying that the decision maker could think more in terms of other objectives, or possibly seek more input, or even other options.

## Natural Disaster and Financial Risk Management

Risk is the probability of an adverse event occurring with the potential to result in loss to exposed element. Natural hazards are meteorological or geological phenomena that due to their location, frequency, and severity, have the potential to affect economic activities. A natural event that results in human and economic losses is an environmental problem contributed by the development in the region. Natural catastrophe risk is generally characterized by low frequency and high severity, though the level of severity varies quite significantly. The extent of the development contributes to the financial vulnerability to the catastrophic effects of the natural disaster. On the same token, the vulnerability of a firm from hazard events depends on the size of its investment and revenue exposures in the region. Natural hazards can be characterized by location, timing, magnitude and duration. The principal causes of vulnerability include imprudent investments and ineffective public policies.

Natural disaster losses are the result of mismanaged and unmanaged disaster risks that reflect current conditions and historical factors.[17] Disaster risk exposure comes from the interaction between a natural hazard (the external risk factor) and vulnerability (the internal risk factor).[18] Proactive disaster risk management requires a comprehensive process that encompasses a comprehensive pre-disaster evaluation involving the three broad steps involving the following activities:

- identification of the potential natural hazards and evaluation of investment at risk;
- risk reduction measures to address the vulnerability, and
- risk transfer to minimise financial losses.

The need to integrate disaster risk management into investment strategy is necessary to manage corporate value and reduce risk in the future. These should be supported by effective governance (e.g. policies, planning, etc.), supplemented by effective information and knowledge sharing mechanisms among different stakeholders.

First, **risk identification** involves creating an awareness and quantification of risk through understanding vulnerabilities and exposure patterns. The process also includes analysis of the risk elements and the underlying causes of the exposure. This knowledge is essential for development of strategies and measures for risk reduction. For example, firms operating in an earthquake-prone zone would need to keep abreast of information on real-time seismic patterns complemented with forecasts on expected hazards. This is complemented with the necessary exposure analysis using mapping, modelling and hazard analysis to assess industry and corporate risk. The evaluations should include calculating a probability profile of occurrence and impacts of hazard events in terms of their characteristics and factoring these elements into the firm's decision-making process. Thus, risk identification and analysis provide for informed decision-making on business investment that will effectively reduce the impacts of potential disaster events and prioritization of risk management efforts.

Second, **risk reduction** involves measures to avoid, mitigate or prepare against the destructive and disruptive consequences of hazards to minimize the potential financial impact. The mitigation measures are actions aimed at reducing the overall risk exposure associated with disasters. This requires an ex-ante business strategy that combines mitigation investments and pre-established financial protection. In this respect, firms can prevent natural disaster losses by avoiding investment in disaster prone regions (i.e. prevention investments) or they may take actions to locate and structure its business operations to avoid heavy investments in disaster prone regions. Such actions require short- and long-term strategic business planning and disaster recovery mechanisms, such as those pertaining to supply chain management. Risk mitigation planning is aimed at taking into account the economic impacts of disasters such as earthquakes. The access to relevant information is important to better-informed decision making and planning. For example, access to hazard information such as frequency, magnitude and trends are required for disaster risk mitigation for corporate investment decisions.

Finally, **risk transfer** mechanisms enable the distribution of the risks associated with natural hazard events such as floods and earthquakes to reduce financial and economic impacts. This might not fully eliminate the firm's financial risk exposure but it allows risk to be shared with other parties. The common risk transfer tool is catastrophic insurance, which allows firms to recover some of their disaster losses and thus managing the financial impacts of disasters. Other financial instruments include catastrophic bonds (cat-bonds) and weather risk management products. The issuance of catastrophe risk linked bonds by insurance or reinsurance companies enables them to obtain coverage for particular risk exposures in case of predefined catastrophic events (e.g. earthquakes). These catastrophe bonds allow the insurance companies transfer risk and obtain complementary coverage in the capital market and increase their capacity to take on more catastrophe risk coverage.

The use of insurance for mitigating financial losses from natural catastrophes is generally lacking in the private sector in developing countries.[19] Catastrophe risk is a public shared risk ("covariate" risk) and collective in nature, therefore, making it difficult to find individual and community solutions.[20] An effective insurance market is essential for financing post disaster recuperation and rehabilitation of firms. In the absence of a sophisticated insurance market, the government normally acts as financier for disaster recovery efforts. Governments can also influence the risk financing arrangements by encouraging the establishment of insurance pools by the local insurance industry and covering higher exposures in the global reinsurance and capital markets.

Property insurance policies for firms in earthquake prone provinces may not be readily available due to inadequate local regulation of property titles, building codes and developmental planning. In this respect, the local governments play an important role in ensuring proper public policies are implemented and regulations enforced to lower premiums and achieve higher insurance coverage in these provinces.

There is a bigger range of instruments for risk financing in the markets today. Other than insurance coverage for disaster risk, new instruments such as catastrophe risk swaps and risk-linked securities are also available in the global capital market. In 1994, the original capital market instrument linked to catastrophe risk called a catastrophe bond was introduced. Since then, more risk-linked securities are available including those providing outright funding commitments to recover economic losses from disasters. These contingent capital instruments are based on estimating the amount of risk involved through risk and loss impact estimates to build a disaster risk profile for the client. The implied risk profile is used to identify and define the risk-linked financial instruments.

## Natural Disaster Risk and Firm Value[21]

The current dynamic business environment embraces the international flow of investment to facilitate success and growth. Firms with sustainable competitiveness and growth are likely to enhance their market value. Business globalisation invariably means that firms become more proactive in scouting for opportunities in foreign markets in order to sustain and build corporate value. Other than the social, economic and political risk factors normally considered in foreign investment evaluations and enterprise risk management processes, firms also need to take into account natural disaster risk. The premiums for catastrophe risk insurance are expensive and there must be a compelling case or economic incentives for firms to establish adequate insurance coverage on their assets. We are interested in the economic impacts of natural catastrophes from a financial management perspective.

The primary objective of the firm is to maximise shareholder wealth and an effective corporate risk management program enhances corporate value. The existent literature contains a respectable body of theories and general acceptance in the market that corporate value can be created with the proper understanding and management of risk. There is a perception of risk associated with investments and traditional finance suggests such perceptions imply that there must be a reward in the form of a risk premium for investors to take on this risk. The firm as a corporate investor is no different in that it also requires a risk premium for assuming risk. The magnitude of the firm value depends on how efficient and effective it can manage its risk exposure. From a firm value versus risk management perspective, it is possible to construe the firm's value as a function of all relevant risk factors.

While the frequency and severity of natural hazards are dictated by the natural phenomenon itself, the losses caused can be controlled by understanding and managing the business development and population density according to the vulnerability of the geographical location. Business development and population density tend to have a positive correlation and therefore natural catastrophe risk has profound social and economic impacts on the local inhabitants and economy.

Contemporary enterprise risk exposure modelling tends to ignore natural hazards and focus on estimating the severity and frequency of financial or operational exposures. The global warming phenomenon has brought about a heightened awareness of many environmental risks that may affect business. Hence, there is a need for firms and policy makers to model, monitor and measure the risk exposure from natural hazards and prepare to manage the potential impacts.

The impacts from a natural catastrophe include the loss of property, life, injury, business interruption and loss of profit. From a firm's perspective, the financial impact on its market value can be mathematically specified as:

$$\text{\textit{Firms value at risk}} = f\,(\textit{hazard}, \textit{vulnerability}) \tag{1}$$

From Eq. (1), the firm's value at risk from natural phenomena is a function of hazard and vulnerability. Equation (1) integrates the impact on the firm's value from natural phenomena and their consequence or exposure. The natural disaster risk management process has to be managed properly from the beginning therefore, it is important that firms improve the evaluation, coordination, efficiency and control of business development and management process to minimize such risks. The issues in this context are the considerations and measures that are available to firms in the natural disaster risk management process. Vulnerability in turn is a function of three factors:

$$Firms\ vulnerability = f\ (fragility, resilience, exposure) \tag{2}$$

Effective risk management requires attention to three factors—hazards, exposure, and vulnerability. Primary disaster impacts include potential physical damage to production facilities and infrastructure. But there also are often secondary impacts, to include business interruption form lack of materials and information, especially in interacting supply chain networks. Risk is a function of hazard and vulnerability, while vulnerability is a function of fragility, resilience, and exposure.[22]

Coase's theory of the firm stresses that the impetus for the emergence of business corporations is the specialised institutional structure that comes into being to reduce the transaction costs.[23] Since the threat of natural disasters, like the volatility of financial prices, implies potential transaction costs to the firm, it is imperative to manage catastrophe risk as it can affect the cost of capital, the cost of production, and revenues. Financial theory suggests that rational firms would hedge their risk exposure to remove the variability in their cash flows. The significance of this view is that by removing variability, firms enhance the predictability in cash flows allowing them to invest in future projects without uncertainty about the negative impact of price fluctuations. The manifestations of variability as a result of a natural catastrophe are disruptions to the firm's supply chain, production, logistics, manpower and clientele. The management issues to be addressed in relation to catastrophe risk management using risk transfer instruments are moral hazard and adverse selection. Moral hazard occurs when the firm fails to implement preventive measures after the risk transfer has taken place and reports excessive losses. Adverse selection happens if the firms uses inside knowledge about the exposure to obtain more favorable terms in the risk transfer policy from the issuing company.

The firm's overall exposure to natural catastrophes like earthquake need to be analyzed based on the region's vulnerability to assess the collective need for risk mitigation arrangements. Therefore, it is necessary to identify and map the major catastrophe risks that affect the region and assess how the business can be organised by adopting a risk neutral structure and/or how to obtain aggregate risk-financing arrangements.

The financial impact of natural disasters is determined by the frequency of an event occurring and by the severity of the resulting loss. The vulnerability to natural catastrophes can be reduced significantly through risk mitigation to lessen the impact of disasters. The catastrophe risk exposures in individual investment projects can be mitigated using a project-based approach to manage catastrophe risk through risk transfer such as insurance to reduce specific project exposures. Risk can also be reduced through corporate planning by building earthquake resistant structures, implementing risk neutral logistics or supply chain, market diversification and other such actions that minimise the overall asset at risk of the firm.

## Financial Issues

Natural disasters can cause serious financial issues for firms as they affect the efficient management and performance of their assets and liabilities. The structural risks associated with natural disasters constitute one of the major sources of risk for most enterprises.[24] Disaster hazards can cause damages and losses to firms in partial or total destruction of assets and disruptions in service delivery. Natural disasters also cause macroeconomic effects in the economy as a whole and can bring significant changes in the macroeconomic environment. The effects of a natural disaster can interact with some of the normal risks faced by firms, including strategic management, operational, financial and market risks. These effects will reveal corporate vulnerabilities related to poor financial decisions.

The following financial issues in relation to risk management are analysed in this section:

- systematic and unsystematic risk exposure
- investment evaluation and planning
- investment to meet strategic demands
- financial risk management and compliance

Firms are constantly trying to develop more efficient models to evaluate the size and scope of risk exposure consequences using risk modelling approaches such as shareholder value at risk (SVA), value at risk (VAR) and stress testing.

## Systematic and Unsystematic Risk

The overall corporate risk can be divided into *alpha* (the competency of the company's management or unsystematic risk) and *beta* (the market or systematic risk). The *alpha* risk is of an idiosyncratic nature can be eliminated by diversifying the investment portfolio, leaving *beta* as the main variable. The risk exposure of a firm can come from the political, economic or operating environments. The operating environment refers more specifically to the idiosyncratic internal and external environments in which the firm conducts it business and the inherent risks to the firm. In this context, the natural disaster risk posed by earthquakes and floods would fall within the definition of external environment. The implication of disaster risk in the internal environment would be related to the internal processes and resources available to manage this risk.

In terms of unsystematic effects of natural disasters like an earthquake, losses related to disruptions in service delivery are the result of a combination of the direct damages to the firm's assets institution and its human resource. The better prepared a firm is in risk managing its resources the lesser the impact of damages and losses to its assets and facilitate in post-disaster business recovery. Systematic risk effects to the firms can be illustrated by damages to the overall infrastructure in the region causing major disruptions to its operations even if the firm is reasonable unscathed at the micro level.

Government normally intervenes in disaster risk management to mitigate systemic risk as damage from disasters tends to be large and locally covariate and the remedial actions are targeted at the provision of public goods, such as infrastructure. The World Bank (2000) suggests that governments are more effective in covering covariant risks, while most idiosyncratic or unsystematic risks may be handled better by private providers. [25]

## Investment Evaluation

An investment evaluation is conducted when a firm is considering a major expenditure. The variables taken into consideration are the cash flows, growth potential and risk associated with the project. The common tools used in investment evaluation are the net present value and internal rate of returns methods. Both these methods incorporate a parameter to measure the risk exposure inherent in the project. As the basic tenet of financial management is one of risk-return optimization. A central feature in modern risk management is the issue of risk and return relationship in investment decisions. The basic link between risk and return says that greater rewards come with greater risk and firms investing in a high natural disaster prone area would need to acknowledge this in their investment. This acknowledgement of catastrophe risk in investment evaluation is similar to accounting for political or economic risks of a country.

The price of risk is commonly referred to as the risk premium. A firm as the investor would demand a risk premium commensurate with the risk characteristics of their investment for the higher risk exposure of operating in a region with greater natural disaster risk. The risk premium to compensate for potential disaster risk can be built into the risk equation by factoring in liquidity risk from destabilizing cash fluctuations, and default or credit risk. Moreover, liquidity risk and credit risk interact under disaster conditions escalating risk premium and thus the cost of capital. This will impact on firms after the disaster when they go back into the capital markets to raise credit to rebuild their business.

Natural disasters typically trigger operational risks resulting in disruptions to cash flows and possible default of loan obligations to creditors. However, firms with efficient liquidity management will minimize the disaster effects on cash flows. The nature and magnitude of the disaster and clients' profile are factors that will influence the severity of cash flow disruptions and the ensuing credit risk. The firm can manage a credibility problem and spiralling cost of capital from a disaster if it made prior financial arrangements with creditors. These effects may lead to short term liquidity crises and heightened cost of capital in the medium term for firms. Credit risk is particularly heightened by a disaster due to disruptions to cash flows and serious loss of assets used as collaterals for loans. Unless prior arrangements are in place for creditors to mitigate repayment risks and redress the deterioration in the quality of securities, firms may face delinquency actions and loss of financial facilities.

## Strategic Investment

Firms can reduce cash flow variability through business portfolio diversification by engaging in different investments, different locations and activities whose returns are not perfectly correlated. In the context of natural disaster risk management, strategic investment refers to making a financial commitment in a location after considering the risk implications and the available investment alternatives. That is, investment in risky environments must be consistent and sensitive to the risk and return profile of the firm. For instance, making a decision to invest in a new supply chain process in a disaster prone area may require looking at risk neutral alternatives. The risk neutral option may be more costly but would be appropriate if the new supply chain is to service the entire firm's operations. A Cost Effectiveness Analysis (CEA) technique can be used to compare the monetary costs of different options that provide the same physical outputs.

The commercial challenges after a natural disaster are the resumption and maintenance of client services and the financial viability of the business. Firms are caught unprepared and will struggle during a disaster to provide emergency and recovery services to their clients without adversely affecting its own financial position. The strategic perspective of disaster effects is on the adequacy of organisational and financial planning on the part of management in relation to the firm's business growth and the resultant structural design. Firms that have experienced rapid growth but do not comprehensively plan and design their business model around a disaster contingency plan are likely to be more affected by a disaster. Rapid business expansion without a appropriately well designed business model, planned investments and logistics addressing disaster risk will likely experience exacerbated problems during a disaster.

## Risk Management and Compliance

To fully address corporate risk exposure with respect to natural disasters, companies need a comprehensive risk management process that identifies and mitigates the major sources of risk. Formulating a detailed risk program with capabilities for risk identification, assessment, measurement, mitigation, and transfer is necessary in a complete risk management strategy. A comprehensive corporate risk management process requires effective techniques that provide a systematic evaluation of risks, which then enables risk managers to make judgments on acceptable risks. Such a process should allow insight into primary areas of uncertainty by identification of the risk factors, highlighting likely outcomes of events and measuring the possible financial impact on the company. The process must also have built-in techniques that can provide a cost-benefit analysis of hedging options as a basis for prioritizing risk strategies. Through the risk management process, a company is able to set its risk tolerance level and any unwanted exposure may be avoided or hedged and the company is left bearing the risk it is willing to assume.

A firm-wide risk management system, using tools like the value at risk (VaR) model, which is capable of capturing the aggregate effect of financial risk exposure to financial, is important to enhance the company's overall market value. The VAR model summarizes the value at risk in a worst case scenario of possible loss under normal conditions.

## Conclusions

The severe climatic changes brought about by global warming are evident by the freezing temperature which caused damages amounting to billions of dollars in China in February 2008. The rapidly changing built environment in China also means that new risk assessment models need to be developed to accurately reflect and risk assess the real impact. Financial risk modelling and management using computer simulations incorporating probabilistic and statistical models would be valuable for evaluating potential losses from future natural catastrophes for better managing potential losses. Firms operating in high natural disaster risk areas should use risk modelling for investment evaluation, risk mitigation, disaster management and recovery planning as part of the overall enterprise wide risk management strategy. They also need to identify new business strategies for operating in disaster prone regions and financial instruments to manage risk.

Governments play an important role in financial markets in encouraging financial institutions to support borrowers in risk reduction and to mitigate the impacts of natural disasters.

## Notes

1. Mueller, R.S. III (2004). The FBI, *Vital Speeches of the Day* 71:4, 106–109.
2. Hristidis, V., Chen, S.-C., Li, T., Luis, S. Deng, Y. (2010). Survey of data management and analysis in disaster situations. *The Journal of Systems and Software* 83:10, 1701–1714.
3. Thompson, S., Altay, N., Green, W.G. III, Lapetina, J. (2006). Improving disaster response efforts with decision support systems, *International Journal of Emergency Management* 3:4, 250–263.
4. Lee, J.-K., Bharosa, N., Yang, J. Janssen, M., Rao, H.R. (2011). Group value and intention to use – A study of multi-agency disaster management information systems for public safety, *Decision Support Systems* 50:2, 404–414.
5. Amailef, K., Lu, J. (2011). A mobile-based emergency response system for intelligent m-government services, *Journal of Enterprise Information Management* 24:4, 338–359.

6. Santella, N., Steinberg, L.J., Parks, K. (2009). Decision making for extreme events: Modeling critical infrastructure interdependencies to aid mitigation and response planning, *Review of Policy Research* 26:4, 409–422.
7. Aleskerov, F., Say, A.L., Toker, A., Akin, H.L., Altay, G. (2005). A cluster-based decision support system for estimating earthquake damage and casualties, *Disasters* 3, 255–276.
8. www.sahana.lk/overview accessed 2/22/2010.
9. Morelli, R., Tucker, A., Danner, N., de Lanerolle, T.R., Ellis, H.J.C., Izmirli, O., Krizanc, D. and Parker, G. (2009) Revitalizing computing education through free and open source software for humanity, *Communications of the ACM* 52:8, 67–75.
10. www.sahana.lk/overview accessed 8/2/2016; Wikipedia, Sahana FOSS Disaster Management System, accessed 8/2/2016.
11. Tesfamariam, S., Sadiq, R., Najjaran, H. (2010). Decision making under uncertainty – An example for seismic risk management, *Risk Analysis* 30:1, 78–94.
12. Ibid.
13. Karvetski, C.W., Lambert, J.H., Keisler, J.M., Linkov, I. (2011). Integration of decision analysis and scenario planning for coastal engineering and climate change, *IEEE Transactions on Systems, Man, and Cybernetiocs – Part A: Systems and Humans* 41:1, 63–73.
14. Ibid.
15. Briggs, C.A., Tolliver, D. and Szmerekovsky, J. (2012). Managing and mitigating the upstream petroleum industry supply chain risks: Leveraging analytic hierarchy process. *International Journal of Business and Economics Perspectives* 7(1), 1–12.
16. Edwards, W. (1977). How to use multiattribute utility measurement for social decisionmaking, *IEEE Transactions on Systems, Man, and Cybernetics*, SMC-7:5, 326–340.
17. Alexander, D. 2000, *Confronting Catastrophe: New Perspectives on Natural Disasters*, Oxford University Press, New York.
18. Cardona, O. 2001, Estimación Holistica del Riesgo Sísmico Utilizando Sistemas Dinámicos Complejos. Barcelona, Spain: Centro Internacional de Métodos Numéricos en Ingeniería (CIMNE), Universidad Politécnica de Cataluña.
19. Guy Carpenter & Company 2000, *The World Catastrophe Reinsurance Market*, New York.
20. Comfort, L. 1999, Shared Risk: Complex Systems in Seismic Response, Pergamon, New York.
21. Extracted from Oh, K.B., Ho C. and Wu. D. Natural disaster and financial risk management. Int. J. Emergency Management, Vol. 6, No. 2, 2009.
22. Merz, M., Hiete, M., Comes, T. and Schultmann, F. (2013). A composite indicator model to assess natural disaster risks in industry on a spatial level. Journal of Risk Research 16(9), 1077–1099.
23. Coase, R. H. 1937, 'The Nature of the Firm', *Econometrica*, no. 4, pp. 386–405, repr. in G.J. Stigler, and K.E. Boulding, (eds.), 1952, *Readings in Price Theory*, Homewood, Ill.
24. Sebstad, J. and M. Cohen. 2000. "Microfinance, Risk Management, and Poverty: Synthesis of Field Studies Conducted by Ronald T. Chua, Paul Mosley, Graham A.N. Wright, Hassam Zaman", Study submitted to Office of Microenterprise Development, USAID, Washington, D.C.
25. World Bank 2000, *World Development Report 2000/2001: Attacking Poverty*, Oxford University Press, New York.

# 14 Sustainability and Enterprise Risk Management

The challenge of environmental sustainability is important not only as a moral imperative, but also a managerial responsibility to operate profitably. Environmental sustainability has become a critical factor in business, as the threats to environmental degradation from carbon emissions, chemical pollution, and other sources has repeatedly created liability for firms that don't consider the environment, as well as regulatory attention. Legislators and journalists provide intensive oversight to operations of any organization. There are many cases of multi-billion dollar corporations brought to or near to bankruptcy by responsibilities for things like asbestos, chemical spills, and oil spills. As the case of the fire and collapse of the Dhaka garment factory in April 2013 attests, global supply chains create complex relationships that place apparently unaware supply chain members such as Nike at great risk, not only legally, but also in terms of market reputation.

Global warming is here, with notable temperature rise exceeding what appears to be sustainable since 1980.[1] This places ecosystem pressure, creating additional risks to property through greater storm magnitude since the 1960s. Natural disasters are increasing in financial magnitude, due to increased population and development. There are many predictions of more intensive rainfall, stronger sotrms, and increased sea levels along with simultaneous drought.

Other risks arise from:

- Medical risks from disease to include Zika virus, West Nile virus, malaria, and others.
- Boycott risk from supply chain linkages to upstream vendors who utilize child labor (affecting Nike) or unsafe practices (Dhaka, Bangladesh).
- Evolving understanding of scientific risks such as asbestos, once thought a cure for building fire, now a major risk issue for health.
- Hazardous waste, such as nuclear disposal
- Oil and chemical spills



D.L. Olson, D.D. Wu, *Enterprise Risk Management Models*, Springer Texts in Business and Economics, DOI 10.1007/978-3-662-53785-5_14

Risk arises in everything humans attempt.[2] Life is worthwhile because of its challenges. Doing business has no profit without risk, rewarding those who best understand systems and take what turns out to be the best way to manage these risks. We will discuss risk management as applied to production in the food we eat, the energy we use to live, and the manifestation of global economy, supply chains.

## What We Eat

One of the major issues facing human culture is the need for quality food. Two factors that need to be considered are first, population growth, and second, threats to the environment. We have understood since Malthus that population cannot continue to grow exponentially without severe changes to our ways of life. Some countries, such as China, have been proactive in controlling population growth. Other areas, such as Europe, seem to find a decrease in population growth, probably due to societal consensus. But other areas, to include India and Africa, continue to see rapid increases in population. Some think that this will change as these areas become more affluent (see China and Europe). But there is no universally acceptable way to control population growth. Thus we expect to see continued increase in demand for food.

Agricultural science has been highly proactive in developing better strains of crops, through a number of methods, including bioengineering and genetic science. This led to what was expected to be a green revolution a generation ago. As with all of mankind's schemes, the best laid plans of humans involve many complexities and unexpected consequences. North America has developed means to vastly increase production of food free from many of the problems that existed a century ago. However, Europe, and even Africa, are concerned about new threats arising from genetic agriculture.

A third factor complicating the food issue is distribution. North America and the Ukraine have long been fertile producing centers, generating surpluses of food. This connects to supply chains, to be discussed below. But the issue is the interconnected global human system with surpluses in some locations and dearth in others. Technically, this is a supply chain issue. But more important really is the economic issue of sharing spoils, which ultimately lead to political issues. Contemporary business with heavy reliance on international collaborative supply chains leads to many risks arising from shipping (as well as other factors). Sustainable supply chain management has become an area with heavy interest.[3]

Water is one of the most widespread assets Earth has (probably next to oxygen, which chemists know is a related entity). Rainwater used to be considered pure. The industrial revolution managed the unintended consequence of acid rain. Water used to be free in many places. In Europe, population density and things like the black plague made beer a necessary health food. In North America, it led to the bottled water industry. Only 30 years ago paying for water would have been considered the height of idiocy. Managing water is recognized as a major issue.[4] Water management also ultimately becomes an economic issue, leading to the political arena.

## The Energy We Use

Generation of energy in its various forms is a major issue leading to political debate concerning tradeoffs among those seeking to expand existing fuel needs, often opposed by those seeking to stress alternative sources of energy. Oil of course is a major source of current energy, but involves not only environmental risks[5] but also related catastrophe risks[6] and market risks.[7] The impact of oil exploration on the Mexican rain forest[8] has been reported and cost risks in alternative energy resources studied.[9]

Mining is a field traditionally facing high production risks. Power generation is a major user of mine output. Cyanide management has occurred in gold and silver mining in Turkey,[10] and benzene imposes risks.[11] Life cycle mine management has been addressed through risk management techniques.[12] The chemical industry also is loaded with inherent risks. Risk management in the chemical industry has been discussed as well.[13]

## The Supply Chains that Link Us to the World

Supply chain risk management involves a number of frameworks, categorization of risks, processes, and mitigation strategies. Frameworks have been provided by many, some focusing on a context, such as supply chain[14] or small-to-medium sized enterprises[15]. Some have focused around context, such as food[16] or pharmaceutical recalls, or terrorism.[17] Five major components to a framework in managing supply chain risk have been suggested:[18]

- Risk context and drivers.

  Risk drivers arising from the external environment will affect all organizations, and can include elements such as the potential collapse of the global financial system, or wars. Industry specific supply chains may have different degrees of exposure to risks. A regional grocery will be less impacted by recalls of Chinese products involving lead paint than will those supply chains carrying such items. Supply chain configuration can be the source of risks. Specific organizations can reduce industry risk by the way the make decisions with respect to vendor selection. Partner specific risks include consideration of financial solvency, product quality capabilities, and compatibility and capabilities of vendor information systems. The last level of risk drivers relate to internal organizational processes in risk assessment and response, and can be improved by better equipping and training of staff and improved managerial control through better information systems.
- Risk management influencers

  This level involves actions taken by the organization to improve their risk position. The organization's attitude toward risk will affect its reward system, and mold how individuals within the organization will react to events. This attitude can be dynamic over time, responding to organizational success or decline.

- Decision makers

  Individuals within the organization have risk profiles. Some humans are more risk averse, others more risk seeking. Different organizations have different degrees of group decision making. More hierarchical organizations may isolate specific decisions to particular individuals or offices, while flatter organizations may stress greater levels of participation. Individual or group attitudes toward risk can be shaped by their recent experiences, as well as by the reward and penalty structure used by the organization.
- Risk management responses

  Each organization must respond to risks, but there are many alternative ways in which the process used can be applied. Risk must first be identified. Monitoring and review requires measurement of organizational performance. Once risks are identified, responses must be selected. Risks can be mitigated by an implicit tradeoff between insurance and cost reduction. Most actions available to organizations involve knowing what risks the organization can cope with because of their expertise and capabilities, and which risks they should outsource to others at some cost. Some risks can be dealt with, others avoided. One view of the strategic options available include the following six broad generalizations:[19]
  - Break the law
  - Take the low road
  - Wait and see
  - Show and tell
  - Pay for principle
  - Think ahead

The first option, breaking the law, apart from ethical considerations, poses serious risks in terms of ability to operate and can lead to jail.

The second implies doing the absolute minimum required to comply with laws and regulations. This approach satisfies legal requirements, but environmental laws and regulations change, so modified behavior will probably be required in the future and will probably be much more expensive than earlier consideration of sustainability factors.

The wait and see option would see firms preparing for expected regulatory changes as well as consumer behavior and competitor strategies. Thus option 3 is more proactive than the prior two options.

Show and tell presumes that the organization is addressing environmental issues but not fully publicizing these activities. Show and tell implies an honest portrayal of environmental performance, as opposed to "greenwashing" where public relations is used to present a misleading report. Show and tell has the deficiency that if problems do arise, or if false accusations are made, firm reputation can suffer.

Pay for principle involves sacrificing some financial performance in order to meet ethical and environmental standards. It implies financial sacrifice.

Think ahead involves proceeding based on principle as well as business logic. Benefits include gaining competitive advantage and protecting against future legislation, seeking to be at the leading edge of sustainability.

Which of these broad general options is appropriate of course depends on firm circumstances, although there is little justifiable support for options 1 and 2.

## The Triple Bottom Line

Organizational performance measures can vary widely. Private for-profit organizations are generally measured in terms of profitability, short-run and long-run. Public organizations are held accountable in terms of effectiveness in delivering services as well as the cost of providing these services. One effort to consider sustainability and other aspects of risk management is the triple bottom line (TBL), [20] considering financial performance, environmental performance, and social responsibility.

$$TBL = f\ (F, E, SR, cost) \tag{1}$$

All three areas need to be considered to maximize firm value. In normal times, there is more of a focus on high returns for private organizations, and lower taxes for public institutions. Risk events can make their preparation in dealing with risk exposure much more important, focusing on survival.

## Sustainability Risks in Supply Chains

As we covered in Chap. 1, supply chains involve many risks imposing disruptions and delays due to problems of capacity, quality, financial liquidity, changing demand and competitive pressure, and transportation problems. By their nature, supply chains require networks of suppliers leading to the need for reliable sources of materials and products with backup plans for contingencies. Demands are at the whim of customers in most cases. There are endogenous risks somewhat within a firm's control, as well as exogenous risks. These can also be viewed by the triple bottom line. Sustainability aspects arise in both endogenous and exogenous risks, as shown in Table 14.1:

Table 14.2 in turn describes exogenous risks and possible responses with practices to implement them.

Tables 14.1 and 14.2 both highlight the variety of things that can go wrong in a supply chain, as well as some basic responses available. Each particular circumstance would of course have more specific appropriate practices available to adequately respond.

**Table 14.1** Endogenous risks related to the triple bottom line[21]

| Endogenous | Risk | Response | Practice |
|---|---|---|---|
| Environmental | Accident | Prevent<br>Mitigate<br>Reduce<br>Cooperate<br>Insure | Locate away from heavy population<br>Emergency response plans<br>Quick admission of responsibility<br>Work with suppliers to identify sources<br>Work with insurers to prevent & mitigate |
| | Pollution | Avoid<br>Mitigate<br>Reduce | Use clean energy, avoid polluting<br>Monitor and reduce emissions<br>Sustainable waste management |
| | Legal compliance | Assure<br>Control<br>Share | Legal policies, disseminate<br>Monitor compliance<br>Sustainability audits with suppliers |
| | Product/package waste | Prevent<br>Mitigate<br>Cooperate | Apply lean management practices<br>Recycle<br>Design products with sustainable packaging |
| Social | Labor | Avoid<br>Prevent<br>Mitigate | Shun sources using child labor<br>Fair wages/reasonable hours<br>Quick admission of responsibility |
| | Safety | Prevent<br>Mitigate<br>Insure | Training<br>Adequate medical access<br>Work with insurers to prevent & mitigate |
| | Discrimination | Prevent<br>Mitigate<br>Transfer | Equal opportunity practices<br>Complaint handling system<br>Legal services and public relations |
| Economic | Antitrust | Avoid<br>Reduce<br>Mitigate | Avoid investing in unstable regions<br>Build local relationships<br>Create extra capacity |
| | Bribery<br>Corruption | Prevent<br>Cooperate | Train management<br>Work with legal authorities |
| | Price fixing<br>Patents | Prevent<br>Mitigate<br>Insure | Follow licensing laws<br>Use whistleblowing<br>Work with supply chain partners |
| | Tax evasion | Prevent | Follow tax laws |

**Table 14.2** Exogenous risks related to sustainability[22]

| Exogenous | Risk | Response | Practice |
|---|---|---|---|
| Environmental | Natural disaster | Reduce<br>Mitigate<br>Insure | Have alternative sources available<br>Resilient contingency plan<br>Insure when risk unavoidable |
| | Weather | Prevent<br>Mitigate<br>Reduce<br>Insure | Built flexible supply chain, forecast<br>Resilient contingency plan<br>Water recycling<br>Insure when risk unavoidable |
| Social | Demographic | Mitigate<br>Reduce | Agile product design<br>Proactively advertise |
| | Pandemic | Reduce<br>Mitigate | Strong health procedures in place<br>Monitor in real-time |
| | Social unrest | Mitigate<br>Insure | Maintain good local relations<br>Have alternative sources, evacuation plans |
| Economic | Boycotts | Prevent<br>Reduce<br>Retain | Provide quality product<br>Public relations<br>Accept risk if cost is low |
| | Litigation | Avoid<br>Prevent<br>Insure | Quality control<br>Responsive public relations<br>Follow laws and regulations |
| | Financial crisis | Avoid<br>Insure | Keep informed<br>Have contingency sources |
| | Energy | Mitigate<br>Transfer | Improve environmental audits<br>Hedge |

## Models in Sustainability Risk Management

The uncertainty inherent in risk analysis has typically been dealt with in two primary ways. One is to either measure distributions or to assume them, and to apply simulation models. Rijgersberg et al.[23] gave a discrete-event simulation model for risks involved in fresh-cut vegetables. The management of risks in the interaction of food production, water resource use, and pollution generation has been studied through Monte Carlo simulation.[24]

The other way to treat risk is to utilize other models (optimization; selection) with fuzzy representations of parameters. Multiple criteria models have been widely applied that consider risk in various forms. Analytic hierarchy process is commonly used in a fuzzy context.[25] The related analytic network process (ANP) has been presented in design of flexible manufacturing systems.[26] Another multiple criteria approach popular in Europe is based on outranking principles. Fuzzy models of this type have been applied to risk contexts in selecting manufacturing systems[27] and in allocating capacity in semiconductor fabrication.[28] These are only representative of many other multiple criteria models considering risk.

## Sustainability Selection Model

We can consider the triple bottom line factors of environmental, social, and economic as a framework of criteria. Calabrese et al.[29] gave an extensive set of criteria for an analytic hierarchy process framework meant to assess a company's sustainability performance. We simplify their framework and demonstrate with hypothetical assessments. We follow the SMART methodology presented in Chap. 3.

## Criteria

Each of the triple bottom line categories has a number of potential sub-criteria. In the environmental category, these might include factors related to inputs (materials, energy, water), pollution generation (impact on biodiversity, emissions, wastes), compliance with regulations, transportation burden, assessment of upstream supplier environmental performance, and presence of a grievance mechanism. This yields six broad categories, each of which might have another level of specific metrics.

In the social category, there could be four broad sub-criteria to include labor practices (employment, training, diversity, supplier performance, and grievance mechanism), human rights impact (child labor issues, union relations, security), responsibility to society (anti-corruption, anti-competitive behavior, legal compliance), and product responsibility (customer health and safety, service, marketing, customer privacy protection). This yields four social criteria. Some of the specific metrics at a lower level are in parentheses.

The economic category could include economic performance indicators (profitability), market presence (market share, product diversity), and procurement reliability (three economic criteria).

## Weight Development

Weights need to be developed. AHP operates within each category and then relatively weighting each category, but a bit more accurate assessment would be obtained by treating all criteria together. We thus have 13 criteria to weight. This is a bit large, but this application was intended by Calabrese et al. as a general sustainability assessment tool (and they had 91 overall specific metrics). We demonstrate with the following weight development using swing weighting in Table 14.3:

The total of the swing weighting assessments in column 3 is 730. Dividing each entry in column 3 by this 730 yields weights in column 4.

**Table 14.3** Swing weighting for sustainability selection model

| Criterion | Rank | Compared to 1st | Weight |
|---|---|---|---|
| Env1—Input sustainability | 1 | 100 | 0.137 |
| Soc2—Human rights impact | 2 | 90 | 0.123 |
| Econ2—Market presence | 3 | 85 | 0.116 |
| Env2—Pollution control | 4 | 80 | 0.110 |
| Soc3—Responsibility to society | 5 | 70 | 0.096 |
| Soc1—Labor practices | 6 | 60 | 0.082 |
| Env3—Compliance with regulations | 7 | 50 | 0.068 |
| Econ1—Profit | 8 | 45 | 0.062 |
| Econ3—Procurement reliability | 9 | 40 | 0.055 |
| Soc4—Product responsibility | 10–11 | 30 | 0.041 |
| Env4—Transportation sustainability | 10–11 | 30 | 0.041 |
| Env5—Upstream supplier performance | 12–13 | 25 | 0.034 |
| Env6—Grievance mechanism | 12–13 | 25 | 0.034 |

**Table 14.4** Firm assessment of performance by criteria

| Criterion | Firm 1 | Firm 2 | Firm 3 |
|---|---|---|---|
| Env1—Input sustainability | Very good | Average | Low |
| Soc2—Human rights impact | Good | Excellent | Low |
| Econ2—Market presence | Average | Average | Very good |
| Env2—Pollution control | Excellent | Good | Low |
| Soc3—Responsibility to society | Good | Excellent | Low |
| Soc1—Labor practices | Good | Excellent | Good |
| Env3—Compliance with regulations | Good | Good | Good |
| Econ1—Profit | Average | Low | Very good |
| Econ3—Procurement reliability | Good | Average | Excellent |
| Soc4—Product responsibility | Very good | Excellent | Good |
| Env4—Transportation sustainability | Excellent | Very good | Good |
| Env5—Upstream supplier performance | Very good | Good | Good |
| Env6—Grievance mechanism | Excellent | Very good | Low |

## Scores

We can now hypothesize some supply chain firms, and assume relative performances as given in Table 14.4 in verbal form. Firm 1 might emphasize environmental concerns. Firm 2 might emphasize social responsibility. Firm 3 might be one that stresses economic efficiency with relatively less emphasis on environmental or social responsibility.

We can convert these to numbers to obtain overall ratings of the three firms. We do this with the following scale:

**Table 14.5** Performance Index Calculation

| Criteria | Weight | Firm 1 | Firm 2 | Firm 3 |
|---|---|---|---|---|
| Env1—Input sustainability | 0.137 | 0.9 | 0.5 | 0.2 |
| Soc2—Human rights impact | 0.123 | 0.7 | 1.0 | 0.2 |
| Econ2—Market presence | 0.116 | 0.5 | 0.5 | 0.9 |
| Env2—Pollution control | 0.110 | 1.0 | 0.7 | 0.2 |
| Soc3—Responsibility to society | 0.096 | 0.7 | 1.0 | 0.2 |
| Soc1—Labor practices | 0.082 | 0.7 | 1.0 | 0.7 |
| Env3—Compliance with regulations | 0.068 | 0.7 | 0.7 | 0.7 |
| Econ1—Profit | 0.062 | 0.5 | 0.2 | 0.9 |
| Econ3—Procurement reliability | 0.055 | 0.7 | 0.5 | 1.0 |
| Soc4—Product responsibility | 0.041 | 0.9 | 1.0 | 0.7 |
| Env4—Transportation sustainability | 0.041 | 1.0 | 0.9 | 0.7 |
| Env5—Upstream supplier performance | 0.034 | 0.9 | 0.7 | 0.7 |
| Env6—Grievance mechanism | 0.034 | 1.0 | 0.9 | 0.2 |
| **Firm score** | | **0.762** | **0.724** | **0.501** |

| | |
|---|---|
| Excellent | 1.0 |
| Very good | 0.9 |
| Good | 0.7 |
| Average | 0.5 |
| Low | 0.2 |

These numbers yield scores for each firm that can be multiplied by weights as in Table 14.5:

## Value Analysis

In this case, Firms 1 and 2 perform relatively much better than Firm 3, but of course that reflects the assumed values assigned. Note that one limitation of the method is that the more criteria, the tendency is to have higher emphasis. There were only three economic factors, as opposed to six environmental factors. Even though the weights could reflect higher rankings for a particular category (here the last four ranked factors were environmental), there is a bias introduced. The six factors for environmental issues here may account for Firm 1 slightly outperforming Firm 2. The overall bottom line is that one should pay attention to all three triple bottom line categories. The performance index demonstrated here might be used by each firm to draw their attention to criteria where they should expend effort to improve performance.

## Conclusions

There is an obvious growing move toward recognition of the importance of sustainability. This is true in all aspects of business. We reviewed some of the risks involve in the supply chain context, and considered risk management in a framework including context and drivers, influences, decision maker profiles, and general categories of response.

The triple bottom line is a useful way to focus on the role of sustainability in business management. This chapter included a review of enterprise risk categories along with common responses. We also demonstrated a SMART model, and suggested value analysis considerations. Earlier in the book we provided modeling examples where we emphasize the tradeoffs among choices available to contemporary decision makers. But it must be realized that sustainability is not necessarily counter to profitability. Wise contemporary decision making should seek to emphasize attainment of sustainability, social welfare, and profitability. Admittedly it is a challenge, but it is important for success of society that this be accomplished.

## Notes


1. Anderson, D.R. and Anderson, K.E. (2009). Sustainability risk management. *Risk Management and Insurance Review* 12(1), 25–38.
2. Olson, D.l., Birge, J.R., and Linton, J. (2014). Introduction to risk and uncertainty management in technological innovation. *Technovation* 34(8), 395–398.
3. Seuring, S. and Műller, M. (2008). From a literature review to a conceptual framework for sustainable supply chain management. *Journal of Cleaner Production* 16(15), 1699–1710.
4. Lambooy, T. (2011). Corporate social responsibility: Sustainable water use. *Journal of Cleaner Production* 19(8), 852–866.
5. Ng, D. and Goldsmith, P.D. (2010). Bio energy entry timing from a resource based view and organizational ecology perspective. *International Food & Agribusiness Management Review* 13(2), 69–100.
6. Meyler, D., Stimpson, J.P. and Cutghin, M.P. (2007). Landscapes of risk. *Organization & Environment* 20(2), 204–212.
7. Pulver, S. (2007). Making sense of corporate environmentalism. *Organization & Environment* 20(1), 44–83.
8. Santiago, M. (2011). The Huasteca rain forest. *Latin American Research Review* 46, 32–54.
9. Zhelev, T.K. (2005). On the integrated management of industrial resources incorporating finances. *Journal of Cleaner Production* 13(5), 469–474.
10. Akcil, A. (2006). Managing cyanide: Health, safety and risk management practices at Turkey's Ovacik gold-silver mine. *Journal of Cleaner Production* 14(8), 727–735.
11. Nakayama, A., Isono, T., Kikuchi, T., Ohnishi, I., Igarashi, J., Yoneda, M. and Morisawa, S. (2009). Benzene risk estimation using radiation equivalent coefficients.*Risk Analysis: An International Journal* 29(3), 380–392.
12. Kowalska, I.J. (2014). Risk manasgement in the hard coal mining industry: Social and environmental aspects of collieries liquidation. *Resources Policy* 41, 124–134.
13. Műller, G. (2015). Managing risk during turnarounds and large capital projects: Experience from the chemical industry. *Journal of Business Chemistry* 12(3), 117–124.

14. Khan, O. and Burnes, b. (2007). Risk and supply chain management: Creating a research agenda. *International Journal of Logistics Management* 18(2), 197–216; Tang, C. and Tomlin, B. (2008). The power of flexibility for mitigating supply chain risks. *International Journal of Production Economics* 116, 12–27.
15. Nishat Faisal, M., Banwet, D.K. and Shankar, R. (2007). Supply chain risk management in SMEs: Analysing the varriers. *International Journal of Management & Enterprise Development* 4(5), 588–607.
16. Roth, A.V., Tsay, A.A., Pullman, M.E. and Gray, J.V. (2008). Unraveling the food supply chain: Strategic insights from China and the 2007 recalls. *Journal of Supply Chain Management* 44(1), 22–39.
17. Williams, Z., Lueg, J.E. and LeMay, S.A. (2008). Supply chain security: An overview and research agenda. *International Journal of Logistics Management* 19(2), 254–281.
18. Ritchie, B. and Brindley, C. (2007). An emergent framework for supply chain risk management and performance measurement. *Journal of the Operational Research Society* 58, 1398–1411.
19. Rosenberg, M. (2016). Environmental sensibility: A strategic approach to sustainability. *IESE Insight* 29, 54–61.
20. Elkington, J. (1997). *Cannibals with Forks*. Capstone Publishing Ltd.
21. Giannakis, M. and Papadopoulos, T. (2016).. Supply chain sustainability: A risk management approach. *International Journal of Production Economics* 17(part 4), 4555–470.
22. Ibid.
23. Rijgersberg, H., Tromp, S., Jacxsens, L. and Uyttendaele, M. (2009). Modeling logistic performance in quantitative microbial risk assessment. *Risk Analysis* 30(1), 10–31.
24. Sun, J., Chen, J., Xi, Y. and Hou, J. (2011). Mapping the cost risk of agricultural residue supply for energy application in rural China. *Journal of Cleaner Production* 19(2/3), 121–128.
25. Chan, F.T.S., Kumar, N., Tiwari, M.K., Lau, H.C.W. and Choy, K.L. (2008). Global supplier selection: A fuzzy-AHP approach. *International Journal of Production Research* 46(14), 3825–3857.
26. Kodali, R. and Anand, G. (2010). Application of analytic network process for the edesign of flexible manufacturing systems. *Global Journal of Flexible Systems Management* 11(1/2), 39–54.
27. Saidi Mehrabad, M. and Anvari, M. (2010). Provident decision making by considering dynamic and fuzzy environment for FMS evaluation. *International Journal of Production Research* 48(15), 4555–4584.
28. Kang, H.-Y. (2011). A multi-criteria decision-making approach for capacity allocation problem in semiconductor fabrication. *International Journal of Production Research* 49(19), 5893–5916.
29. Calabrese, A., Costa, R., Levialdi, N. and Menichini, T. (2016). A fuzzy analytic hierarchy process method to support materiality assessment in sustainability reporting. *Journal of Cleaner Production* 121, 248–264.

# Environmental Damage and Risk Assessment

# 15

Among the many catastrophic damages inflicted on our environment, recent events include the 2010 Deepwater Horizon oil spill in the Gulf of Mexico, and the 2011 earthquake and tsunami that destroyed the Fukushima Daiichi nuclear power plant. The Macondo well operated by British Petroleum, aided by driller Transocean Ltd. and receiving cement support from Halliburton Co. blew out on 20 April 2010, leading to eleven deaths. The subsequent 87 day flow of oil into the Gulf of Mexico dominated news in the U.S. for an extensive period of time, polluted fisheries in the Gulf as well as coastal areas of Louisiana, Mississippi, Alabama, Florida, and Texas. The cause was attributed to defective cement in the well. The Fukushima nuclear plant disaster led to massive radioactive decontamination, impacting 30,000 km$^2$ of Japan. All land within 20 km of the plant plus an additional 2090 km$^2$ northwest were declared too radioactive for habitation, and all humans were evacuated. The Deepwater Horizon spill was estimated to have costs of $11.2 billion actual containment expense, another $20 billion in trust funds pledged to cover damages, $1 billion to British Petroleum for other expenses, and risk of $4.7 billion in fines, for a total estimated $36.9 billion.[1] The value of total economic loss at Fukushima range widely, from $250 billion to $500 billion. About 160,000 people have been evacuated from their homes, losing almost off of their possessions[2].

The world is getting warmer, changing the environment substantially. Oil spills have inflicted damage on the environment in a number of instances. While oil spills have occurred for a long time, we are becoming more interested in stopping and remediating them. In the United States, efforts are under way to reduce coal emissions. US policies have tended to focus on economic impact. Europe has had a long-standing interest in additional considerations, although these two entities seem to be converging relative to policy views. In China and Russia, there are newer efforts to control environmental damage, further demonstrating convergence of world interest in environmental damage and control.

We have developed the ability to create waste of lethal toxicity. Some of this waste is on a small but potentially terrifying scale, such as plutonium. Other forms of waste (or accident) involve massive quantities that can convert entire regions



D.L. Olson, D.D. Wu, *Enterprise Risk Management Models*, Springer Texts in Business and Economics, DOI 10.1007/978-3-662-53785-5_15

into wasteland, and turn entire seas into man-made bodies of dead water. Siting facilities and controlling transmission of commodities lead to efforts to deal with environmental damage lead to some of the most difficult decisions we face as a society.

Recent U.S. issues have arisen from energy waste disposal. Nuclear waste is a major issue from both nuclear power plants as well as from weapons dismantling.[3] Waste from coal plants, in the form of coal ash slurry, has proven to be a problem as well. The first noted wildlife damage from such waste disposal occurred in 1967 when a containment dam broke and spilled ash into the Clinch River in Virginia.[4] Subsequent noted spills include Belews Lake, North Carolina in 1976, and the Kingston Fossil Plant in Tennessee in 2008. Lemly noted 21 surface impoundment damage cases from coal waste disposal, five due to disposal pond structural failure, two from unpermitted ash pond discharge, two from unregulated impoundments, and twelve from legally permitted releases.

Some waste is generated as part of someone's plan. Other forms arise due to accident, such as oil-spills or chemical plant catastrophes. Location decisions for waste-related facilities are very important. Dangerous facilities have been constructed in isolated places for the most part in the past. However, with time, fewer places in the world are all that isolated. Furthermore, moving toxic material safely to or from wherever these sites are compounds the problem.

Many more qualitative criteria need to be considered, such as the impact on the environment, the possibility of accidents and spills, the consequences of such accidents, and so forth. An accurate means of transforming accident consequences into concrete cost results is challenging. The construction of facilities and/or the processes of producing end products involve high levels of uncertainty. Enterprise activities involve exposure to possible disasters. Each new accident is the coincidence of several causes each having a low probability taken separately. There is insufficient reliable statistical data to accurately predict possible accidents and their consequences.

## Specific Features of Managing Natural Disasters

Problems can have the following features:

1. Multicriteria nature

   Usually there is a need for decision-makers to consider more than mere cost impact. Some criteria are easily measured. Many, however, are qualitative, defying accurate measurement. For those criteria that are measurable, measures are in different units that are difficult to balance. The general value of each alternative must integrate each of these different estimates. This requires some means of integrating different measures based on sound data.
2. Strategic nature

The time between the making of a decision and its implementation can be great. This leads to detailed studies of possible alternative plans in order to implement a rational decision process.

3. Uncertain and unknown factors

   Typically, some of the information required for a natural disaster is missing due to incomplete understanding of technical and scientific aspects of a problem.

4. Public participation in decision making

   At one time, individual leaders of countries and industries could make individual decisions. That is not the case in the twenty-first century.

   While we realize that wastes need to be disposed of, none of us want to expose our families or ourselves to a toxic environment.

## Framework

Assessing the value of recovery efforts in response to environmental accidents involves highly variable dynamics of populations, species, and interest groups, making it impossible to settle on one universal method of analysis. There are a number of environmental valuation methods that have been developed. Navrud and Pruckner[5] and Damigos[6] provided frameworks of methods. Table 15.1 outlines market evaluation approaches.

There are many techniques that have been used. Table 15.1 has three categories of methods. **Household production function** methods are based on relative demand between complements and substitutes, widely used for economic evaluation of projects including benefits such as recreational activities.

The **Travel Cost Method** assumes that the time and travel cost expenses incurred by visitors represent the recreational value of the site. This is an example of a method based on revealed preference.

**Hedonic price analysis** decomposes prices for market goods based on analysis of willingness-to-pay, often applied to price health and aesthetic values. Hedonic price analysis assumes that environmental attributes influence decisions to consume. Thus market realty values are compared across areas with different environmental factors to estimate the impact of environmental characteristics. Differences are assumed to appear as willingness to pay as measured by the market. An example of hedonic price analysis was given of work-related risk of death and worker characteristics.[7] That study used US Federal statistics on worker fatalities and

**Table 15.1** Methods of environmental evaluation

| Household production function methods | Revealed preference | Travel cost method |
|---|---|---|
| Hedonic price analysis | Revealed preference of willingness to pay | Benefit transfer method |
| Elicitation of preferences | Stated preference | Contingent valuation |

worker characteristics obtained from sampling 43,261 workers to obtain worker and job characteristics, and then ran logistic regression models to identify job characteristic relations to the risk of work fatality.

Both household production function methods and hedonic price analysis utilize revealed preferences, induced without direct questioning. Elicitation of preferences conversely is based on stated preference, using hypothetical settings in contingent valuation, or auctions or other simulated market scenarios. The benefit transfer method takes results from one case to a similar case. Because household production function and hedonic price analysis might not be able to capture the holistic value of natural resource damage risk, contingent valuation seeks the total economic value of environmental goods and services based on elicited preferences. Elicitation of preferences seek to directly assess utility, to include economic, through lottery tradeoff analysis or other means of direct preference elicitation.

**Cost-benefit analysis** is an economic approach pricing every scale to express value in terms of currency units (such as dollars). The term usually refers to social appraisal of projects involving investment, taking the perspective of society as a whole as opposed to particular commercial interests. It relies on opportunity costs to society, and indirect measure. There have been many applications of cost-benefit analysis around the globe. It is widely used for five environmentally related applications,[8] given in Table 15.2:

The basic method of analysis is cost-benefit analysis outlined above. Regulatory review reflects the need to expand beyond financial-only considerations to reflect other societal values. Natural Resource Damage Assessment applies cost-benefit analysis along with consideration of the impact on various stakeholders (in terms of compensation). Environmental costing applies cost benefit analysis, with requirements to include expected cost of complying with stipulated regulations. Distinguishing features are that the focus of environmental costing is expected to reflect a marginal value, and that marginal values of environmental services are viewed in terms of shadow prices. Thus when factors influencing decisions change, the value given to environmental services may also change. Environmental accounting focuses on shadow pricing models to seek some metric of value.

Cost-benefit analysis seeks to identify accurate measures of benefits and costs in monetary terms, and uses the ratio benefits/costs (the term benefit-cost ratio seems more appropriate, and is sometimes used, but most people refer to cost-benefit analysis). Because projects often involve long time frames (for benefits if not for costs as well), considering the net present value of benefits and costs is important.

**Table 15.2** Environmental evaluation methods

| | |
|---|---|
| Project evaluation | Extended cost-benefit analysis—normative |
| Regulatory review | Metric other than currency—normative |
| Natural Resource Damage Assessment | Stakeholder consideration—compensatory |
| Environmental costing | Licensing analysis |
| Environmental accounting | Ecology-oriented |

We offer the following example to seek to demonstrate these concepts. Yang[9] provided an analysis of 17 oil spills related to marine ecological environments. That study applied clustering analysis with the intent of sorting out events by magnitude of damage, which is a worthwhile exercise. We will modify that set of data as a basis for demonstrating methods. The data is displayed in Table 15.3:

This provides five criteria. Two of these are measured in dollars. While there might be other reasons why a dollar in direct loss might be more or less important than a dollar lost by fisheries, we will treat these at the same scale. Hectares of general ocean, however, might be less important than hectares of fishery area, as the ocean might have greater natural recovery ability. We have thus at least four criteria, measured on different scales that need to be combined in some way.

## Cost-Benefit Analysis

Cost-benefit analysis requires converting hectares of ocean and hectares of fishery as well as affected population into dollar terms. Means to do that rely on various economic philosophies, to include the three market evaluation methods listed in Table 15.1. These pricing systems are problematic, in that different citizens might well have different views of relative importance, and scales may in reality involve significant nonlinearities reflecting different utilities. But to demonstrate in simple form, we somehow need to come up with a way to convert hectares of both types and affected population into dollar terms.

**Table 15.3** Raw numbers for marine environmental damage

| Event | Direct loss ($million) | Fishery loss ($million) | Polluted ocean area hectares | Polluted fishery area (hectares) | Population affected (millions) |
|---|---|---|---|---|---|
| 1 | 60 | 12 | 216 | 77 | 20.47 |
| 2 | 11 | 14 | 53 | 10 | 2.20 |
| 3 | 31 | 14 | 217 | 48 | 14.65 |
| 4 | 36 | 11 | 105 | 40 | 11.48 |
| 5 | 14 | 17 | 69 | 12 | 4.65 |
| 6 | 16 | 16 | 17 | 3 | 1.96 |
| 7 | 15 | 15 | 164 | 25 | 13.77 |
| 8 | 38 | 13 | 286 | 90 | 23.94 |
| 9 | 8 | 15 | 24 | 0 | 3.88 |
| 10 | 26 | 13 | 154 | 41 | 16.40 |
| 11 | 9 | 16 | 59 | 15 | 6.40 |
| 12 | 19 | 12 | 162 | 55 | 18.82 |
| 13 | 27 | 11 | 68 | 11 | 8.15 |
| 14 | 18 | 16 | 38 | 4 | 6.44 |
| 15 | 14 | 15 | 108 | 13 | 12.89 |
| 16 | 11 | 17 | 6 | 3 | 5.39 |
| 17 | 5 | 20 | 32 | 0 | 3.99 |

We could apply tradeoff analysis to compare relative willingness of some subject pool to avoid polluting a hectare of ocean, a hectare of fishery, and avoid affecting one million people. One approach is to use marginal values, or shadow prices to optimization models. Another approach is to use lottery tradeoffs, where subjects might agree upon the following ratios:

Avoiding 1 ha of ocean pollution equivalent to $0.3 million

Avoiding 1 ha of fishery pollution equivalent to $0.5 million

Avoiding impact on 1 million people equivalent to $6 million

Admittedly, obtaining agreement on such numbers is highly problematic. But if it were able to be done, the cost of each incident is now obtained by adding the second and third columns iof Table 15.2 to the fourth column multiplied by 0.3, the fifth column by 0.5, and the sixth column by 6. This would yield Table 15.4:

This provides a simple (probably misleadingly simple) means to assess relative damage of these 17 events. By these scales, event 8 and event 1 were the most damaging.

Wen and Chen[10] gave a report of cost-benefit analysis to balance economic, ecological, and social aspects of pollution with the intent of aiding sustainable development, National welfare, and living quality in China. They used GDP as the measure of benefit, allowing them to use the conventional approach of obtaining a ratio of benefits over costs. Cost-benefit analysis can be refined to include added features, such as net present value if data is appropriate over different time periods.

**Table 15.4** Cost-benefit calculations of marine environmental damage demonstration

| Event | Direct loss ($million) | Fishery loss ($million) | Polluted ocean ($million) | Polluted fishery ($million) | Population affected ($million) | Total ($million) |
|---|---|---|---|---|---|---|
| 1 | 60 | 12 | 64.8 | 38.5 | 122.82 | 298.12 |
| 2 | 11 | 14 | 15.9 | 5 | 13.2 | 59.1 |
| 3 | 31 | 14 | 65.1 | 24 | 87.9 | 222 |
| 4 | 36 | 11 | 31.5 | 20 | 68.88 | 167.38 |
| 5 | 14 | 17 | 20.7 | 6 | 27.9 | 85.6 |
| 6 | 16 | 16 | 5.1 | 1.5 | 11.76 | 50.36 |
| 7 | 15 | 15 | 49.2 | 12.5 | 82.62 | 174.32 |
| 8 | 38 | 13 | 85.8 | 45 | 143.64 | 325.44 |
| 9 | 8 | 15 | 7.2 | 0 | 23.28 | 53.48 |
| 10 | 26 | 13 | 46.2 | 20.5 | 98.4 | 204.1 |
| 11 | 9 | 16 | 17.7 | 7.5 | 38.4 | 88.6 |
| 12 | 19 | 12 | 48.6 | 27.5 | 112.92 | 220.02 |
| 13 | 27 | 11 | 20.4 | 5.5 | 48.9 | 112.8 |
| 14 | 18 | 16 | 11.4 | 2 | 38.64 | 86.04 |
| 15 | 14 | 15 | 32.4 | 6.5 | 77.34 | 145.24 |
| 16 | 11 | 17 | 1.8 | 1.5 | 32.34 | 63.64 |
| 17 | 5 | 20 | 9.6 | 0 | 23.94 | 58.54 |

## Contingent Valuation

Contingent valuation uses direct questioning of a sample of individuals to state the maximum they would be willing to pay to preserve an environmental asset, or the minimum they would accept to lose that asset. It has been widely used in air and water quality studies as well as assessment of value of outdoor recreation, wetland and wilderness area protection, protection of endangered species and cultural heritage sites.

Petrolia and Kim[11] gave an example of application of contingent valuation to estimate public willingness to pay for barrier-island restoration in Mississippi. Five islands in the Mississippi Sound were involved, each undergoing land loss and translocation from storms, sea level rise, and sediment. A survey instrument was used to present subjects with three hypothetical restoration options, each restoring a given number of acres of land and maintaining them for 30 years. Scales had three points: status quo (small scale restoration), pre-hurricane Camille (medium restoration), and pre-1900 (large scale restoration). Dichotomous questions were presented to subjects asking for bids set at no action, 50 % baseline cost, 100 %, 150 %, 200 %, and 250 %. These were all expressed in one-time payments to compare with the level of restoration, asking for the preferred bid and thus indicating willingness to pay.

Carson[12] reported on the use of contingent valuation in the Exxon Valdez spill of March 1989. The State of Alaska funded such as study based on results of a 39 page survey, yielding an estimate of the American public's willingness to pay about $3 billion to avoid a similar oil spill. This compared to a different estimate based on direct economic losses from lost recreation days (hedonic pricing) of only $4 million dollars. Exxon spent about $2 billion on response and restoration, and paid $1 billion in natural resource damages.

## Conjoint Analysis

Conjoint analysis has been used extensively in marketing research to establish the factors that influence the demand for different commodities and the combinations of attributes that would maximize sales.[13]

There are three broad forms of conjoint analysis. **Full-profile analysis** presents subjects with product descriptions with all attributes represented. This is the most complete form, but involves many responses from subjects. The subject provides a score for each of the samples provided, which are usually selected to be efficient representatives of the sample space, to reduce the cognitive burden on subjects. When a large number of attributes are to be investigated, the total number of concepts can be in the thousands, and impose an impossible burden for the subject to rate, unless the number is reduced by adoption of a fractional factorial. The use of a fractional design, however, involves loss of information about higher-order interactions among the attribute. Full profile ratings based conjoint analysis, while setting a standard for accuracy, therefore remains difficult to implement if there are many attributes or levels and if interactions among them are suspected. Regression models with attribute levels treated with dummy variables are used to identify the preference function, which can then be applied to products with any combination of attributes.

**Hybrid conjoint models** have been developed to reduce the cognitive burden. An example is **Adaptive Conjoint Analysis** (ACA), which reduces the number of attributes presented to subjects, and interactively select combinations to present until sufficient data was obtained to classify full product profiles.

A third approach is to **decompose preference** by attribute importance and value of each attribute level. This approach is often referred to as trade-off analysis, or self-explicated preference identification, accomplished in five steps:

1. Identify unacceptable levels on each attribute.
2. Among acceptable levels, determine most preferred and least preferred levels.
3. Identify the critical attribute, setting its importance rating at 100.
4. Rate each attribute for each remaining acceptable level.
5. Obtain part-worths for acceptable rating levels by multiplying importance from step 3 by desirability rating from step 4.

This approach is essentially that of the simple multiattribute rating theory.[14] The limitations of conjoint analysis include profile incompleteness, the difference between the artificial experimental environment and reality. Model specification incompleteness recognizes the nonlinearity in real choice introduced by interactions among attributes. Situation incompleteness considers the impact of the assumption of competitive parity. Artificiality refers to the experimental subject weighing more attributes than real customers consider in their purchases. Instability of tastes and beliefs reflects changes in consumer preference.

For studies involving six or fewer attributes, full-profile conjoint methods would be best. Hybrid methods such as Adaptive Conjoint Analysis (ACA) would be better for over six attributes but less than 20 or 30, with up to 100 attribute levels total; and self-explicated methods (trade-off analysis of decomposed utility models) would be better for larger problems. The trade-off method is most attractive when there are a large number of attributes, and implementation in that case makes it imperative to use a small subset of trade-off tables.

Conjoint analysis usually provides a linear function fitting the data. This has been established as problematic when consumer preference involves complex interactions. In such contingent preference, what might be valuable to a consumer in one context may be much less attractive in another context. Interactions may be modeled directly in conjoint analysis, but doing so requires (a) knowing which interactions need to be modeled, (b) building in terms to model the interaction (thereby using up degrees of freedom), and (c) correctly specifying the alias terms if one is using a fractional factorial design. With a full-profile conjoint analysis with even a moderate number of attributes and levels, the task of dealing with interactions expands the number of judgments required by subjects to impossible levels, and it is not surprising that conjoint studies default to main-effects models in general. Aggregate-level models can model interactions more easily, but again, the number of terms in a moderate-sized design with a fair number of suspected contingencies can become unmanageable. Nonlinear consumer preference functions could arise due to interactions among attributes, as well as from pooling data to estimate overall market response, or contextual preference.

Shin et al.[15] applied conjoint analysis to estimate consumer willingness to pay for the Korean Renewable Portfolio Standard. This standard aims at reducing carbon emissions in various systems, to include electrical power generation, transportation, waste management, and agriculture. Korean consumer subjects were asked to tradeoff five attributes, as shown in Table 15.5:

There are $3^5 = 243$ combinations, clearly too many to meaningfully present to subjects in a reasonable time. Conjoint analysis provides means to intelligently reduce the number of combinations to present to subjects in order to obtain well-considered choices that can identify relative preference. One sample choice set is shown in Table 15.6:

Attributes were presented in specific measures as well as the stated percentages given in Table 15.6. The fractional factorial design used 18 alternatives out of the 243 possible, divided into six choice sets, including no change. None of these had a dominating alternative, thus forcing subjects to tradeoff among attributes. There were 500 subjects. Selections were fed into a Bayesian mixed logit model to provide estimated consumer preference.

When preference independence is not present, Clemen and Reilly[16] discuss options for utility functions over attributes. The first approach is to perform direct assessment. However, too many combinations lead to too many subject responses, as with conjoint analysis. The second approach is to transform attributes, using

**Table 15.5** Conjoint structure for Korean carbon emission willingness to pay

| Attribute | Low level | Intermediate level | High level |
|---|---|---|---|
| Electricity price | 2 % increase | 6 % increase | 10 % increase |
| $CO_2$ reduction | 3 % decrease/year | 5 % decrease/year | 7 % decrease/year |
| Reduction in unemployment | 10,000 new jobs/ year | 20,000 new jobs/ year | 30,000 new jobs/ year |
| Power outage | 10 min/year | 30 min/year | 50 min/year |
| Forest damage | 530 $km^2$/year | 660 $km^2$/year | 790 $km^2$/year |

**Table 15.6** Sample questionnaire policy choice set

| Attribute | Policy 1 | Policy 2 | Policy 3 | Do nothing |
|---|---|---|---|---|
| Electricity price | 2 % increase | 6 % increase | 6 % increase | 0 increase |
| $CO_2$ reduction | 7 % decrease | 5 % decrease | 7 % decrease | 0 increase |
| Reduction in unemployment | 30,000 new jobs | 20,000 new jobs | 30,000 new jobs | No new jobs |
| Power outage | 50 min/year | 10 min/year | 30 min/year | No decrease |
| Forest damage | 660 $km^2$/year | 660 $km^2$/year | 530 $km^2$/year | No reduction |

measurable attributes capturing critical problem aspects. Another potential problem is variance in consumer statement of preference. The tedium and abstractness of preference questions can lead to inaccuracy on the part of subject inputs.[17] In addition, human subjects have been noted to respond differently depending on how questions are framed.[18]

## Habitat Equivalency Analysis

Habitat equivalency analysis (HEA) quantifies natural resource service losses. The effect is to focus on restoration rather than restitution in terms of currency. It has been developed to aid governmental agencies in the US to assess natural resource damage to public habitats from accidental events. It calculates natural resource service loss in discounted terms and determines the scale of restoration projects needed to provide equal natural resource service gains in discounted terms in order to fully compensate the public for natural resource injuries.

Computation of HEA takes inputs in terms of measures of injured habitat, such as acres damaged, level of baseline value of what those acres provided, losses inferred, all of which are discounted over time. It has been applied to studies of oil spill damage to miles of stream, acres of woody vegetation, and acres of crop vegetation.[19] The underlying idea is to estimate what it would cost to restore the level of service that is jeopardized by a damaging event.

**Resource equivalency analysis** (REA) is a refinement of habitat equivalency analysis in that the units measured differ. It compares resources lost due to a pollution incident to benefits obtainable from a restoration project. Compensation is assessed in terms of resource services as opposed to currency.[20] Components of damage are expressed in Table 15.7:

Defensive costs are those needed for response measures to prevent or minimize damage. Along with monitoring and assessment costs, these occur in all scenarios. If resources are remediable, there are costs for remedying the injured environment as well as temporary welfare loss. For cases where resources are not remediable, damage may be reversible (possibly through spontaneous recovery), in which case welfare costs are temporary. For irreversible situations, welfare loss is permanent.

**Table 15.7** Resource equivalency analysis damage components[21]

| Condition | Remedial | Irremediable |
|---|---|---|
| Reversible | Defensive costs<br>Costs of monitoring & assessment<br>Remediation costs<br>Interim welfare costs | Defensive costs<br>Costs of monitoring & assessment<br>Interim welfare costs |
| Irreversible | Defensive costs<br>Costs of monitoring & assessment<br>Remediation costs<br>Interim welfare costs | Defensive costs<br>Costs of monitoring & assessment<br>Permanent welfare losses |

HEA and REA both imply adoption of compensatory or complementary remedial action, and generation of substitution costs.

Yet a third variant is the **value-based equivalency** method, which uses the frame of monetary value. Natural resource damage assessment cases often call for compensation in non-monetary, or restoration equivalent, terms. This was the basic idea behind HEA and REA above. Such scaling can be in terms of service-to-service, seeking restoration of equivalent value resources through restoration. This approach does not include individual preference. Value-to-value scaling converts restoration projects into equivalent discounted present value. It requires individual preference to enable pricing. This can be done with a number of techniques, to include the travel cost method of economic valuation.[22] Essentially, pricing restoration applies conventional economic evaluation through utility assessment.

## Summary

The problem of environmental damage and risk assessment has grown to be recognized as critically important, reflecting the emphasis of governments and political bodies on the urgency of need to control environmental degradation. This chapter has reviewed a number of approaches that have been applied to support decision making relative to project impact on the environment. The traditional approach has been to apply cost-benefit analysis, which has long been recognized to have issues. Most of the variant techniques discussed in this chapter are modifications of CBA in various ways. Contingent valuation focuses on integrating citizen input, accomplished through surveys. Other techniques focus on more accurate inputs of value tradeoffs, given in Table 15.1. Conjoint analysis is a means to more accurately obtain such tradeoffs, but at a high cost of subject input. Habitat equivalency analysis modifies the analysis by viewing environmental damage in terms of natural resource service loss.

Burlington[23] reviewed natural resource damage assessment in 2002, reflecting the requirements of the US Oil Pollution Act of 1990. The prior approach to determining environmental liability following oil spills was found too time consuming. Thus instead of collecting damages and then determining how to spend these funds for restoration, the focus was on timely, cost-effective restoration of damaged natural resources. An initial injury assessment is conducted to determine the nature and extent of damage. Upon completion of this injury assessment, a plan for restoration is generated, seeking restoration to a baseline reflecting natural resources and services that would have existed but for the incident in question. Compensatory restoration assessed reflects actions to compensate for interim losses. A range of possible restoration actions are generated, and costs estimated for each. Focus is thus on cost of actual restoration. Rather than abstract estimates of the monetary value of injured resources, the focus is on actual cost of restoration to baseline.

## Notes


1. Smith, L.C., Jr., Smith, L.M. and Ashcroft, P.A. (2011). Analysis of environmental and economic damages from British Petroleum's Deepwater Horizon oil spill, *Albany Law Review* 74:1, 563–585.
2. http://www.fairewinds.org/nuclear-energy-education/arnie-gundersen-and-helen-caldicott-discuss-the-fukushima-daiichi-meltdowns
3. Butler, J. and Olson, D.L (1999). Comparison of Centroid and Simulation Approaches for Selection Sensitivity Analysis, *Journal of Multicriteria Decision Analysis* **8**:3, 146–161
4. Lemly, A.D. and Skorupa, J.P. (2012). Wildlife and the coal waste policy debate: Proposed rules for coal waste disposal ignore lessons from 45 years of wildlife poisoning. *Environmental Science and Technology* 46, 8595–8600.
5. Navrud, S. and Pruckner, G.J. (1997). Environmental valuation – To use or not to use? A comparative study of the United States and Europe. *Environmental and Resource Economics* 10, 1–26.
6. Damigos, D. (2006). An overview of environmental valuation methods for the mining industry, *Journal of Cleaner Production* 14, 234–247.
7. Scotton, C.R and Taylor, L.O. (2011). Valuing risk reductions: Incorporating risk heterogeneity into a revealed preference framework, *Resource and Energy Economics* 33, 381–397.
8. Navrud and Pruckner (1997), op cit.
9. Yang, T. (2015). Dynamic assessment of environmental damage based on the optimal clustering criterion – Taking oil spill damage to marine ecological environment as an example. *Ecological Indicators* 51, 53–58.
10. Wen, Z. and Chen, J. (2008). A cost-benefit analysis for the economic growth in China. *Ecological Economics* 65, 356–366.
11. Petrolia, D.R. and Kim, T.-G. (2011). Contingent valuation with heterogeneous reasons for uncertainty, *Resource and Energy Economics* 33, 515–526.
12. Carson, R.T. (2012). Contingent valuation: A practical alternative when prices aren't available, *Journal of Economic Perspectives* 26:4, 27–42.
13. Green, P.E. and Srinivasan, V. (1990). Conjoint analysis in marketing: New developments with implications for research and practice, *Journal of Marketing Science* 54:4, 3–19.
14. Olson, D.L. (1996). *Decision Aids for Selection Problems*. New York: Springer-Verlag.
15. Shin, J., Woo, J.R., Huh, S.-Y., Lee, J. and Jeong, G. (2014). Analyzing public preferences and increasing acceptability for the renewable portfolio standard in Korea, *Energy Economics* 42, 17–26.
16. Clemen, R.T. and Reilly, T. (2001). *Making Hard Decisions*. Pacific Grove, CA: Duxbury.
17. Larichev, O.I. (1992). Cognitive validity in design of decision-aiding techniques, *Journal of MultiCriteria Decision Analysis* 1:3, 127–138.
18. Kahneman, D. and Tversky, A. (1979). Prospect theory: An analysis of decision under risk, *Econometrica* 47, 263–291.
19. Dunford, R.W., Ginn, T.C. * Desvousges, W.H. (2004). The use of habitat equivalency analysis in natural resource damage assessments, *Ecological Economics* 48, 49–70.
20. Zafonte, M. and Hamptom, S. (2007). Exploring welfare implications of resource equivalency analysis in natural resource damage assessments, *Ecological Economics* 61, 134–145.
21. Defancesco, E., Gatto, P. and Rosato, P. (2014). A 'component-based' approach to discounting for natural resource damage assessment, *Ecological Economics* 99, 1–9.
22. Parsons, G.R. and Kang, A.K. (2010). Compensatory restoration in a random utility model of recreation demand, *Contemporary Economic Policy* 28:4, 453–463.
23. Burlington, L.B. (2002). An update on implementation of natural resource damage assessment and restoration under OPA. *Spill Science and Technology Bulletin* 7:1–2, 23–29.

CPSIA information can be obtained
at www.ICGtesting.com
Printed in the USA
LVHW082104111119
637008LV00009B/109/P